D1233279

The Four Days
of Courage

The Untold Story of the People
Who Brought Marcos Down

BRYAN JOHNSON

West Berkeley Branch Library
1125 University Avenue
Berkeley, CA 94702

THE FREE PRESS
A Division of Macmillan, Inc.
NEW YORK

BERKELEY PUBLIC LIBRARY

W
95 9.9
J63f

Copyright © 1987 by Bryan Johnson

All rights reserved. No part of this book may be reproduced or transmitted in any form or by any means, electronic or mechanical, including photocopying, recording or by any information storage and retrieval system, without permission in writing from the Publisher.

The Free Press
A Division of Macmillan, Inc.
866 Third Avenue, New York, N.Y. 10022

First American Edition 1987

Printed in the United States of America

printing number

1 2 3 4 5 6 7 8 9 10

Library of Congress Cataloging-in-Publication Data
Johnson, Bryan
   The four days of courage.
    1. Philippines—History—Revolution, 1986. I. Title.
DS686.62.J64 1987   959.9'046   87-7589
ISBN 0-02-916571-7

8900820

CONTENTS

To Vangie, Ramona, and Jesse

FOREWORD

The Toronto *Globe and Mail* was stuck with a delinquent Peking correspondent back in the 1979–81 era. My territory was supposed to extend from Heilongjiang to Hainan, and my duties included steaming down the Yangtze on a barge and drinking milk tea in a Mongolian yurt. Instead, I kept sending bulletins about a political prisoner in the Philippines named Benigno Aquino or about child prostitution in Manila. The *Globe*'s "China man" was perpetually AWOL, and forever on the phone from Bicol, Davao, or Baguio – trying to convince an exasperated foreign editor that the day's big news was in some Philippine boondock.

It seemed eccentric behavior at the time. The *Globe and Mail*, after all, had been North America's window on China for twenty years. And the Middle Kingdom had made world headlines with its audacious democracy movement and the big-character posters at Xidan Wall.

My arrival in the autumn of 1979, however, coincided with the crackdown on the young dissidents. I got there in time to make friends with a few poets and polemicists, and then to report on the trumped-up "trials" that sent them to hard-labor camps. My enduring memory of China is of the freezing night I sat by a curb and watched workers rip down all the posters, repaint the Xidan wall a dirty white, and set up billboard ads for face cream and fork-lift trucks. Peking was grim, grey, and cold. On a good day, a journalist might persuade a Chinese citizen to reveal something interesting – and thereby get himself arrested. The bad days were worse.

The Philippines was under martial law at that time, but taking the Peking-Manila flight was like going from prison camp to summer camp. My first sensation was the wet, warm breeze of Manila Bay against the chapped lips of a Peking winter. A kid at the airport grabbed my bag and tried to run off with it. When I caught hold of his T-shirt, he flashed the biggest smile I had seen in months. "Hi, Joe," he said. "You wanna taxi?" The ten-year-old con artist found me a cab and a hotel, in return for a Shakey's pizza covered in pineapple and anchovies. He pencilled two dozen Tagalog phrases into my notebook, wished me luck, and disappeared out the door. This, I realized, was not China.

About 3 a.m. that first night, a building burned to the ground while I downed a San Miguel beer and talked politics at an outdoor café across the street. The fire trucks took forever to arrive, but only a shoeshine boy seemed to mind. "I have just two T-shirts," he explained, "and one is at the laundry inside that building." The patrons laughed, tossed him some pesos, ordered more beer, and made plans to watch the sun rise over the burning embers. This was *definitely* not China.

That first impression of vivacity has ripened over the years, and developed a tinge of sadness. But the Philippines turned out to be even more entrancing than I imagined. It is a journalist's paradise, where everyone is accessible, nothing remains secret for long, and even the wildest rumors seem plausible. Within days of my arrival I had talked on the phone to a soft-spoken suburban housewife named Corazon Aquino, and sat for a two-hour lecture by the country's First Lady. Imelda Marcos drew a cross on a blackboard and labelled the four points: "God, The People, Love, and Me". Before the bizarre dissertation was over, she had explained to us how God loved her, the people loved God, she loved the people . . . and wrapped the whole diagram up in a four-petal flower.

"That's my philosophy of life," Imelda rhapsodized, extending two flaccid arms to heaven. No one doubted it for a moment.

The Philippine magic, however, is more than just a stream of good news stories. It begins with a landscape plucked from a South Seas fantasy, and it winds a seductive path toward the country's national treasure: the *Filipina*. "In the Philippines," swears one aged Jesuit priest, "God and the women are the same. We see God in the women. They speak of the same values, the same world. . . ."

That romantic notion was backed with hard evidence during the Four-Day Revolution in February 1986. But my own version had nothing to do with stopping tanks. In 1981 I was transformed from a 31-year-old confirmed bachelor to a dazzled husband in about a month. Back in Peking, before my wife could join me, I would walk through the dusty market near Tian an Men Square, trying to translate Mandarin store signs into Tagalog. I was, literally and figuratively, hooked on the Philippines.

The next few years were supposed to be spent writing weekend feature articles for the *Globe* in Toronto. But there was always a reason to spend the winter in Asia: whether covering a Pierre Trudeau tour, acting as guest speaker on a Singapore–Hong Kong cruise ship, or simply hopping a plane to the Philippines.

In 1985 my editor bowed to the inevitable and formalized a winter-in-Asia arrangement. So I was in Manila two months before the February 7, 1986, presidential election, and stayed long after the rebellion that flung Ferdinand Marcos to Hawaii on one bounce. That astonishing drama kept my byline on the front page for weeks, and eventually led me to search for the story behind the story.

This book is a fusion – at times, I am afraid, it may seem an uncomfortable one – of first-person narrative and journalistic history. I was trembling beside the tanks when the nuns stopped them cold, was strolling past Colonel Balbas as he got the "Fire on target!" order from above, and stood at the Palace walls as U.S. helicopters saved Marcos from the mob at the barricades. Inevitably those vivid scenes are written from memory.

But the bulk of this story was gathered in three months of intensive interviews after the rebel victory. Nearly ninety key players on both sides were interviewed, some of them three or four times. A scheduled one-hour session with the Reformist colonels became an all-day marathon that emptied a case of San Miguel and sparked many return visits. My interview with "General" June Keithley, the high-pitched voice of Radio Bandido, evoked some astonishing revelations. And my sessions with the wry Cardinal Jaime Sin ranged from slapstick comedy to rapt, damp-eyed silence.

The witnesses sometimes contradicted each other, forcing follow-up interviews and a search for other sources. Most of these disparities resulted from honest mistakes; but occasionally someone was obviously lying. Those instances are pinpointed where they seem important.

I have not cluttered the book with my own comings and goings during those four hectic days. For readers who are interested, the Midtown Hotel is just two blocks from the Associated Press office where I sent my stories to Toronto, so there was a chance for a quick nap and a meal every twenty-four hours. Monday morning was a journalist's nightmare, as I was trapped inside a taxi on the wrong side of the barricades, desperately trying to report the rebel helicopter assault on Malacañang Palace. I kept dashing into stores and private homes, trying to use the phone, but the overseas lines were all plugged. Finally the cab driver hurdled a sandbag barrier and got me there on deadline.

My publisher keeps reminding me that I am writing for Western readers, and insists upon explanations for things you might find confusing about the Philippines. (For example, to assist readers in understanding the geography and order of so many incidents, we have included a map of Manila at the start of the illustration section, and a Chronology of Events at the end of the book.) But my true intention is not well hidden. At heart, this book is for the Filipinos who staged the astounding rebellion – and, perhaps even more so, for those who refused to obey the orders to crush it. There were heroes, and villains, on both sides. I hope this book has helped to find them.

Bryan Johnson
January, 1987

I *A CONTAGIOUS COURAGE*

THEY RAN *TOWARDS* THE DANGER. When the crunch came, when that first column of Marine tanks smashed through a concrete wall and churned across a vacant field, the Filipinos around me hesitated for just a moment. "Jesus Christ!" yelled a kid in a blue T-shirt, heading instinctively for the machines, "they're trying to get around us!" The anonymous young man vaulted the six-foot wall and disappeared. Within seconds, two dozen others had followed. By the time all nine tanks had formed up for the attack, they were engulfed in a human sea.

People Power reacted with courage to its first sight of firepower, but it was a courage of trembling lips and of eyes brimming with tears. The thousands of nuns, housewives, school kids, ordinary people, and hard-core activists were brave enough to lay their bodies under the treads of tanks – but most were too terrified to look at them. They fixed their gaze on the scrubgrass, or cast imploring glances to the sky, while the stench of exhaust choked them and coated them with filth.

Why did the ground shake so violently? Was it the pulsating roar of the tanks, or was it all of us trembling together? People clasped hands instinctively and inched forward. Nuns clung to their rosaries, thrusting them heavenward, squeezing their eyes shut, reciting the Sorrowful Mysteries too fast for anyone to follow. And all the while, halted by the barricade of lying, sitting, kneeling people, the tanks continued to roar at full throttle.

It was an eternity, perhaps five minutes, before one tank hatch popped open with a metallic clank and a Marine looked out. Muffled radio messages could be heard from inside. More hatches opened, and other soldiers clambered out onto their machines in camouflage fatigues, encased in criss-crossed ammunition belts with bullets the size of fountain pens. These were combat soldiers, just arrived from the guerrilla war zones in Mindanao. They had a reputation as the country's toughest sons-of-bitches and now they played that role to the hilt. The crowd's chants of "Co-ry! Co-ry! Co-ry!" were met by stone faces or outright sneers. Those who pressed forward to offer cigarettes and flowers were dissuaded by Armalite assault rifles, pointed without waver towards the human barricade.

The Ferdinand Marcos forces in that first confrontation seemed uniformed clones of the President himself: deadly, ruthless, and utterly contemptuous of the average Filipino. They had rolled out of Fort Bonifacio like a conquering army on a routine mopping-up exercise – exuding haughty indifference as they squatted beside 50-caliber machine guns and dandled M-16s on their knees. And why not? The military split that Sunday afternoon was 200,000-to-500 in favor of Marcos. His loyal soldiers had nothing to fear from Juan Ponce Enrile and General Fidel Ramos, much less the unarmed rabble who supported them.

On February 22, 1986, Defense Minister Enrile and Deputy Chief of Staff Ramos had announced their breakaway from the twenty-year dictatorship of President Marcos. Enrile had been a loyal administrator during the darkest years of the martial-law regime, and Ramos was a Marcos cousin considered too rigid and upright to support a coup attempt. But the two men had blinked soberly into TV lights and told the world they believed Marcos had cheated in recent presidential elections. Their small band of military supporters, virtually defenseless that first night, were saved only by the indecision and overconfidence of the Marcos generals. But now, after dithering all morning as the civilian crowd grew, Chief of Staff General Fabian Ver had finally dispatched two thousand Marines to sweep the rebels out of their redoubt.

Word of the attack flashed over the Catholic radio station Veritas, and the citizen defenders prepared to make their stand at Ortigas Avenue. Traffic had been nearly normal there just minutes before as an advance group of vigilantes started to fill sandbags and build a knee-high barricade. Now the intersection received an adrenalin rush of pure panic. Thousands made a dash from the nearby Camp Crame (pronounced Crah-may) rebel base and frantically began to reinforce the pathetic barrier. People surged into the path of oncoming traffic. Cars skidded to a halt as astonished drivers found a crowd dragging trees, buses, and burning tires across the road. Someone who had brought a PA system from Crame and set it atop a red station wagon began to direct cars and taxicabs into open spots in the barricade. "Hi," said the vigilantes. "We need your car. The tanks are coming. Please flatten the tires." Amazingly, almost everybody leapt out and started tearing off valve caps.

Laughter erupted when a grey-haired man in a cream-colored

Mercedes-Benz obediently slid one million pesos' worth of German engineering into the front ranks, then waved an L-sign – the trademark of Cory Aquino's *Laban* party – out of the window. Bus drivers had no choice. Passengers poured through doors and even windows as the belching blue diesels slowed, and began stabbing the tires with knives. Two women on one commandeered bus pleaded to be allowed through. They were visiting a sick sister, they protested. They *must* get to Baclaran. "Sorry, misses," said an efficient college boy in his late teens, "but we really need the bus. We're all in this together, hah?"

Outside, the man on the PA offered unsettling last-minute advice: "Please listen carefully," he ordered gravely. "I pray to God that you will not have to follow these instructions, but, just in case, they are very important. When the tanks come, if they should start firing into the crowd . . . well, we hope it will not happen but, if it does, it will be very important not to panic. . . . We do not want anyone to be trampled." A young woman tousled the feathery black hair of the baby in her arms, and eased away from the front lines.

Rosary beads were flying through fingers now, as nuns gathered in small prayer circles and sank to their knees. The shouted final instructions, the warnings about tear gas, and the noise of a tractor-trailer being dragged into place all died away. Now there was only a gentle hiss as the entire crowd stared south down the broad expanse of Epifanio de los Santos Avenue (EDSA) and let out its breath.

The Marine tanks came thundering over a small rise and into plain view, then slowed to a crawl when they spotted the barrier. They loomed on the horizon, their engines vibrating underfoot even at EDSA and Ortigas, about 600 yards away. There was an ominous pause, as if the grey monsters themselves were slowly pondering the situation. Suddenly their metal tracks began chewing up the asphalt in reverse. "They're retreating!" someone yelled. "They're going back." But no. The whole column reared back and made a ninety-degree turn to the right. Then the leader gunned its engines and – "Oh no. Christ, no!" – pandemonium broke out along the human barricade.

There is a huge open field at the intersection's southeast corner, a scrub-covered wasteland used for carnivals. It is bounded by a six-foot fence of whitewashed cement blocks, a barrier the civilians had assumed was impenetrable. The tanks treated it as a minor irritant. The first one slowed just slightly before pulverizing the wall and grinding into the field. Eight more went clattering in behind.

The armored column should have kept rolling. It could have crashed through the far wall and rumbled back onto Ortigas, leaving the civilians behind and perhaps changing the course of the four-day Philippine revolt. Instead, the tanks paused briefly to get their bearings and map out a new plan. Those few seconds were all that People Power needed to make its fateful decision: forward, over the wall, into the breach.

"The strange thing is that nobody ever talked about tactics," says Sister Anunciata, a Good Shepherd nun who spent the entire three days guarding the rebel camp with her frail sixty-year-old body. "Or maybe it's more accurate to say that *everybody* did. We all talked among ourselves about how to approach the soldiers, but there was no master plan. Some of us were veterans of many demonstrations and street actions, but the nuns who stopped the tanks were mostly first-timers. They weren't given lessons on how to do it. Frankly, many of them were very naive and frightened. Somehow, they just did the right thing."

People Power's plan was instantaneous and unspoken, perhaps a creation of the collective unconscious. But it is not difficult to put into words. "Yes, Mr. Marcos," two million Filipinos were saying to their president, "we will run when confronted with your tanks, soldiers, machine guns, and artillery. But we'll run right *at* them. We will dare them to shoot us, and when they hesitate we'll push close enough to stare your gunners in the eye. We won't fight the soldiers; we'll smother them. We won't storm your palace and hang you from a tree, as you deserve. We will just sit here until you come to your senses and have the grace to leave."

There are echoes of Mahatma Gandhi in that strategy, but it is more properly credited to Benigno "Ninoy" Aquino, the man shot dead in 1983 on the Manila airport's tarmac. Passionate demonstrations and inflammatory speeches raged for months following the opposition leader's brutal assassination. And though his widow, Corazon, did not lead the protests, she played a crucial role at every major rally. After the politicians had rent the air with clenched fists and epithets, Cory would step forward for a few gentle remarks about her husband. Day after day she ended the rallies with a solemn recital of the same quotation.

"Ninoy always said that courage and cowardice had one thing in common," Cory told the angry crowds. "They are both contagious. We can all be cowards, or we can all be heroes together."

That seemed a platitude, but it proved to be a powerful prophecy. The 75-hour Philippine revolution was an eerie inversion of fear, the mirror image of mass panic. It was the antithesis of the Chinese cultural revolution, yet strangely similar. In my years in China, I had seen the results of the Red Guards' shared mania for lopping the heads off Buddhas. Filipinos caught the opposite disease: an infectious bravery, a near-manic willingness to throw flesh against steel, to smother military might with their own vulnerability. Total weakness, they discovered, has tremendous moral strength.

That courage puzzles even those who lay down before the tanks. "I didn't feel brave. I just felt *scared*," recalls Agapito "Butz" Aquino, brother of the slain Ninoy and a veteran organizer of street protests. "My first impulse was to get up and run. But then I looked at those tiny nuns on both sides, and they weren't going anywhere. It just wouldn't have been macho to chicken out."

In their stubborn defiance of Marcosian firepower, others felt the hand of God, or some deep yearning of the Filipino psyche. "It may sound like we were all doing heroic acts, but it was more like dealing with some inner feelings in the spiritual realm," says Robert Chabeldin, one of the EDSA vigilantes. "To this day, I cannot explain where we all got that sense of spirituality. I thought by joining the barricades I was being one of them, and them being part of me. That in sharing those moments of challenge, we had achieved a breakthrough in national consciousness. It is difficult to explain it. You have to experience it to know what it is about."

Something else, too, was hidden in the bravery – a dark secret that foreigners did not detect until later. We stood among them at EDSA, and shivered alongside them when the Sikorsky gunships swooped down towards us on Monday morning. But only Filipinos themselves realized that they were shedding a shameful legacy. While the world press celebrated the revolt as a heroic triumph, Philippine newspapers reacted as if a leper colony had just been healed by a miracle:

"We have redeemed ourselves before the world," exulted an editorial in the *Manila Times*. "We have asserted our rights as free men. No one will ever refer to our race as being made up of so many millions of cowards again."

The prestigious Catholic journal *Veritas* was even more specific about this national inferiority complex. "There was a time not so very long ago," said the weekly, "when we were despised by other peoples. Why did we allow a man to ride roughshod over us, trample over our human rights, and not do anything about it? We were, our detractors said, a nation of 54 million cowards ruled by one – pardon the language – bastard. But not anymore. The four days in February forever divested us of that unflattering appellation."

Fifty-four million cowards? It was astounding to hear such racial slurs from the country's own opinion-makers. Certainly the international community had made the Philippines a pariah for some time. But the distaste was aimed at Ferdinand Marcos and a larcenous government system best described as a "kleptocracy". Filipinos were seen as victims, not cowards. As recently as two weeks before the revolt, observers had flocked from all over the world to scrutinize the February 7 presidential election. The dominant conclusion: Marcos is a thug, but the love for democracy in his Third World nation seemed little short of phenomenal.

The world's judgement was obviously not shared by Filipinos themselves. In their own minds they were cowards for blowing that last legal chance to throw off the dictator. Their self-loathing was nursed privately, too painful to be spoken at the time. But it was confessed openly, tearfully, in the wild aftermath of Marcos's fall from power. The ransacking of Malacañang Palace was more than a celebration: it was an act of national exorcism.

Such feelings are not difficult to understand in a land that has been subjugated since the sixteenth century. Ferdinand Magellan, the famous circumnavigator, planted the Spanish flag near Samar island in 1521. He was followed by Miguel Lopez de Legazpi and a band of *conquistadores* wielding both swords and crosses. They named the 7,107 islands Las Filipinas after their king, Philip II, and made Manila the great port of Southeast Asia – where galleons laden with Mexican silver met Chinese junks loaded with silk and jade.

Though the Spanish had discovered a healthy tribal culture with its own laws and language and a bustling regional trade, they immediately recast the archipelago in their image. Its natives were baptized and renamed en masse, creating an instant nation of Lopezes, Aquinos, and Marcoses. But the names were a mere convenience for the conquerors' Latin tongues, not a sign of equality. The Spaniards set up a rigid new social pecking order based on absolute racism, with the light-skinned Europeans as lords and masters of the Malay serfs. Eventually a mixed breed of wealthy *ilustrados* emerged to form the close-knit landowner class that controls the country's wealth even today. The Marcos family were borderline outsiders to this club, which helps explain the President's relentless destruction of family dynasties and creation of his own band of "crony capitalists" after his assumption of power in 1965.

Filipinos never adjusted to their colonial status, but they never managed to throw it off, either. The 377 years of Spanish rule witnessed more than one hundred revolts, many of them bloody and brave, none entirely successful. The tide of rebellion rose to a crescendo after the execution of national hero Jose Rizal in 1896. But fate, and the Spanish-American War, brought an even lighter-skinned master steaming into Manila Bay. The Filipino rebels were waging war against the Spaniards on land when Yankee commodore George Dewey caused great rejoicing by routing the Spanish navy in 1898. The cheers died when, by the Treaty of Paris, the Philippines was handed to the United States as a prize of war.

Few Americans know anything of the barbarous campaign that followed, but Filipinos have not forgotten. Young General Emilio Aguinaldo declared the First Philippine Republic in 1899, and was immediately attacked by a U.S. army still thirsty for blood. The triumphal Spanish-American conflict had lasted a bare three months – ''not war enough to go around'', as Teddy Roosevelt complained. Now the U.S. forces would get a chance to bag their limit.

''We started across the creek in mud and water up to our waists, but we did not mind it a bit,'' wrote Private Hambleton of the 1st Washington Volunteer regiment, some sixty years before the My Lai massacre. ''Our fighting blood was up and we all wanted to kill 'niggers'. This shooting human beings is a hot game, and beats rabbit hunting all to pieces. We charged them, and such a slaughter you never saw. We killed them like rabbits – hundreds, yes, thousands of them. Everyone was crazy.''

Another American soldier, A. A. Barnes of the 3rd Artillery Regiment, wrote home after helping slaughter one thousand men, women, and children in the destruction of Titia: ''I am probably growing hard-hearted, for I am in my glory when I can sight my gun on some dark skin and pull the trigger.''

After two years of fighting, dozens of such massacres, and 250,000 deaths, General Aguinaldo was forced to surrender and swear allegiance to the Stars and Stripes. U.S.–Philippine relations were off to a grand start.

This Southeast Asian nation has seldom been a regional aggressor, but its strategic position – stretching 1,100 miles between Taiwan and Borneo, smack in the South China Sea lane, directly on the sea route to Japan, and just off the east coast of Vietnam – has always ensured an unfair share of turmoil. The Philippines was just about to receive its long-awaited independence from the United States when the Second World War brought a Japanese occupation force and General Douglas MacArthur's famous ''I shall return!'' pledge. Thereafter, the Philippines was a central focus of the War in the Pacific, and the scene of a great naval battle in Leyte Gulf. The siege at Corregidor, and the war's grisliest death march, were endured before the country was "liberated". Finally, when it had been devastated by brutal occupation and its picturesque capital reduced to a heap of rubble, the Philippines became a republic on July 4, 1946.

But the country's "hamburgerization" had only begun. While other emerging Asian nations were rooted in Confucianism, Buddhism, and racial homogeneity, Filipinos worshipped an eclectic set of Western gods: Jesus Christ, Hollywood, and the U.S. army jeep. Even today, the ubiquitous "jeepney" (an elongated jeep painted in clashing pastels, with a herd of nodding silver horses on its hood) is the prime mode of public transport. And though Filipinos come from solid Malay-Chinese racial stock, they are far too flashy and "Westernized" to be fully embraced by their Asian regional brothers. "They may look like us," a Thai diplomat once told me, during a Manila meeting of the Association of Southeast Asian Nations, "but they *think* like foreigners."

That is a half-truth, or less, but it's easy to see why a Thai would think so. Apart from a Muslim minority in the south, the Philippines is a fanatically Christian nation with an English-speaking educational system influenced by both Jesuits and Americans. So, such crucial Western concepts as democracy and individualism – which baffle the Chinese, the Indonesians, and the Vietnamese – need no translation here. They are adopted word-for-word as Thomas Jefferson set them down, repeated with the fidelity of a U.S. high-school civics textbook. Freedom of the press took a battering under Marcos, who jailed publishers and padlocked papers that cast doubts on his dubious war record, but the concept is much cherished and celebrated by Manila's free-wheeling independent newspapers. Filipinos are happy to debate politics until dawn over Asia's best beer in "Taglish", an eclectic mix of Tagalog and colloquial Americanisms. "Mag-relax tayo sa beach bukas" means "We'll relax tomorrow at the beach." My wife regularly orders "isang sideorder nang bacon" with her breakfast. Like her, most Filipinos are so fluently bilingual they grab whichever word comes to mind, and stuff it into a sentence. Some of the "English" newspapers even write their stories that way.

This can be infuriating for newcomers, forever on the verge of grasping what is being said, and the frustration extends far beyond mere language. The Philippines *seems* so Westernized that foreigners are easily fooled into thinking they understand the place. Only later do they realize that it is a thoroughly Asian culture, as inscrutable in its own way as Japan or Thailand.

A system called *utang na loob*, for example, is the unwritten iron law that guides social behavior. The phrase can be translated as "debt of honor" or "debt of gratitude", but no English term captures its subtle implications. A solemn obligation is incurred for any favor, whether it is an hour of babysitting or rescue from financial ruin. The practice touches all strata of society, and dictates responses even in the highest reaches of government and commerce. "It is sometimes abused and becomes a burden," my closest Filipino friend explains, "but in essence it's very, very positive, the main reason we're such a friendly and open society. A favor is almost *never* refused in the Philippines, simply because people know they can expect the same when it comes their turn to ask. Foreigners don't like the sound of it, because they don't like to be in debt to anyone. For us, it is a good feeling. It means we always have people around who'll help us out."

And just to make sure they are surrounded by allies, Filipinos draw almost anyone they know into their big, warm extended families. A young seamstress might address an older co-worker as *ate*, or "big sister", creating an immediate allegiance. The millions of bustling, officious middle-aged ladies are called *tita* ("auntie") by half the people they know. Even outsiders are quickly woven into the social fabric: I was a regular customer at a small Manila restaurant for just three weeks before the waitresses began calling me *kuya*, or "older brother".

Binding ties continue to grow even tighter. In a country where most people have a half-dozen brothers and sisters, and twice that many "aunties", Filipinos still spend their lives creating a new set of relatives. Hence the *padrino*, or godfather, system, observed here with more passion and fidelity than in the Latin countries of its origin. To be a child's godfather makes you the *compadre* of its parents – a relationship nearly as close as that of brothers. Filipinos abbreviate the term to *Pare*, and sometimes extend it to close friends who are not godfathers. The ties created by such terms are virtual blood knots, with a depth of honor and responsibility never experienced by most Westerners.

In political terms, it is impossible to overestimate the impact of the *padrino* system on the nation's power structure. Ferdinand Marcos once admitted that he was godfather to at least twenty thousand children, and required a staff of twenty merely to keep track of their birthdays and gifts. That gave him an army of *compadres* to do his bidding – men to whom he, in turn, owed incalculable favors.

Those who have never been to the Philippines may feel that they know nothing of the country, when in fact its spectacular beauty is imbedded in their mind's eye. The world's best film-makers have disguised it as every-thing from Vietnam to Indonesia, in movies such as *Apocalypse Now* and *The Year of Living Dangerously*. That dark, mysterious jungle and swirl-ing river. The little village on stilts with coconut-fringed beaches, where the helicopters swooped down spraying bullets and classical music. The bright green mountainside rice terraces, and the crystal-clear waters with old boats bleaching in the sun. The crowded cities with putrid slums, open sewers, visible waves of stifling heat, beggars, thieves, laughing whores, and rowdy bars . . . that is the Philippines.

It is a tropical paradise for some, a South Seas dream come true; a foreigner with any money at all can easily find a deserted beach and a beautiful woman. In fact, Manila's nightlife makes Sodom and Gomorrah seem like Salt Lake City – and at Bible-era prices, too. "I love the poverty here," an American tourist once told me without a hint of irony. "It makes everything so goddam cheap." This endorsement came while the man was sitting in the Blue Hawaii bar, a rollicking emporium of beer, music, and available ladies that might draw daily shuttles from Kennedy Airport if its existence were widely known.

The unrepentant Yankee tourist was exactly right. Poverty *is* the country's dominant feature, the genesis of everything from Manila's throb-bing Ermita strip to the emaciated children on Negros island. A national economic council has set the official poverty line at $1,000 (U.S.) per year for a family of six, a level exceeded by only one-quarter of the population. That smiling teenage waitress at your local bar has a great job: she earns two dollars a day for twelve to fourteen hours' work, seven days a week. Jeepney drivers make slightly more for battling through diesel fumes in furnace-oven heat for an average eighty hours a week. Almost anyone else would gladly trade places with them. Even college-educated school-teachers can – and, tragically, do – earn far more as maids in Hong Kong than in instructing their own countrymen.

And that, of course, is the middle class. The majority live far below, down where this "tropical paradise" dissolves into Hell, and families spend their lives foraging for plastic bags on a steaming garbage dump called the Smokey Mountain. You might pity the ten-year-old hustlers and child prostitutes who sleep in Rizal Park – but not after you visit the homes they have run away from, and find their parents sleeping among rats, roaches, and pools of stale urine. The lifeblood of the Tondo slum, the source of water for drinking, cooking, and washing, is a soup of floating excrement called the Pasig River. The Leveriza area has twenty-five thousand people living on one-fifth of a square mile without any sanitation and with only intermittent electricity. "The children are finished before they're two years old," says Sister Christina Tan, a nun who lives among them. "Their minds just slow down from lack of food, until they almost stop. We do what we can, but mostly we watch the life drain out of them." By comparison, a park bench is five-star accommodation.

This is the country from which President Marcos and his wife Imelda managed to extract approximately ten billion dollars, or three times the annual Gross National Product – a sum that won them recognition in the *Guinness Book of World Records* as the planet's premier thieves. The First Lady's family and an assortment of other presidential cronies made off with a similar amount, pushing the total deep into eleven figures. It is – and always was – clear that not only were they stealing just dollars, they were also stealing lives.

That alone is enough to justify the 75-hour uprising that overthrew Marcos. But it is only part of the explanation. The President was unpopular and corrupt, yet firmly in control until August 1983, when he received the first of two secret kidney transplants. While Marcos lay gravely ill, someone close to him staged the clumsy and brutal shooting that left Ninoy Aquino face down on the airport tarmac. The bullet-ridden body of a supposed "communist assassin" was dumped beside him, but nobody bought that ruse. What followed was a thirty-month enactment of a Shakespearean tragedy, with the First Couple cast as Macbeth and his lady, and the slain Ninoy as Banquo's ghost.

Poor as the Philippines was, it became poorer. Through 1984 and 1985, capital flight, international queasiness, and tumbling commodity prices whacked nearly ten per cent off the GNP. By November 3, 1985, when Mr. Marcos announced a "snap" presidential election – on the David Brinkley TV show, no less, as an apparent afterthought – both his White House allies and the International Monetary Fund were howling for reforms. Worse, frightened Filipino businessmen were staging gigantic rallies down the central boulevard of Manila's chic Makati financial district.

The President was not receptive to complaints about money problems, since his only financial difficulty lay in remembering all the fictitious names and signatures for his Swiss bank accounts. (When the hordes stormed the Palace after his departure, they found scraps of practice paper on his desk, with the signature "William Saunders" written over and over.) Marcos had more dollars than he could hide, and a government printing press that was churning out enough pesos to buy another term in

Malacañang. He knew how to win elections. Besides, the fractious opposition parties seemed certain to split their vote between two candidates. So a supremely confident Marcos told the whole world to "come and see our democracy at work". Two international observer groups and at least 1,500 foreign media accepted the invitation.

It was a marvellous snow job, a clever ploy to upgrade his shabby international image. But somehow this political masterstroke rebounded in the President's face. Many say Corazon Aquino charmed the Filipino people with her simple honesty, and channelled two decades of resentment into a tidal wave of outrage. Mrs. Aquino herself, who prayed at her husband's grave and meditated in a convent before accepting the nomination, believes that God simply gathered up the Philippines in his own hands. "It was a fight between good and evil," she says evenly. "Of *course* He intervened. I believe He actually came down and walked among us during those days."

Whatever the cause, the result was miraculous. A housewife without a shred of experience ran head-on into the Marcos election machine, and demolished it. The President used every weapon honed in decades of dirty Philippine polls: switching of the voters lists, massive vote-buying, intimidation by thugs with clubs or guns, ballot-box stealing and stuffing, even outright murder. Still, an independent citizens' watchdog group and most foreign observers are convinced he lost the election, possibly by a landslide. After all the other cheating, the ruling KBL (the Tagalog acronym that was applied to the New Society Movement) party had to blatantly fiddle the returns before a slim victory could be declared by the Marcos-controlled National Assembly.

The fraud was apparent to everyone except Ronald Reagan, who contradicted his own State Department by suggesting there might have been "cheating on both sides". But while most foreigners bowed to the inevitability of another Marcos term, something stirred deep inside the nation. "We were heartsick, disgusted, horrified," says Rene Cayetano, an MP from the President's own party. "I voted for Marcos and supported him, and even *I* felt sick to my stomach. Just imagine how angry the people were who voted for Cory."

It was the last straw, the final insult. Defense Minister Juan Ponce Enrile's own son Jackie sat down and wrote his father a letter: "I will never fathom how such a great man can stoop to such lowness as to cheat all of us out of our right to choose. . . . I can no longer support such a man." The computer operators at the government's own vote-counting centre stalked out, clutching floppy disks that proved the results had been skewed.

They ended up in Baclaran Church at 3 a.m., tearfully pouring out their story to the world press and a pop-eyed group of U.S. congressional observers. The country's Catholic bishops met, and launched a stinging attack by the Church on the State. The Marcos election victory was "tantamount to a forcible seizure", the clerics decided. The resulting government thus had "no moral basis" to rule.

What happened next is known to everyone . . . but to almost no one.

2 THE HIDDEN PLOT

THERE WERE NO REPORTERS in the northern Sierra Madre mountains, a few weeks before the revolt, to record the gigantic fireball that leapt into the sky and shot flames far beyond the treetops. The few young military officers who watched from behind rocks just grinned and shook one another's hands. Their 100-pound incendiary bombs worked like a charm. This was going to be some kind of a goddam barbecue.

At a "safehouse" in a Manila suburb, Lt.-Col. Eduardo "Red" Kapunan was making little x's on a scale model of Malacañang (pronounced Malacan-*yang*) Palace. It was a magnificent model, the size of a Ping-Pong table, accurate to the slightest detail. But Kapunan's wicked sense of humor had recently taken over; he had raided a toy department and come home with fistfuls of tiny plastic soldiers, tanks, cars, and guns, then set them artfully in their actual spots along the Palace defense perimeter. Other members of the Reform the Armed Forces Movement (RAM) found the toys a bit much, but Kapunan enjoyed the added realism. The stores did not sell toy plastic firebombs, so the colonel just marked nine x's where the explosives would be planted. One of them was painted on a toy car outside the front door of General Fabian C. Ver, Chief of Staff of the Armed Forces of the Philippines.

Meanwhile, General Ver's own men were making daily trips to a horrid little island in Manila Bay off the tip of Corregidor. It is a jagged piece of rock called Caballo, without fresh water or vegetation, and it is usually surrounded by sharks. Indeed, it bears an uncanny resemblance to the island of Alcatraz – a likeness that had not escaped the President's loyal military henchman. Ver's men were erecting crude barracks, a cookhouse, and a few large water barrels. They had also commandeered a pair of old-fashioned navy landing craft, huge flat-bottomed boats of Second World War vintage. The scows were smelly and rusted, but they would hold a lot of people and could be used as processing centres. That would be important when "Operation Everlasting" went into effect. It was one thing to round up all the President's political and military opponents, quite another to keep them isolated. Caballo Island was an inspired choice. Cory Aquino, Cardinal Jaime Sin, and dozens of others would be safe there, far from the prying eyes of international media and the human-rights busybodies.

These ominous events occurred just beyond the reach of the press and the Filipino people. But their submerged shape was slowly rising into view. By Thursday, February 20, 1986, a military information officer had gathered reporters from the anti-Marcos media and told them to stand by, because something "big" was coming. The next day, opposition politician Aquilino Pimentel leaned over the table in a Manila coffee shop and handed me a front-page story. "Cory [Aquino] is trying to keep the military out of it," he said, just before joining her on a trip to Cebu. "We're afraid they're going to take power. If they do, who knows if they'll ever give it back? This could be the end of democracy here."

On the afternoon of Saturday, February 22, the boil finally burst. Defense Minister Enrile and Deputy Chief of Staff Lt.-Gen. Fidel V. Ramos barricaded themselves inside Camp Aguinaldo with about two hundred armed men. At 6 p.m., the two astonished the world by publicly breaking with President Marcos and pledging their lives to his overthrow. Enrile told a press conference he was "morally convinced that it was Mrs. Aquino who was elected by the Filipino people". He told his countrymen to "wake up to what is happening in our land" and confessed to knowledge of 350,000 fake ballots in his native Cagayan region alone. Now, he claimed, Marcos was going to concoct a fake coup attempt, then use it to arrest all his opponents. Already, roundup orders had been issued for Enrile's men. His own arrest would surely follow. The "rebels" had assembled purely in self-defense.

The reaction from President Marcos was surprisingly slow in coming. He did not appear on television until four hours later, when a thin human barricade had already begun to form around the rebel camp. The President's version of events was utterly different: Enrile was not "resigning" at all, said Marcos. The minister's top military aides were part of a coup d'état that had been sniffed out and broken by Palace security. To prove it, Marcos brought forward Captain Ricardo Morales – Imelda's own security escort – who, white as a sheet and barely able to speak, confessed his role in an elaborate coup attempt.

The rebels laughed off the charge as another of the President's fantastic lies. "There is no Ricardo Morales in the Philippine military," huffed Enrile, and the vast majority of Filipinos readily believed him.

Civilians flocked to the barricades by the hundreds of thousands, until two million eventually protected the rebel camp with their bodies. They quaked in fear beneath the metal treads of Loyalist tanks, fell back under tear-gas attacks, and cowered in the spinning shadows of helicopter gunships. But when the military balance of power swung to the Enrile-Ramos faction, they won the greatest victory in their nation's history. The hated dictator gathered up his loot and ran, a thief in the night.

He is now in Hawaii, a shrivelled little rich man in an ill-fitting black suit and a pale-blue golf cap. His wife, our lady of the 2,700 pairs of shoes, is an international laughing-stock.

So much, and remarkably little else, is known for certain about the 75-hour revolution. The army of excellent journalists who covered the uprising spent a couple of weeks after the event digging for its "inside" story. We each published one version or another, many of them tremendously exciting – and none of them came even close to the truth.

But that was not our fault. The young Reform the Armed Forces (RAM) officers who in fact masterminded the revolt had spent more than a year in a systematic "disinformation" campaign, carefully lulling President Marcos into a false security while they tested their firebombs out in the hills. The Reformists became masters of the "cover story", wrapping every move in labyrinthine layers of deceit. They always had clever fallback positions, "inside" tidbits that could be leaked to the anti-Marcos press. But those, too, were meticulous lies. So it was with a delicious irony on the fateful Saturday night that the rebel officers realized that all of us in the press believed *their* version.

"Yeah," grins Captain Ricardo Morales, who was indeed Imelda's military escort and most certainly was part of a plot to seize the Palace, "it was a wonderful moment in our history. For once in his life, Marcos was telling the truth. And nobody believed him. Nobody in the whole world believed him."

The Reformists painted President Marcos as the aggressor and themselves as peaceful defenders. As always, the story had a grain of truth. The President's guest list for Caballo Island did include Enrile, Ramos, and the key RAM officers. But that roundup was still a few days away when the balloon went up on Saturday afternoon. The rebels' own preemptive raid on the Palace – a bloody blitzkrieg that would have fried alive the entire Presidential Security Command – was set for 2 a.m. Sunday morning. By dawn, according to the secret plan, the country would have woken to find its First Family prisoners in their own Palace, and a friendly Reformist officer beaming from their TV sets. He would announce the creation of a "provisional" ruling council, with none other than Juan Ponce Enrile among its members. Free and fair elections were supposed to follow.

Now the plot was discovered and the script had changed – so the rebels were forced to ad-lib a whole new scenario. But since no one believed Marcos, their main problem was to keep a straight face while reciting the most outlandish falsehoods.

"We lied like hell," smiles Colonel Kapunan, intelligence chief of the "special operations group" which was Enrile's personal security force. "We were saying 'No, that's a lot of baloney' to everything Marcos said. We didn't want anyone to believe the President, because, if we confirmed it, that would make us look malicious. A lot of people would have sympathized with us anyway. Many Filipinos *wanted* the army to try a coup against Marcos. But we couldn't afford to alienate others or give him any credibility. It was decided to lie."

Kapunan was the designer of the coup plot, the guardian of its much-cherished scale model, and the man who discovered that the plan had been compromised by a last-minute security leak – and who later found the source of the leak. He was also singled out by President Marcos on the Saturday night TV broadcast as one of the key plotters.

"When I heard my name on TV, I put on the most innocent face I knew how," he says. "Right after Marcos said that, I talked to a newspaperman and said, 'Oh, come on. How can that be true? I'm in the air force. I'm not an infantryman. How could I possibly lead an attack?' Everyone nodded their heads and wrote it down. I've still got the clipping."

Lt.-Col. Oscar "Tito" Legaspi, another member of both the coup plot and Enrile's security group, took less delight in play-acting his role as innocent victim. "I kind of hated to lie to you guys about it," he says now. "I never thought we had anything to be ashamed of. The real shame would be if nobody in the military had the guts to throw Marcos out. But we couldn't take any chances. The odds were really against us at that point, and the main thing we had in our favor was public sympathy. We couldn't gamble on losing it."

That is why I and my colleagues spent so much of our time filing fiction from the scene of the Philippine revolt. But it does not explain what happened later. In the midst of that glorious national celebration, many fine Western journalists put their best efforts into uncovering the true story. Meanwhile, at least half the Filipino literary community set off on a race to create inspiring instant books on the subject. Millions of words clattered over the Telex wires and rolled off printing presses . . . while the Reformists debated among themselves whether to come clean. By the time they decided to do so, the foreigners had gone home, and the instant Filipino histories were already sitting on bookshelves.

The result is a massive misunderstanding of the revolt, still, all over the world, and even among the nation's most informed people. Prominent Filipino businessmen, church leaders, and government officials were astonished during my research interviews to hear that I had also spoken to Ricardo Morales. ''You mean he actually exists?'' gasped the principal of one Catholic college. ''Does he look anything like the guy that Marcos put on TV?'' It is still difficult to convince most Filipinos that RAM was going to incinerate the Palace guard – although the group's own leaders now freely admit it.

The rebel cover stories were just too delicious, too crammed with ''inside'' stuff, to be forgotten. Once they had been reported around the world and enshrined within hard covers, they developed a life of their own. My own experience is typical. There was plenty of interest in the news bulletins that blazed across the Toronto *Globe and Mail*'s front page for weeks. But the highest praise was reserved for the ''deep background'' story I filed three days after the fall of Malacañang – a terrific piece of fiction whispered in my ear by the rebels during those heady post-revolution days:

> MANILA – Trade Minister Roberto Ongpin threw a tantrum last Saturday, when he discovered that someone had arrested his bodyguards. And by that slim thread, the regime of President Ferdinand Marcos began to unravel.
>
> The arrests meant nothing to Mr. Ongpin, except his personal inconvenience. But someone listening to him complain in a Manila hotel coffeeshop knew exactly what was happening:
>
> The rumors were true. Mr. Marcos was going to concoct a fake coup attempt and use it to arrest all military and political opponents, then declare martial law.
>
> It was time to run and hide. Or stand and fight.
>
> That is the fateful scenario which kicked off last week's lightning Filipino rebellion, according to detailed accounts that have begun to leak from the major participants. They now admit there was indeed a military action planned against Mr. Marcos. But they say it was not a Palace coup, and it was not scheduled to start until today.
>
> ''We were going to seize some military bases in the prov-

inces, places where we were already in the majority," says one Reformist officer. "Then the pressure was supposed to grow, little by little, from those secure areas. Nobody was going to attack Malacañang, and nothing was scheduled until Feb. 28."

Mr. Marcos, however, apparently got wind of the plan, and hatched a devastating counter-blow of his own. He would seize some military men loyal to Defense Minister Juan Ponce Enrile, then force confessions of involvement in a coup d'état and assassination plot against the First Couple. That would be used to arrest Mr. Enrile, deputy chief of staff Gen. Fidel Ramos and, eventually, the then-opposition leader Corazon Aquino and her top aides.

"That was the intelligence report we got," said the Reformist. "But nobody knew whether to believe it."

Then came the sudden arrest of Mr. Ongpin's bodyguards – all loyal Enrile men – and the defense minister's security staff quickly put two and two together. They began a desperate attempt to find their boss before the Presidential Security Command could seize him. . . .

Et cetera, ad nauseam. This was one of about four variations peddled at the time. One stressed a provincial rebellion as the "real" RAM goal; another mentioned an attack on the Palace as a "rescue" plan, but only if Enrile and Ramos were imprisoned there. Still another spoke of a mysterious "Plan B": to establish a "war footing" against Marcos and go down fighting as a "symbolic" gesture to "establish a military tradition for future generations".

All of the stories were, like mine, essentially fairy tales. The RAM officers might be idealists, but they had no intention of offering themselves as sacrificial lambs. "We weren't kidding around," says Colonel Legaspi. "We were going all the way. In fact, we didn't even have a contingency plan for retreat. There was no room for failure, no turning back." Asked how many presidential guards the Reformists expected to kill, the colonel grinned from ear to ear: "Everyone who wasn't on vacation or leave."

Still, the myths die hard. The best Philippine book on the revolt, journalist Cecilio T. Arillo's *Breakaway*, appeared in August 1986 – still repeating the rebels' cover stories as fact and stating flatly that "there was no . . . plot to seize power." The Arillo account, subtitled *The Inside Story of the Four-Day Revolution*, was widely accepted as true and even hailed as the Reformists' own version of the uprising.

Once again, the false impression was not the journalist's fault.

"I'm afraid we're to blame," Red Kapunan conceded, shortly after *Breakaway*'s publication. "There was a big quarrel in our group about what kind of picture we should show. And it hadn't been resolved when Arillo was doing research. Many of our members felt that if we revealed our 'naughty' actions, some people would be afraid of us. They might figure that, if we did it once, we are capable of doing it again. So our intention those first weeks was to present a 'tame' scenario, and not paint ourselves as monsters.

"Personally, I didn't like it. The truth will come out some time. It is better if we just tell it the way it happened. Our members have never agreed to that . . . but some of us have made a personal decision."

In fact, the RAM officers have little to fear from the truth. Their plans were crystal-clear and perfectly in accord with the will of most Filipinos: they would turn Malacañang into a gigantic frying pan, roast the President's security command, and hog-tie the First Family in the Palace basement. Then they would put the Marcoses on trial and hand the government over to a civilian council.

Among those "civilians", however, was a certain defense minister whose own boundless political ambition is now only too well known. And whatever Juan Ponce Enrile chose to dub his ruling "council", the world would have called it a junta. Mr. Enrile denies any specific knowledge of the coup plot, and claims he was informed only on the day of the revolt. But that is nonsense. The Reformists themselves admit that the minister was involved virtually from the outset, and even helped by gathering Palace intelligence during cabinet meetings.

The plan would have worked, too, if a man from a certain foreign embassy had not leaked the whole thing to President Marcos. Now, why on earth would someone do a thing like that? But, first, who are these reformists who planned a military assault, and wound up staging a massive public relations coup?

3 "ALL THE GUYS WILLING TO DIE"

"GRINGO" HONASAN'S OFFICE behind the Philippine defense ministry could be the props department of a Rambo movie. A blue bullet-proof vest hangs from the barrel of a wall-mounted Uzi machine gun. An M-16 assault rifle and a beat-up guitar are propped against a stereo speaker, beside a motorcycle helmet, an old hunting knife, another flak jacket, a pair of Nike running shoes, and one of those sleek, Israeli-made Galil rifles with the black-plastic stocks. Three long shelves of books provide a catalogue of killing: *Psychological Operations in Guerrilla Warfare, Secrets of the Ninja, Forbidden Fighting Techniques of the Ninja, Silencers for Hand Firearms*, a sky-diving book titled *Body Pilot*, and a video cassette called "Rock 'n Roll #1 – Fully Automatic Machine Gun Fun". "More than 20 of the most modern, state-of-the-art automatic weapons are demonstrated in this exciting, action-packed video tape," says the blurb on the box. "Assault rifles, pistols and shotguns from most major manufacturers are featured in actual test-fire situations. 45 minutes, color, w/ freeze frame and slow motion."

The sign on the door says: "My Wife, Yes. My Dog, Maybe. My Gun, Never." Honasan throws it open, crushes your hand in a vice-grip, and flashes a perfect set of teeth. He is wearing a black T-shirt with SNIPER in bold letters across the chest, and a smaller message below: "Mess with the best. Die like the rest. One Shot – One Kill."

This is the revolution's heart-throb, the "cute" rebel, the man one local newspaper dubbed "the Lancelot of the revolt". Quick-witted and armed with a mischievous smile, he has a reputation as a one-man death squad, a ninja without the mask. Honasan carries nth-degree black belts in both *goju*-style karate and an ancient Filipino martial art called *arnis*, and his airborne exploits are legendary: The time he leapt from an airplane with a pet python named Tyffany double-wrapped around his neck. The time he taught a business school course and began by forcing the whole class to jump from a plane. And that time he planned to skydive with his two-year-old son . . . then backed down when Mrs. Honasan threatened divorce.

33

But Gregorio Honasan is not a macho cartoon. Tucked among the deadly bric-a-brac in his office are the *Bhagavad-Gita, The Tibetan Book of the Dead*, a small Karl Marx library, *Bushido: the Warriors' Code*, and a framed photo of the face on the Turin shroud. "I wanted to be a priest when I was young," he shrugs, blushing slightly at the admission. "If my father hadn't convinced me to attend the Academy, you might be interviewing me now about my exploits in stopping tanks with prayers." Instead, he became class president of "Batch '71", the founder of the Reformist Movement, and an architect of Ferdinand Marcos's downfall.

"I never imagined we'd start a revolt," he says. "All we wanted was the restoration of minimum standards of fairness in the military. We begged Marcos to institute just a few very manageable reforms. We were only interested in an army committed to defending the people. The goal was simple: we wanted to recover the lost virginity of the armed forces."

As early as 1982, Honasan began gathering his classmates around boxes of cold San Miguel beer, and drawing up a list of their grievances. The military was rife with corruption, as massive sums of U.S. aid dollars mysteriously evaporated far above the field level. Wounded soldiers took up collections to pay for their medicine, or lay on the battlefield awaiting transportation to hospital. Meanwhile, evacuation helicopters, painted in the blue-and-white presidential colors, ferried Imelda Marcos to her yacht. Military transport planes were to be seen carrying silver Rolls-Royces to birthday celebrations or bringing fresh sod and fruit to adorn lavish garden parties. Yet the soles on the infantrymen's boots were made of virtual cardboard, ammunition was in short supply, and soldiers died needlessly, in hopeless campaigns decreed from above by absentee generals.

The malcontents of Batch '71 were not alone. Other classes held similar gripe sessions, and soon melded into one nameless but determined unit. This embryo group was, however, obsessed with the military niceties, reluctant to seek publicity, and determined to follow the chain of command. Indeed, they made a solemn vow to renounce violence and never to support any coup attempt. But their devastating frankness was in sharp contrast to the toadying of the generals to Marcos.

The Reformists introduced themselves to their fellow officers in February 1985 with a ringing mimeographed manifesto. The paper denounced "the prevailing military culture which rewards boot-licking incompetents and banishes independent-minded professionals and achievers – resulting in an organization with a chronic paralysis of the extremities." The young officers said they had sought leaders among their superiors, but "most, if not all, are too high to be non-partisan, too comfortable to be interested, too wealthy to care. . . ."

Reaction was swift. General Ver's military intelligence unit began sniffing around Defense Minister Ponce Enrile's "special operations group" as senior officers denounced the Reformers in the press. The rebellious talk, they jeered, was the work of "cowards hiding behind a cloak of anonymity".

Such taunts were a slap in the face to the Philippine Military Academy (PMA) grads, who live by West Point's ironclad code of honor. The rebels arrived at the Academy's graduation rites on March 21, 1985, with streamers and T-shirts declaring "We Belong", and daringly unfurled them in front of President Marcos as they broke ranks with their classmates and marched past the reviewing stand in a solid block. The Reformists still didn't have a name, but now there was a defiant message: "We belong to the organization. We're the ones you're looking for. What are you going to do about it?"

Marcos stood rigid and sullen as Honasan, Kapunan, Legaspi, and nearly three hundred other protesters strode past. After delivering the commencement address, he took reporters aside and abruptly dismissed the incident. "Griping in the armed forces is traditional," he sniffed. "All they've done is call it by an esoteric name." That was eleven months, almost to the day, before the gripers drove him from the country.

Defense Minister Enrile, of course, stood beside Marcos on that same reviewing stand, presumably trying to keep a grin off his face. Officially, Enrile played no part in RAM's formation, meeting the dissidents only later for a five-hour grievance session in his capacity as minister. He also denies any advance knowledge of their eventual coup attempt. "No, I did not know," he assured me in a July 1986 interview. "I never asked them about it. They came to me [on Saturday afternoon] and simply said there was an order for our arrest, for the arrest of the members of RAM – including me."

But that is pure fabrication, often contradicted both by the Reformist officers and by Enrile's other statements.

"I knew that I would not be able to get out of government, not probably alive," he told a *Philippine Star* interviewer last year. "So my boys decided to do something about it. They started contacting their classmates, they started talking about the problems of the country. . . . Then things started to develop. They expanded their contacts until finally they told me they were forming a group. And I said go ahead."

Enrile admits purchasing five hundred high-powered Galil assault rifles in 1984, with his own private funds and for his own personal security. A nearly half-million-dollar cache of weapons, for *private use?* "Yeah," says Enrile. "But I gave one hundred to General Ver, to the army . . . essentially on loan to them."

Didn't this raise any official eyebrows?

"No. I told them I needed it for my security. They did not object."

And these guns were placed at RAM's disposal?

"Later on, yes."

The minister's private stockpile actually formed the backbone of the rebel armory on the revolt's first night. And his participation even in minute details of the coup plot is confirmed by many insiders. "Yes, he knew about it," conceded Colonel Kapunan in July 1986, apparently unaware that his boss was still denying it. "In fact, he was helping us with the reconnaissance of the Palace. When he went to a cabinet meeting there, he'd notice the doors and tell us what kind they were . . . what kind of defensive strength. And he was doing most of the political analysis . . . helping decide when we should go [on the coup attack]."

Such contradictions are not surprising, in view of RAM's superb propaganda skills. The Reformists became sitting ducks the instant they unfurled their banners at the PMA, so they developed a knack for protective camouflage. On the surface, RAM seemed to be struggling for survival and thus posed no serious threat to the Marcos government. In truth, the group received massive support throughout the officer corps right from the beginning.

"There was an iceberg-like quality to RAM," as Colonel Legaspi puts it. "Most of it was submerged. There was some noise on the surface to keep the Palace occupied, but most of the real work was done very quietly, underneath. We wanted them to underestimate our strength. At press conferences, we were saying, 'Never, never, never will we rise in arms against the government' " – Legaspi laughs heartily – ". . . and he believed it, too, that Marcos."

The President, in fact, was the target of RAM's most outlandish snow job. His enormous ego concerning military matters was well known, aptly illustrated by the chestful of "medals" he'd accumulated since taking office. Marcos would fervently recount tales of his Second World War exploits at social gatherings, and always stressed his personal affinity with the armed forces. So, when they were finally granted a chance to present their grievances in May 1985, the Reformists arrived bearing a stack of the President's own books.

They had held a day-long dialogue with Enrile, and spent nearly four hours briefing General Ramos on their concerns. But the Palace visit turned into a 45-minute monologue. "Marcos was the only one talking," recalls Kapunan. "He told us that he was once a soldier himself and knew how we felt. It was just the old bullshit, and then it was over. We were supposed to leave." Instead, Kapunan rose and held up a copy of *The Filipino Ideology*, one of many ghost-written inspirational histories supposedly produced by the noted author Ferdinand E. Marcos. The rebel colonel spun a rhapsodic tale of how the group had found inspiration in the book, and had adopted it as their guide. Would the President be so kind as to autograph a few copies, and dedicate them to the Reform Movement?

Marcos could barely keep his feet on the ground. He glided among the soldiers with a broad smile and a felt-tipped pen, patting backs, offering words of encouragement, and scrawling kindly messages inside the front covers: "May this modest volume of mine serve as your guide. . . ." The Reformists rushed off to their Xerox machines and churned out hundreds of copies. For months thereafter, they would wave them under the noses of Marcos generals who opposed them. "That gave us some credibility," grins Kapunan, savoring the irony. "We could show those copies around and say we had his approval. It was all there in black and white, dedicated to RAM."

And, back then, the Reformists still needed the boost. Many officers sympathetic to their aims had shunned them as naive dreamers courting disaster. Others had dismissed them as an outgrowth of Enrile's transparent political ambitions. In the shadow world of Philippine politics, some officers even thought RAM was an outright hoax, a Marcos ploy to show the Americans that he tolerated military dissent.

Meanwhile, the group's inner core gradually dropped away from the main body. "RAM had made commitments about non-violence," explains Tito Legaspi, "and what we had in mind was going to be *very* violent. So there had to be another group. We called ourselves the 'Fourth Classmen' [the Academy term for first-year plebs] and went about our work secretly. We'd recruit people, but only as we needed them, and then we kept them compartmentalized. Even people who were very much involved in the plan didn't know what we were doing. All they knew was their own part."

The shift from benign to "naughty" was so smooth that Reformist insiders no longer remember who first suggested driving President Marcos out of his Palace. Four of the rebels were meeting in June 1985 to review the progress of the RAM movement when somebody pounded a fist on the table and angrily blurted out what everyone was thinking: "This is all bullshit. There's no way in the world Marcos is going to hand us anything. If we really want reforms, we'll have to take them. The only thing that bastard understands is power."

There was no ominous pause, no thunderbolt from the sky. The quartet of young colonels simply nodded their assent and buckled down to work: What is the tactical situation at the Malacañang Palace? How is the defense set up? Who've we got on the inside? Who might be persuaded to betray Marcos? Or was it entirely insane to consider penetrating the most heavily defended fortress in Southeast Asia?

Malacañang is a sprawling white wedding cake of a building, surrounded by a huge park, a ten-foot fence, and five battalions of the crack Presidential Security Command (PSC). It was once a governor's mansion and later the graceful hub of Manila high society. But the Marcoses had sealed the balconies behind bullet-proof glass and turned most of the second-floor windows into walls. No airplane was allowed to fly over the Palace, and roads leading to it were under heavy guard at all times.

"Everybody thinks of our decision as very dramatic," shrugs Colonel Legaspi, one of the those who sat around the table that night. "But it was just a natural progression. We're military people, so you can't remove the option of an armed move. It's natural for us to make use of what we are trained for. At the start, we just wanted to know if we *could* do it – if it was militarily feasible – before deciding to go ahead. But once we began making plans and realized it was possible . . . there was no more doubt. We never really made the big decision. It was inevitable, and unanimous. Once we saw it would work, there was no question of abandoning it."

By no coincidence at all, three of the original plotters were key members of Enrile's elite security group: Legaspi, intelligence wizard Red Kapunan, and the minister's swashbuckling security chief, Gringo Honasan. The fourth was Lt.-Col. Victor Batac of the Philippine Constabulary, a close aide to General Fidel Ramos.

Nor is there anything strange about the absolute unanimity of the coup instigators. All were 37-year-old graduates of the Philippine Military Academy, battle-tested young officers who'd marched out arm-in-arm at the head of the excellent Class of '71. They were now hardened veterans of the guerrilla wars against the Communists in Mindanao and northern Luzon – field commanders with at least four years in the jungle, who had returned to important jobs in Manila. They roamed the country on security missions, blending into the crowd in their blue jeans, T-shirts, and shaggy hair, with a stubby Colt or Luger stuffed in a hip holster. Together they had killed dozens of men, "but honorably, professionally, on the field of battle, in line with a job description which requires us to both kill, and die, on command," as the defiant Gringo Honasan later put it. They were proud of themselves and their cool professionalism, but sickened by the low estate of the Philippine military. They were also united in a visceral contempt for Chief of Staff General Fabian Ver, his three officer sons, and the coterie of rich, corrupt, over-age generals he had placed in charge of the army, navy, and air force.

"The Ver boys were never professional soldiers, including the father," sneers Colonel Honasan. "They have been pretending to be soldiers all these years. You saw it clearly during the revolution. Very young officers, some of them fresh out of the Academy, were out-thinking one president, one four-star general, and a dozen other generals with braid all over their hats. Tactically, General Ver is an incompetent. He came up through the intelligence ranks. His forte is shuffling dossiers and information. He had never commanded anything bigger than a platoon."

The Reformist officers had long been aware of Ver's shortcomings. But the extent of his bungling was not grasped until they had dared to dream the impossible. The colonels began their coup talk with the same attitude as other Filipinos: regarding Malacañang as an impregnable stronghold, surrounded by excellent troops with the best weapons in the military. A closer look, however, revealed astonishing mistakes at every military level.

"At first we thought it was hopeless," concedes Red Kapunan. "But the more we explored, the more we realized General Ver had made a complete misapprehension of the military situation. With all those fiercely loyal, overstaying generals, he and Marcos figured they had control of the armed forces. But these guys were bureaucrats, not commanders, and Marcos was alienating the real fighters by keeping the old guys on. The officers next in line hated him, for depriving them of their chance.

"When push came to shove, all the guys willing to die were on our side. His only true military loyalists were over-aged paper-pushers. We recognized that almost from the outset. Our first priority was to assess everyone's loyalties, and we were amazed to discover how few good people Marcos and Ver could really count on. They never did realize that . . . until they were in Honolulu."

What's more, the rebels noticed a gaping flaw in the Palace defense. General Ver had poured some of the army's best talent into the PSC and ensured its loyalty by putting his son Irwin in charge. But he had relied on sheer force of numbers and had opted almost exclusively for a perimeter defense. Five battalions, bristling with tanks and machine guns in Malacañang Park, were stationed across the Pasig River from the Palace. There was plenty of security along the high walls that surround the whole compound. But the Palace itself was lightly guarded, with no more than two dozen sentries covering the doors and hallways, many of whom spent their time drinking coffee and watching basketball in the guard room.

That seemed only a minor weakness, with such a huge reaction team just 200 yards across the river. But it planted "naughty" seeds in the fertile strategic mind of Colonel Kapunan. Suppose someone worked out a way to capture the armed camp and train its guns on the Palace? Suppose a small squad simultaneously stormed the First Family's living quarters. And, just to let fantasies run wild, let's imagine the attackers had allies *inside* Malacañang – including, say, Imelda's own military escort.

"We arranged a kind of welcoming committee," smiles Captain Ricardo Morales, who, after the revolt, joined his fellow conspirators on Defense Minister Enrile's security team. "The attackers couldn't just run from bedroom to bedroom with a gun, trying to find Imelda. It was my job to know where everybody was."

"Inside the Palace," recalls Colonel Legaspi, "we paid very, very special attention to that little girl Aimee [the Marcoses' ward] and also [grandson] Borgy. We knew that little girl was in there and took special precautions to get her to a safe place. The problem was the guards inside. We didn't know how they'd react. Our teams going in were prepared for anything. We were even willing to absorb extra casualties to make sure the kids and the Marcoses didn't get killed."

Dozens of attack plans were considered, ranging from elaborate diversions to full-scale assaults. Even most Reformists aware of the coup plot believed it would be mainly bloodless. But the core group quickly discarded that notion. From the outset they adopted the "bloody option", starting with huge incendiary bombs planted right beside the Palace armory. "We worried about it a lot," says Legaspi, "but we knew that was the only way. We decided to blow holes in the wall so anyone who wanted to run could get away. And we wouldn't chase them. But that was our only concession. Anyone who fought back was going to die."

This was the final coup plan, distilled by Colonel Kapunan from various earlier versions:

At 9 p.m. Saturday night, two uniformed men in a PSC look-alike patrol car would enter Malacañang Park with nine 100-pound incendiary bombs. These were double-box creations, in which a mixture of diesel fuel and soapsuds in one container would be touched off by two timing devices and a pack of C-4 explosive in another. "At the test in the mountains, the flames went about thirty feet high with a radius of five metres," says Kapunan. "It was a very impressive sight. The stuff has basic napalm characteristics . . . it sticks to walls and burns. Two of them would destroy a one-storey building completely." And nine would do considerably more damage.

The Presidential Security camp is divided into two parts, with General Ver's headquarters, the intelligence building, an armory, and most of the PSC barracks on one side. That south section would become an inferno. The main car bomb was to be set between Ver's house and a fuel depot, putting an immediate end to the chief of staff. Other bombs would be distributed around the barracks, for maximum killing power.

At 1 a.m., an hour before the bombs went off, Colonel Gringo Honasan and a thirty-man attack squad would infiltrate the north end of the camp with inside help. After crossing the river in three rubber boats, they would be met outside the Palace by the "reception committee" of Palace insiders, including Captain Morales.

"As soon as Gringo reports he's well in place, that's when I make my move," says Kapunan, who was to lead 120 men against the PSC compound. This group included six tank crews, plus M-60 tripod machine guns and a few anti-tank weapons. When the bombs erupted on the south side at 2 a.m., Kapunan's men would storm the other end, capturing the motor pool, the Scorpion tanks, and the V-150 armored vehicles while raining bullets on the remaining PSC barracks. Tank cannons would be trained on the Palace. The combination of machine-gun bullets and the fire storm in honor of General Ver was expected to cause widespread panic, so any PSC soldiers left alive would be encouraged to flee through gaps in the wall. "We had Molotov cocktails, too, because there was a shortage of anti-tank weapons," says Kapunan. "And we'd turn machine guns on the barracks because . . . well, because we didn't have any classmates in the PSC barracks."

"Red would absorb the brunt of the defense," says navy captain Felix Turingan, another RAM plotter, "because he was on that side of the river. If he didn't destroy the armory, he'd have been in trouble. But we figured their four or five battalions were too big for a small place. We counted on a lot of chaos, with all those officers giving conflicting orders."

Honasan's men would burst through the Palace doors the instant the bombs blew. With Morales leading the way, his group should hit the

Marcos bedrooms in seconds – depending on the length of the fire fight in the hallways. The rebels expected the defenders to rush to the windows when they heard the blast, then be cut down before they could recover. The tanks poised across the river should dissuade the survivors from mounting any serious resistance.

The Marcos family were to be captured alive, at all costs. "We wanted them alive to answer for their crimes," explains Legaspi. "If Marcos was killed, there's the chance he could become a martyr if we lost. Also, the image around the world would have been bad."

While his buddies took the Palace, Colonel Legaspi himself was to capture Villamor Air Base, the key military airfield a few miles across Manila. This plan was entirely different: minimum bloodshed, maximum deception, and a much larger attacking force. A contingent of 260 Philippine Constabulary officers would arrive Saturday afternoon, ostensibly en route to the provinces. They would book themselves into the camp overnight to catch an early C-130 transport plane. Surreptitiously the PC rebels would drop teams in strategic buildings and make ready to seize the gates. By 4 p.m., one hundred unarmed soldiers from Enrile's home province – dubbed the Cagayan Hundred – would arrive in trucks. Without weapons, they would arouse no suspicion, but their firearms would soon land in a Fokker jet. Before nightfall, the Hundred would go to a secluded hangar and reclaim their guns.

"Our plan was more fun than Red's," laughs Legaspi. "About 9 p.m. we'd just gather around the swimming pool and drink beer, waiting for the bomb attack at Malacañang. About 1:30 a.m. we'd send someone to air force headquarters with a few plates of *pancit* [noodles] and invite the guards to eat. While they were eating, our guys would just take their guns and explain the situation: they could go on eating, or they could get shot. Take your pick."

The rebels were sure Villamor could be captured peacefully. Air force defectors would secure the flight line with bullhorns – simply by announcing the coup and asking others to join. There were plenty of guns to enforce the order, but little likelihood of a shoot-out. Meanwhile, two teams would secure the house of air force commanding general Vicente Piccio, a fervent Marcos Loyalist. "We had prepared Telexes calling for an emergency meeting at headquarters," says Legaspi. "The idea was deceit. We were trying to fool everybody. But if Piccio smelled a rat, we were prepared to invite him to the meeting at the point of a gun."

Simultaneously, smaller assault teams would seize Maharlika Broadcasting, the government's notorious television propaganda network, and other key media outlets. By 4 a.m, hundreds of rebel reinforcements would begin landing at Villamor Air Base and move to surround the presidential Palace. By dawn, reassuring Reformist colonels would go on the air with the news. They would announce the formation of a new ruling "council", and call for civilians to form a protective barrier around Malacañang – the army's own putative version of People Power.

But this "temporary" government remains the question mark of the coup plot. The Reformist core is now happy to reveal its attack plans, yet turns guarded and defensive when questioned closely about the proposed civilian council. "We knew people would be suspicious," concedes Captain Turingan. "We could call it by any name we wanted, but the whole world would call it a junta."

With Juan Ponce Enrile in the driver's seat, that is hardly surprising. The Defense Minister's endless political ambitions had been apparent for years as he jockeyed with other KBL party stalwarts to succeed Marcos. Nor was there any secret about his sudden loss of power in 1983, when the President pointedly shifted military control to his trusted bodyguard General Ver. Filipinos would be wary of any council run by Enrile – a suspicion, it turned out, richly justified by his post-revolutionary behavior.

The Reformists insist they "selected" the minister for the ruling council. "We had to have him there, because we know him," as Colonel Legaspi puts it. "We knew what his aspirations were. We knew he wanted the same things we did." The more likely scenario is that Enrile chose himself, and used the daring young colonels of his security group to carry out the plan. Both the Reformists and their minister deny that. But Enrile admits he gave the nod to forming RAM in the first place. He supplied the rebels with his own five hundred Galils and even scouted the Palace for weaknesses. At the very least, the two sides must have "selected" each other.

Other members of the ruling junta could not be informed of their selection, for obvious reasons of secrecy. But they had been chosen and would have been "secured" during the Palace attack. Proposed members included Cory Aquino (the plan was formed in the summer of 1985, months before she became a candidate), Cardinal Jaime Sin, Prime Minister Cesar Virata, and Rafael Salas, a Filipino expatriate who had become a high-level bureaucrat at the United Nations. Virata was picked as the least offensive representative of the Marcos government, a semi-political technocrat. Salas had been executive secretary to Marcos before breaking with the authoritarian president; more important, he was Enrile's political mentor and *compadre*, his early guide through the white-water rapids of Philippine politics.

By October 1985 the plan was finished and the coup tentatively set for December. Preparations began in earnest as the Reformists quietly set up radios to monitor the Palace and began briefing their attack teams. They left the precise attack date to Enrile, since he was best placed to gauge the political timing for the appropriate moment.

But Ferdinand Marcos tossed the revolutionaries a wicked curve ball. He was not due for re-election until 1987, and had repeatedly denied rumors he might call an early "snap" poll. On November 3, however, he dropped an election bombshell while blinking into the TV lights on a satellite hook-up with the David Brinkley show. He was "thinking" of putting his mandate to the test, Marcos casually told a startled American TV audience. Such a move was entirely unconstitutional, but the objections were brushed aside. Within days, the President confirmed the news to his own citizens: there would be a presidential election on February 7, 1986.

"Maybe it was stupid of us," says Colonel Kapunan, "but we gave him the benefit of the doubt. Everyone was saying it was the last chance for democracy in the Philippines. Thousands of foreign press and observers were coming. Who could tell? Maybe he was sincere. You know, hope springs eternal. So we put our plans on hold. We decided to give him one last chance."

Meanwhile, RAM took advantage of the immense international scrutiny to kick its movement into high gear. The Reformists held press conferences to announce "Kamalayan '86" (it means "awareness"), a campaign to foster integrity within the armed forces and to curtail the flagrant abuses of past elections. Since the military had always been the main tool of Marcos's ballot-busting tactics, the campaign drew worldwide media coverage. The press also enjoyed the subsequent fencing matches, in which RAM would announce a consciousness-raising "prayer meeting", only to have General Ver cancel it. Various generals met the group to convey ill-concealed threats from above – which the Reformists delighted in leaking to the opposition press.

But even the most seasoned observers considered RAM a mere irritant to the all-powerful Marcos-Ver axis. When questioned about their movement's strength, the young colonels would shift uneasily and admit they had only 2,000 of the 13,000-man officer corps, and none of the 230,000 enlisted men. Naturally, they would "never, never, never" consider any military move against the President.

This aw-shucks performance was a complete charade.

"The election was just a cover," admits Red Kapunan. " 'Kamalayan '86' was actually a mobilization exercise. The press conferences were full of disinformation, mostly to make the people in Malacañang feel comfortable. The campaign just gave us an excuse to move around the country and make contacts."

In the guise of working for free and fair elections, the RAM brain trust made three swings across the Philippines, visiting sympathizers in even the most remote battle zones. "It was a tremendous boon to us," says Captain Turingan. "We brought new [military] units to our side, and had a chance to meet with the civilian opposition groups. We were thinking of People Power even back then, although nobody called it that. The response was overwhelming. A lot of them *volunteered* the idea of overthrowing the government. They were *urging* it on us. We didn't have to sell it at all. With some of the units, it was more subtle. Indirectly, they were telling us: 'You have to move against Marcos sooner or later. When the time comes, we'll support you.' "

The blood-spattered election day was a severe test for the reform group. Their spy radios intercepted Marcosian orders for ballot-box snatching and intimidation missions, but there was little RAM could do about it. In the shoot-'em-up southern island of Mindanao, a few Reformist lieutenants threatened to ambush any colleagues who engaged in fraud. And some young officers were forced to brandish their guns in Manila's business district when goons tried to destroy a voting centre.

Mostly, they sat tight-lipped, watched the corruption, and waited. President Marcos had been given his last chance, and had muffed it. Now it was their turn.

4 THE CARDINAL AND THE CHURCH

FOUR DAYS AFTER the dirtiest election in Philippine history, the De La Salle College gymnasium in suburban Manila felt like a great, domed tomb. Hundreds of listless volunteers still manned computers and tote boards for NAMFREL, the National Citizens' Movement for Free Elections, the watchdog group that had marshalled half a million people in a vain attempt to ensure honest polls. But the proud idealists in the "Bantay ng Bayan" ("Guardian of the Nation") T-shirts had been reduced to a dispirited rump. The Marcos media had mocked and smeared them, preparing the way for the President to shut down their inconveniently independent vote count. The last chance for Philippine democracy was slipping away, and its champions were being ground into the muck.

But that gloomy Tuesday morning suddenly came alive as a rumor swept the cavernous NAMFREL centre: "The Cardinal is coming. He will defend us against Marcos." Within minutes a crush of newsmen around the entrance signalled his imminent arrival. Three hundred faces glowed with expectation. "It's true," beamed an excited teenage girl, unconsciously squeezing my arm numb. "Our Cardinal is coming."

Archbishop of Manila Jaime Cardinal Sin burst through the door like a portly film star, resplendent in a white robe, a phalanx of Church security men plowing a path before him. The more aggressive ballot-counters struggled to touch his garments or to kiss his ring, while women clasped hands to their breasts and began to weep. A few of the faithful thrust papers towards him, and he hurriedly scrawled two dozen autographs with a black felt pen. The treasured papers showed "J. Card. Sin", preceded by a small cross.

He had not mounted the stage or uttered a word, but the atmosphere was already one of barely controlled hysteria.

The beleaguered NAMFREL leader, Jose Concepcion, mounted a central observation post and informed his troops how much "their" Cardinal truly loved them. It was only an hour since Concepcion had called the official residence at Villa San Miguel and asked if there might be time for a visit this week. "The next call I got," he beamed, "was from Cardinal Sin's secretary. She said, 'I hope you are ready for him, because he has already gone out the door. He's on his way.' " The applause was thunderous. Only the night before, most of the nation had watched in helpless rage as poor Concepcion was devoured by Marcos media wolves. He had spent two hours on the government-controlled Maharlika television network, under attack by a bully-boy panel of paid hacks and dubious election "experts". They had peppered him with accusations, sneered at his replies, and demanded to know "Who gave NAMFREL the right to speak for the people?"

The Cardinal had obviously been watching, too. He took the microphone from Concepcion with exaggerated gravity, and embraced him warmly. Then he paused for a few seconds, until the bustling computer centre fell silent as a cathedral. Suddenly his ample jowls shook with passion and his voice boomed off the domed ceiling. "You members of NAMFREL, you are the answers to my prayers," he intoned. "The other day, when the President started accusing you, I got mad. So I sat down and wrote him a letter. I said, 'Mr. President, if you keep on slandering these good people, I will have to stand up publicly and call you a liar!' "

It was very nearly a declaration of war. Church vs. State. Sin vs. Marcos, one on one. The crowd sucked in its breath for just an instant, then rattled the gymnasium with an exultant howl. The "beaten" NAMFREL workers were leaping onto chairs and tables for a better view, shaking hands and pounding each other on the back. "Now we've got a chance," said the schoolgirl beside me, who was trying to copy down the Cardinal's speech in a three-ring notebook. Two enormous tears splashed down and splattered the ink all over her page.

His words were gobbled up just as eagerly by the huge foreign-press contingent, which reported the event as if Jaime Sin had seized upon NAMFREL as a visible symbol of resistance to Marcos. In fact he was actually coming to the rescue of his own creation. It had been the Cardinal who urged Concepcion, a wealthy businessman and prominent Catholic lay leader, to form the National Citizens' Movement for Free Elections nearly two years before, then provided him with an elite corps of priests and nuns to act as recruiters and organizers. Though the group's executives appeared to be "civilians", they were in fact devout laymen who "think of our NAMFREL work as a Christian apostolate," in the words of committee chairman Ben Lozare. "We use the bishops to verify possible members, to weed out the saboteurs and infiltrators. And in a lot of areas, where Marcos controls everything, the laymen prefer that the local

NAMFREL chairman be a priest. That way, he is less likely to be threatened or even assassinated."

The same philosophy carried over to the February 7 election watch when the so-called "NAMFREL Marines" were organized as a crack trouble-shooting unit: a SWAT team dispatched to scenes of violence and intimidation. The "Marines" were made up of six hundred of the tiniest, meekest, and holiest-looking nuns that Joe Concepcion could find.

"We don't fight fire with fire," one volunteer told me. "NAMFREL fights fire with God."

But Marcos was a determined and ruthless opponent. In an attempt to counter NAMFREL's charges of election fraud, the government media had even shown scenes of nuns purportedly "stealing" ballot boxes – boxes they were actually trying to keep away from armed Marcos goons. Worse, the crude slander and constant mud-slinging seemed to be working. It had already drawn the idiotic "cheating on both sides" remark from Ronald Reagan, and sensationalist Tagalog tabloids were carrying the same message to poor and semi-literate Filipinos across the country.

Cardinal Sin was not about to absorb such barbs in silence, and now he was declaring war, here in the gymnasium. He waited for the joyful bedlam to die down, then swept his right hand across the Operation Quick Count centre in a gesture that seemed to bless every man, woman, child, and computer terminal in the room. By the time he was finished extolling their virtues, even the lowliest NAMFREL number-runner must have felt like a candidate for canonization.

"I know the truth about you!" shouted the Cardinal. "I know you are doing your best to restore the freedom and dignity of the Filipino people. I know how much courage you have shown, and how much you have suffered in the recent elections. The Bible says much about the virtue of suffering . . . and you, you members of NAMFREL, have shown me how to suffer. I am inspired by you, and sometimes I am ashamed. I should be the one to inspire you, but it is the other way around. Some of you have died for your country, but now I ask you to go forth and *live* for your country!"

He continued in that vein for fifteen minutes, speaking without notes, yet never at a loss for a majestic phrase, his delivery punctuated by ominous pauses and stirring tremolos. Now the Cardinal was set for the grand finale, a blood pledge of fidelity between the Church and NAMFREL. "In you," he told the volunteers, hand extended in benediction, "lies the Spirit, and may the Lord bless you. We will abide with you. We will support you to the very end. Thank you so much."

By this time there was no holding the crowd. The Cardinal's polite security men were no longer a match for the delirious mob that swept over them in waves. But the chaos took a benevolent, utterly Filipino, form. After crashing through the defenders, the first assault wing threw on its brakes to keep from bowling over their precious, corpulent Cardinal. They wanted to touch him, kiss him, embrace him . . . but only oh-so-gently. So the second and third waves were held back by their own companions. "Don't harm our Cardinal!" came the cry. Instinctively a hundred pushers and shovers made the sign of the cross, and tried to look terribly contrite.

Foreigners took little note of this tender tug-of-war, abruptly thrusting microphones in the church leader's face and shouting questions above the din. "Is this an endorsement of NAMFREL's count? Do you think Cory Aquino won the election? Will you denounce the official results as fraud?" But the Cardinal was preoccupied, offering his ring to the faithful with one hand while using the other to scrawl "J. Card. Sin" on the hats, tags, and slips of paper pushed towards him. He somehow arrived at the Radio Veritas table, where he was slated to deliver a pro-NAMFREL speech to the nation. The noisy journalistic scrum made that impossible, so Jaime Sin switched on a puckish smile and filled everyone's tape recorder with quotes.

"You cannot truly enjoy Easter Sunday unless you have suffered the pain of Good Friday," he told them, in his strong Visayan accent. "This is our Good Friday, but Sunday is coming soon. Stay here and wait for it. Don't leave us yet. You must stay and see the Resurrection." Uttered by anyone else, such remarks might now be construed as evidence of complicity in the Reformist plot against Marcos. There was the Cardinal, just ten days before the Enrile-Ramos revolt, openly telling the world press to stick around for an explosion. But no, the Cardinal did not have any fore-knowledge – at least not in the normal sense. He was merely repeating the line he had promulgated for weeks: that God would not allow "Evil" to triumph; that prayer and faith would somehow topple the dictator and restore justice.

A bad government, he later explained, is "God's punishment to a nation. We can return to God through repentance and penance. Then the bad leader is removed, because he is considered a scourge, and a good leader is granted. These are the scriptures teaching us this. And so we fasted. I had been all over the country to tell the people about penance. And then, when the people were prepared, I said, 'The result will be clear. The Lord will help us.' It had nothing to do with psychic powers or knowing about the RAM plot. It was purely scriptural, purely spiritual. Call me a good guesser if you want. That's why I told the reporters to remain with us. I knew something was coming from the Lord."

That confidence was sorely tested within seconds of his impromptu NAMFREL press conference. A Radio Veritas announcer drew close to the Cardinal and, ashen-faced, delivered a horrible news bulletin. Evelio Javier, the popular former governor of Antique Province and a prominent Aquino supporter, had been brutally gunned down. A half-dozen killers had peppered him with bullets in a town square that morning, chased him when he fled, and pumped a final coup de grâce into his forehead as he lay dying in a toilet stall.

There is only a small range of standard human reactions to such news. All around the Cardinal, faces were contorted in grief, shock, and outrage. Javier was a brilliant and much-respected politician, a rising star who had been compared to Ninoy Aquino in his own early days. Now the ultimate parallel had been drawn. Javier's assassination was obviously intended to intimidate the opposition, and to silence the outcry against the rigged Marcos victory.

The Cardinal had known Javier very well, but his reaction to the assassination was an extraordinary contrast to that of the rest of us. He twice nodded gently as the radio man recounted the details, then responded with a brief, dismissive wave of his right hand. "Evelio is safe now," he said softly. "He is in a better place." With that, the Cardinal turned to the Radio Veritas microphone, nodded to a technician, and launched into yet another stirring defense of NAMFREL.

I was standing less than three feet away, and the Cardinal's response struck me like a blow to the chest. He was not expressing mere belief in God, but absolute certainty. He did not merely hope and pray that Javier would be all right, he *knew* it for a fact. His facial expression was a strange mix of relief and impatience. "Ah, good," it said. "At least Evelio is all right. One less lamb for the shepherd to worry about. Now let's see what can be done for the rest of the flock." To a Protestant skeptic such as myself, such profound faith was nearly incomprehensible. Until then, I had thought of the Philippine Catholic Church as a wealthy and dogmatic bureaucracy; its opposition to Marcos had seemed mostly symbolic. All that talk of Good vs. Evil and "God On Our Side" was the standard rhetoric of battle, the same absurd claim made by everyone from Hitler to the Ayatollah Khomeini.

But Jaime Sin had put a large dent in my cynicism. Who knows? Maybe God did care about the millions of poor, devout Filipinos pleading for His intercession. One thing was sure: the Javier assassination had failed to intimidate the Cardinal. Far from being frightened, Asia's most powerful Catholic was going calmly about his task in the certain expectation of his country's Resurrection.

This, of course, was not at all the prevailing view among my colleagues in the foreign media. I had dinner two nights later with a rowdy tableful of TV journalists who were debating the wisdom of sticking around any longer. The show was over, they said. We could tell the world what we pleased about election fraud, but Marcos had "won" another six years – and had the raw power to enforce that charade. He controlled the army, a hand-picked judiciary, and a puppet National Assembly. He did not need global approval. Even if Washington pressured him into cosmetic "reforms", the Philippine dictator was hardly about to reform himself out of power.

The logic was compelling, and I mentally ticked off point-by-point agreement. We sat considering this dim future, until someone launched into an unexpected spiel of romantic nonsense about the Catholic Church. "It's just not going to happen that way," he argued. "Cardinal Sin and the Church won't *let* it happen this time. They're not afraid of Marcos, and they're not going to stop until he's gone. These guys aren't fooling around. It isn't politics with them, it's a moral issue: Good versus Evil. They won't just stand by and watch Evil win." We all turned towards the source of this naive paean to the Cardinal, and I was astonished to discover it was me. Obviously the idea had been percolating for two days, and had leapt out virtually unbidden. It was intellectually indefensible, of course, nothing more than a gut reaction to the NAMFREL drama. But, having babbled on about it, I had no choice but to spend the next half-hour trying to spin out a barely plausible scenario.

Marcos had for years criticized the Catholic bishops for their unwarranted intrusions into politics, and had even accused them of harboring Communist sympathizers in their ranks. But he had always been careful to couch the attacks in oblique language, avoiding any direct assault on the Church itself. In a country that is ninety per cent Catholic, where half the female population seems to be named Maria, Lourdes, or Evangeline and no home is complete without a wall shrine to the Santo Niño, the Christ-child, it is political suicide to declare open war on the Roman Church.

So what would happen, I wondered, if the Church declared war on Marcos? The thousands of parish priests had infinitely more credibility than the "barangay" (district) captains and political hacks of the ruling

KBL party machine. What if they simply informed their parishioners that Cory Aquino had won the election and should be regarded as president? What if two million people surrounded Malacañang and demanded Marcos's resignation? What would he do? What *could* he do?

The theory sounded vaguely plausible, but it was in fact shot full of holes. In the first place, such drastic action would almost certainly run afoul of the Vatican. Pope John Paul II could hardly condemn the "liberation theology" of Central America while letting Jaime Sin and an army of nuns lay siege to the presidential Palace in Manila. And, even with the permission of the Holy See, what more could the Philippine Church really do? It had fired its heavy artillery during the election campaign, and had raised only an unsightly bump on the elephantine political hide of Ferdinand E. Marcos.

It was Cardinal Sin, after all, who personally forged the Aquino-Laurel ticket after all hope of unifying the fractious opposition seemed lost. According to his own version, Sin bluntly ordered Salvador Laurel to drop his presidential candidacy and support Cory Aquino. "I said to him, 'Well, you are not very attractive. Cory is more attractive and, if you run, you will lose. First of all, you should unite.' He said 'All right, Cardinal,' and a tear came down, a sign that there was an internal struggle. 'If that is what you like, I'll run as her second.' " In retrospect, the last-minute shotgun wedding was a pivotal step on the road to Hawaii. A split opposition would have been a pushover for Marcos, who could have won his "mandate" with only minor cheating, and thus retained grudging world approval.

Instead, the Cardinal set up a dramatic David-and-Goliath battle for the Philippine presidency, and made clear his own preference for the party carrying the slingshot. "The Church has remained absolutely neutral," he told me three days before the election. "We have never told our parishioners who to vote for. We have only urged them to choose the right kind of leadership . . . the kind that will stop the terrible abuses so many Filipinos have suffered". If that wasn't obvious enough, the 58-year-old churchman allowed himself an ironic smile and recited an old Spanish proverb: "To every pig comes the feast of St. Martin". No, he was not being enigmatic. Asked what he meant, the prelate hastened to explain that pigs are blessed and slaughtered at St. Martin's feast. The "pig" in question? None other than President Marcos. "It is just a figure of speech," beamed Sin, playing with the large wooden beads on his crucifix. "I don't mean to call the President a pig. It simply means that everyone's turn will come. There is an end to everything. We all die, whether we like it or not."

Manila's archbishop was supposedly walking a tightrope between religion and politics. But during the election and subsequent revolt, he leapt off that rope and cracked it painfully across the back of Ferdinand Marcos. A telling example was his strange edict that Filipinos could accept bribes on election day – providing they voted their conscience. Aside from partly sanctioning the practice of vote-buying, the rule also violated the precepts of *utang na loob* (the "debt of gratitude") which bind Philippine society into an exchange of virtual blood debts. According to the code, anyone paid to vote for Marcos simply must do so; anything less would tear at the country's basic social fabric.

"But there really was no *utang na loob* in this case," argues the Cardinal, "because the people were being bribed with their own money. They were poor, they needed it badly, and certain quarters were offering it. We said: 'Take it; it's yours. There's no sin in that. But if you change your vote . . . *then* you have sinned.' "

Nor was the Cardinal alone in his quest for dramatic political change. The Catholic Bishops' Conference met twice during the campaign, and emerged on both occasions with a biting pastoral letter aimed at an unmistakable target. "These elections can become one great offense to God and a national scandal," warned the second missive, published a week before the polls in full-page newspaper ads and recited from every Catholic pulpit. The bishops said God's will had been "flagrantly transgressed in the past", and reeled off a list of Marcos-era skulduggery: "vote-buying, bribery, unwarranted pressures, serious lies, black propaganda, the fraudulent casting, canvassing and reporting of votes, snatching and switching of ballot boxes, physical violence and killing". Despite the President's assurances, moreover, the skeptical churchmen suggested such thuggery was "threatening to escalate to a level never before experienced".

The letters threw Marcos into a rage. He was too clever to counterattack directly, but he set his minions on a concerted drive against the Church. The government's Commission on Elections (Comelec) issued an order prohibiting priests and nuns from engaging in partisan election activities, with threats of fines and long imprisonment. Opposition lawyers noted wryly that no such order had been forthcoming two weeks earlier when a three-million-strong breakaway sect called the Iglesia Ni Kristo issued its formal endorsement of Mr. Marcos. But such ironies went unreported in the dominant "crony" press, which paused in its vilification of NAMFREL and finally opened up on the real target:

"The papacy made a mistake in elevating Jaime Sin to cardinal," charged Teodoro Valencia, a powerful and slavishly pro-Marcos columnist for the crony-owned *Daily Express*. "Only time will tell how much damage he has done to the Catholic Church."

Meanwhile, the object and architect of all this controversy sat behind his walnut desk at the Villa San Miguel, affecting a look of cherubic innocence. "I agree wholeheartedly that priests shouldn't engage in politics," the Cardinal told me, two days after the Comelec order. "What we must do instead is to give guidelines to our people, so they can conduct the election without violence. This is an important human activity, in which we must be deeply involved. It should be the laymen who are engaged in actual politics. Our role is merely to outline the morality governing it. That is absolutely clear. I don't know how they can fail to see it."

As for those provocative pastoral letters, Cardinal Sin had developed an adroit strategy for deflecting criticism. His first line of defense was a simple explanation that "the bishops are only saying certain terrible things are happening, and that these should never happen. That's all. If one party sees itself as the agent of those abuses . . ." The sentence would end with an eloquent shrug. Then would come a conspiratorial wink and the more authentic response. "Did *you* think the letters were too strong?" he'd ask, wide-eyed in mock surprise. "Some people apparently did. Others thought they were too weak. You should hear some of the sermons in the cathedrals. They are much, much stronger."

Indeed they were. At Our Lady of Perpetual Help, a poor parish just outside Camp Aguinaldo, Msgr. Cesar Pagulayan was already telling his flock that the Blessed Virgin would herself rid the country of its hated dictator. This, at least, is what his parishioners now claim, reminding him that he prophesied the February Revolution. The monsignor was too wound up in the anti-Marcos campaign to remember any of his passionate sermons.

"Yes," he grins, "according to some people here, I made certain utterances from the pulpit. I said we should go on praying, not to falter, because I knew God would manifest something for our people. But were they prophecies? I don't know. I can't remember saying those things any more. Maybe they were just strong convictions. I knew the Lord wouldn't just leave us like that. I knew He would do something, send someone to help us."

Msgr. Pagulayan also unearthed a kind of biblical secret weapon to use against Marcos. It began in 1985, when his parish held many special masses to celebrate the Marian Year, the two-thousandth anniversary of Mary's birth. The congregation prayed repeatedly for the Blessed Virgin's intercession in the Philippines, asking her "oh so strongly to help our people fight their oppressors". But, almost by accident, an odd second prayer was adopted by the Perpetual Help congregation.

"Lord, confound the minds of the evil-doers," the monsignor repeats, savoring the words with obvious satisfaction. "Lord, confound the minds of the evil-doers. It comes from the Psalms. I'm not sure how we discovered it, or why we started to say it. But it seemed so perfect for the Philippines and it was such a simple, powerful prayer. We were saying it here a million times before the election and after the election. When the computer tabulators walked out, it seemed like the first answer to our prayer. For me, it was a very clear sign of God's work."

After the election, the walkout of Linda Kapunan (wife of RAM leader Red Kapunan) and thirty other Comelec computer operators on February 9, with their allegations of government cheating, was a crushing blow to the Marcos camp. By no coincidence at all, the Church was up to its clerical collar in that event, too. A group of NAMFREL workers were the first to grasp both the propaganda value of the defection and its inherent dangers. They quickly herded Kapunan's gang into taxis and made for the sanctuary of nearby Baclaran Church. After the press conference and its ensuing uproar, the operators hid in the Kapunan house at Camp Aguinaldo. But they were later moved to a large Church "safehouse" in suburban Quezon City.

"I went inside Linda Kapunan's place in Aguinaldo, and said mass for them all," recalls Msgr. Pagulayan. "I told them they were heroes of the people. I assured them we all loved them, and God blessed them for what they had done. Many of us in the Church felt they were a symbol of God's work. We would do anything we possibly could to help them." Or anything else, for that matter, that would bring down Ferdinand Marcos.

But what more could the Philippine Catholic Church possibly do? Having hand-picked the opposition candidates, fielded a half-million people to oversee the elections, set up an anti-Marcos radio station and weekly journal, castigated the government from the pulpit, ardently prayed for its downfall, and sheltered its enemies, there seemed no stone on heaven or earth left unturned. What next, Cardinal Sin? The Pope's Swiss guards marching on Malacañang? An exorcist to expel Marcos from the accursed body politic?

No, the Church had shot its bolt, and the President was still in command. Tossing in bed at the Midtown Hotel that Thursday night, I silently recanted my restaurant outburst. The Cardinal was indeed a brave, determined, and powerful man. But Marcos was far more powerful, more desperate, and utterly ruthless. Somehow, he would find a way to hang on.

Instead of lying in bed, I should have been out selling my soul to the Devil – just to become a fly on the wall of Cardinal Sin's office. For there, at that precise moment, unfolded one of the most delicious scenes in the history of Church-State relations. Down on her hands and knees on the carpet was none other than Imelda Romualdez Marcos, Minister of Human Settlements, Governor of Metro Manila, Special Presidential Ambassador, and First Lady of the Philippines. She was throwing a tantrum "like a five-year-old", as a close confidant of the Cardinal later put it. "She actually sat down on the floor right there in his office and started flailing her arms and legs about like a small child, crying and beating her fists. Can you believe it?

"The Cardinal was stunned. He just watched her in horror for a few moments, assuming that she would stop. But no, she kept on wailing. Finally he had to pick her up and shake her. He said, 'Imelda, control yourself.' Eventually she stopped crying and ran out the door. Poor Torpigliani" – the papal nuncio, Msgr. Bruno Torpigliani – "had to run out after her."

That scene sounds preposterous, but it happened just as described. No one in the Church wants his name attached to the revelation, but most high-ranking bishops are aware of it, and insiders will gladly recount it in rich detail when assured of anonymity. The Cardinal himself will not reply to a direct question about the Imelda tantrum. He merely smiles wickedly, cocks an eyebrow, puts a finger to his lips, and whispers: "Shhhh."

In retrospect, it is not difficult to understand the First Lady's apoplectic rage. She had been hovering around the Catholic Bishops' Conference for two days as that august body fashioned yet another of its pastoral letters. Obviously this would be a scorching criticism of the corrupt presidential election; that was to be expected by the Marcoses – but not greatly feared. They had weathered the previous broadsides and the worst was now behind them. Imelda's task was to contain the damage, pressuring the two or three pro-Marcos bishops among the 108 in the conference, and smoothing relations with the others. On both days of the 48-hour meeting, her dark-blue limousine had glided up to a side door of the meeting hall, and she had conducted back-seat conferences with confederates. Imelda was followed almost immediately on the second day by Cory Aquino, who sat in a white Toyota waiting for her own insiders to provide a progress report on the pastoral letter.

By Thursday afternoon, Imelda knew that something was terribly wrong. The snatches of phrases being brought to her were not just critical, they were devastating. The bishops had gone far beyond anything in the history of the Philippine Church. They were not preparing merely to slam the Marcos government – this time they would attack it with an ecclesiastical cruise missile.

The letter's introduction was bad enough. The bishops began with the considered judgement that the recent polls "were unparalleled in the fraudulence of their conduct", and listed ways in which the fraud had been perpetrated: the systematic disenfranchisement of voters, the scrambling of the voters list, the "cynical exploiting of the people's poverty" by widespread vote-buying, the deliberate tampering with election returns, accompanied by "intimidation, harassment, terrorism, and murder".

Then, at the bottom of page one, the clerics dropped their first bomb. "These, and other irregularities, point to the criminal use of power to thwart the sovereign will of the people. Yet, despite these evil acts, we are morally certain the people's real will for change has been truly manifested."

The message was unmistakable to any Filipino. The Catholic Church was declaring its moral certainty that Cory Aquino had won the presidency.

Imelda, horrified, had only one place to seek redress. She rushed immediately to a stately mansion on Taft Avenue, surrounded by high stone walls with a locked steel gate and a brass nameplate identifying the Apostolic Nunciature – home and headquarters of papal nuncio Bruno Torpigliani. The Vatican's official representative had been in the Philippines since 1973, through most of the martial-law decade, through half a dozen fraudulent elections, and through the Aquino assassination and the tumultuous "parliament of the streets" that followed. Yet he had remained a loyal friend of the First Lady and the Marcos regime for the full thirteen years. Msgr. Torpigliani was important to Marcos; an Italian who reported directly to the Vatican secretary of state in Rome, he had contradicted the Philippine bishops on virtually every point in his assessment of the 1986 election.

"He bought the Imelda line . . . and hook, and sinker," says a Church insider with extremely close ties to Cardinal Sin. "Torpigliani had been mesmerized by Imelda's charms, though I don't mean, of course, in a sexual way. She is a very persuasive woman, who can make a man feel like he's the only person in the world. And she had spent thirteen years working on the nuncio; he was her personal project. You should have seen the reports he was sending [to Rome] before the election. He told them that it was imperative for Marcos to be re-elected, because Cory could not be a strong president, make reforms, or fight Communism. He said Marcos had already promised reforms, and there was no reason to doubt him. The stuff was just unbelievable."

Even months after the Revolution, any mention of Msgr. Torpigliani still tests the Christian generosity of high-ranking Filipino churchmen. Sin himself is typical; he resorts to acid sarcasm and struggles to remain civil when asked about the Italian's role in the February revolt. The following exchange took place in a June 1986 interview when I questioned the Cardinal about his direct contacts with Rome during the three-day rebellion:

"Well, you can call the Vatican any time," he answered. Then, with an exaggerated grimace and that finger-to-lips gesture: "But the nuncio, of course, is in touch."

"Your Eminence," I persisted, "let me ask you about the nuncio . . ."

"Do not ask me about the nuncio," Sin replied sternly. "It will only endanger our relationship."

Cardinal Sin is willing to discuss the Vatican's involvement in more general terms. He candidly concedes that the Philippine Church waged an uphill battle against Roman reluctance to act, and says the Holy See was desperately trying to pretend that the problem did not exist. "The Vatican usually does not like to rock the boat," he explains. "It doesn't wish to deal with problems. Now, here in the Philippines we had a problem. The Vatican would like to avoid it, but if there is really a problem you cannot just run away. That was our idea. But the Vatican is fomenting collegiality, subsidiarity, and co-responsibility. And we are the bishops here, so we obeyed. And then here came this bigger problem . . . and can we run away from it? No, it cannot be."

It is not politic for Sin to be more specific. But the wily prelate from the Visayas has a foolproof system, in such cases, for getting his real meaning across. He simply refers further questions to his spokesman, Felix Bautista, suggesting that his alter ego might "fill in more details" – which, of course, the editor of the Catholic weekly Veritas was eager and able to do. Bautista is the Cardinal's closest lay confidant, an eloquent political commentator who is also his friend, biographer, speech-writer, and travelling companion. He spends at least two months in Rome every year, accompanying the Cardinal on an endless round of Vatican committee sessions and curial meetings. So he has a comprehensive knowledge of the tug-of-war between "my Cardinal" and Msgr. Torpigliani for the ear of the Holy See.

"My Cardinal knew exactly what Torpigliani was reporting," says Bautista, "because [Vatican secretary of state Cardinal Agostino] Casaroli confronted him. Casaroli said: 'Torpigliani says this and you say the opposite. What's going on?' There was a great battle about it. Cardinal Sin's line to the Pope was: 'Trust me, your Holiness. Trust me. I *know* what is happening here. I am a Filipino.' That was his very simple approach.''

(Torpigliani's own version of these events would doubtless offer a different perspective. But the nuncio maintains strict silence on the matter. He replied to my interview request with a polite written refusal, explaining that he is ''determined to safeguard, at any cost, the mutual charity between all those who were involved in this story . . . convinced as I am that this attitude is the best way to the search for truth.'')

In Rome itself there was unyielding and unsubtle pressure from the Philippine ambassador, Bienvenido Tantoco, whose daily visits amounted to a virtual stake-out of Pope John Paul's office. The Marcoses had not sent just anyone to the Vatican; their personal envoy was one of the First Lady's closest business cronies, a mega-millionaire who had been given the lucrative duty-free store concessions at airports and who owned Rustan's chain of snooty, upscale department stores. His wife, Gliceria, was the very bluest of Imelda's famed inner circle of ''Blue Ladies''. (Blue was the campaign color of the KBL, the New Society Movement, the Marcos-created ruling party.)

''The Pope wouldn't see him often,'' says a bishop from a Western country who was posted to the Vatican. ''But he'd wait around outside and try to strong-arm the various bishops who were going in and out of the pontiff's office. I suppose he was trying to gather a body of support. It was the standard line: priests staying out of politics and Marcos being the only hope to stop communism. Obviously it didn't work very well.''

(The bishops cornered by Ambassador Tantoco may now consider themselves fortunate that he chose not to shove an Uzi submachine gun in their ribs as part of his lobbying effort. Tantoco was arrested in August 1986 by Italian police after they seized a huge cache of arms at his Roman villa. The confiscated arsenal included a dozen high-powered pistols, two Uzis, and about 2,500 rounds of ammunition. The Marcos associate – now an ex-ambassador – also had two bullet-proof vests, electric cattle prods, spiked balls chained to metal sticks, five tear-gas canisters, several radio transmitters, and a large collection of diplomatic license plates. ''This collection,'' understated police captain Ugo Mastrolitto, ''was certainly not for defensive purposes or protection.'')

The furious Vatican in-fighting was at its height as the bishops gathered on February 12 to compose their post-election blockbuster. But if ties between Manila and Rome were strained, Bautista insists there was near-unanimity inside the Philippine Church. "There was almost no discord at all," he says. "One or two bishops said, 'I cannot sign a document like this,' but these were the strongly pro-Marcos bishops. When you realize there are over one hundred bishops, those two were absolutely insignificant. The Cardinal kept a low profile, really. He did not have to pressure anyone. There was a tremendous depth of feeling about it."

Evidently so. As Imelda plotted strategy with Torpigliani, the news from the bishops' conference kept getting worse. Not satisfied with proclaiming Cory Aquino the true election winner, the Catholic bishops proceeded to sweep away the fundamental legitimacy of the Marcos government – and sounded a ringing call for its non-violent overthrow. Their letter said:

> According to moral principles, a government that assumes or
> retains power through fraudulent means has no moral basis. For
> such an access to power is tantamount to a forcible seizure and
> cannot command the allegiance of the citizenry. The most we can
> say, then, about such a government, is that it is a government
> in possession of power. Because of that very fact, that same
> government itself has the obligation to right the wrong it is
> founded on. It must respect the mandate of the people. This is a
> precondition for any reconciliation.
>
> If such a government does not itself freely correct the evil it
> has inflicted on the people, then it is our serious moral obligation
> as a people to make it do so. . . . If we did nothing, we would be
> party to our own destruction as a people. We would be jointly
> guilty with the perpetrators of the wrong we want righted.

Having crossed this Rubicon, the bishops apparently felt there was nothing left to lose. They spent two more pages informing the faithful exactly how to proceed, laying down ground rules for the expulsion of Ferdinand Marcos. It was as if these precise Jesuit minds were leading the average Filipino through a primer on political activism. "The wrong was systematically organized," they instructed. "So must its correction be." But they could not sanction a "bloody, violent means of righting this wrong. . . . The way indicated to us now is the way of non-violent struggle for justice. This means active resistance of evil by peaceful means – in the manner of Christ." Every loyal Church member must form a judgement on the February 7 elections and, if they agreed with the bishops, "we must come together and discern what appropriate actions to take . . . in a creative, imaginative way, under the guidance of Christ's Spirit."

All of the Marcos political heavyweights were occupied elsewhere that Thursday night, pushing a badly tainted election count through the National Assembly so that the President could be proclaimed the winner within legal time limits. Virtually every regional ballot-count bore some outlandish anomaly, but opposition protests were all filed away by speaker Nicanor Yniguez ("Asterisk . . . just place another asterisk on the document") – to be heard only *after* Marcos was sworn into office.

The First Lady had been assigned to handle the Church, and Imelda tackled the crisis with her usual crisp, direct ham-handedness. First, she rounded up reporters from the Philippine press to interview Msgr. Torpigliani on the subject of religious interference in politics. Then she steered Rome's representative to Villa San Miguel – in order to read Cardinal Sin the Vatican riot act. The trio sat late into the night in the Cardinal's second-floor office as Msgr. Torpigliani painstakingly reviewed a list of papal encyclicals, cited precedents, and reminded the Filipino Church leader of the Pope's express order against "liberation theology". Cardinal Sin nodded politely through it all, and said he agreed wholeheartedly with the Pope. Mixing in politics, he assured the Monsignor, was the very last thing the Philippine Church had in mind.

But what about the letter? Imelda demanded.

Oh, *that*. That wasn't interference in politics, said the Cardinal. That dealt strictly with morality: good and evil, public trust, respect for the sovereign will of the people, the moral foundations of society. It said cheating is bad, killing is bad. Those were moral judgements, not political ones. Admittedly there were comments about the kind of governments that had no moral validity. But the letter spoke only of governments in general and did not single out any specific regime. Why? Did the First Lady perhaps have in mind a government that had committed such acts?

Imelda was at the breaking point. According to a source close to the Cardinal, she tearfully pleaded with him not to sign the letter, and to prevail upon the other bishops to remove their signatures. Cardinal Sin replied: "No, Mrs. Marcos. We must release the letter. It is our duty as Christians." The First Lady, who had been standing near the Cardinal's desk, now sank to her knees and appeared for a moment to have fainted. In fact, she had merely regressed fifty years and proceeded to throw a good, old-fashioned nursery-school tantrum. Msgr. Torpigliani remained frozen in the visitor's chair until, picked up and shaken by the Cardinal, Mrs. Marcos eventually ran crying from the room. The nuncio nodded curtly to Cardinal Sin, and stalked out. The two men were not on speaking terms again until April 6, when they briefly and stiffly shook hands at a Rome press conference.

The bishops' letter, issued on February 14, was promptly hailed as the most explicit political document in Philippine Church history, and soon featured in front-page banner headlines around the world. The mainstream Filipino press, however, dwarfed news of the actual document with saturation coverage of Msgr. Torpigliani's opinions and the yowls of outrage from ruling KBL political stalwarts. "I am scared," said assemblyman Rafael Recto. "This statement is inflammatory. If read improperly by people who are hot-headed, they may take the law into their own hands." Labor Minister Blas Ople charged that the churchmen were inciting violence. He said their "rash decision . . . clearly poses an imminent threat to the peace and tranquility of our country during this time when so many are blinded by partisan rage.

"It is not too late," he added ominously, "for the bishops to reconsider."

Marcos, Imelda, and the KBL chieftains all turned their eyes hopefully towards Rome. The good Msgr. Torpigliani fired off urgent messages to John Paul II, asking the infallible arbiter of the Church to crack down hard on his Philippine bishops. For his part, Cardinal Sin simply waited in silence. He'd made his pitch long ago, and could only hope the "trust me, your Holiness" line would hold.

It did, although just barely. The Pope released a lukewarm two-sentence comment on Sunday, February 16, which pointedly ignored the explosive pastoral letter. It wasn't even addressed to the bishops, but "to the church that is in the Philippines . . . [and] all its people." The response was a masterpiece of ambiguity. The Vatican did not want trouble, and would not stand behind its tempestuous Filipino cardinal. Nor, however, would it stand in his way.

Jaime Cardinal Sin was on his own.

5 *"THIS HEIGHT OF TREASON"*

CAPTAIN RICARDO MORALES was not brought into the coup plot until February 15, just seven days before its launching. He was surprised when a friend said Colonel Honasan wanted to see him, and was flabbergasted when Gringo simply laid out the plan and said: "We need you, Dick. Are you with us?"

"I could hardly breathe," recalls Morales, a tall, handsome officer who was on the military fast-track as Imelda Marcos's personal military escort. The army had sent him to business classes at the Asian Institute of Management and had flown him all over the world on the First Lady's trips. At age thirty-one, he was a young man on his way up. And now this smiling colonel had asked him to risk everything, including his life.

"Why did I say yes?" he wonders. "I guess it was because we had lost our self-respect under General Ver. And Gringo . . . well, he has a great reputation, a great combat record. Nobody can pin a thing on him. When he talks, you just naturally trust him. Plus, something this big had to have some support at the top. They had money to spend: buying equipment, uniforms, the Israeli guns. You can't just filch this kind of money without someone knowing. They were buying stuff from abroad, and you can't pay for that with pesos."

Morales agreed to be the "inside man" and lead Honasan to the Marcos bedrooms. But first he had one question. "Sir," he asked the colonel, "are there any political personalities involved in this? I don't want to be drawn into something like that."

"No, Dick," Honasan lied. "It's just the officers."

Morales went home, made a cup of coffee, and wrote a farewell letter to his parents in the southern city of Davao. "Hello all!" it began. "By the time this letter gets to you, things will already have happened that shall affect all of us, as people and as Filipinos. This might be my last chance of communicating with you. . . . I have joined a movement that intends to restore pride, self-respect and democracy to the Filipino and the Motherland. . . . Should I fail, then remember me with pride and understanding. Please don't disown me. . . ."

The headquarters of Defense Minister Enrile's "special operations group" hummed with excitement over the next few days. Coded messages flashed around the country as RAM's provincial allies prepared to seize transport planes and equipment. Guns were ferried in burlap sacks, and there was even a curious little bundle containing five thousand Philippine-flag shoulder patches. With both sides wearing the same uniforms, the patriotic emblems would be the only way to tell the good guys from the bad guys during the Sunday-morning attack.

On Thursday morning, Red Kapunan wrinkled his forehead as he peered inside Malacañang Park. He had memorized its defensive plan, and checked daily for any changes. Now, dammit, there appeared to be an extra battalion inside the compound. Kapunan went back to his office and began making discreet inquiries. He was unusually careful. Only ten days earlier, when thirty-one of the government's own computer operators in charge of tabulating the election had staged their famous walk-out from the vote-counting centre amid charges that Marcos was faking the count, their leader was none other than Red's wife, Linda, and the resulting international publicity had nearly scuttled the whole coup plan. As its architect and team leader, Kapunan could hardly drop out at that point. Nor could he risk endangering others by being seen with them. So he spent the final two weeks in monk-like solitude, scrupulously avoiding RAM's last-minute planning sessions, and doing his job in his own way. Red's assignment was intelligence. From Thursday on, everything he saw pointed to a single conclusion: something had gone terribly wrong.

"At first there were just indicators that we were compromised, nothing definite," he recalls. "The daily reconnaissance showed an unnecessary buildup at Malacañang – right where we were supposed to go. Remember that entry point I showed you on the map? That's where we were coming in, and that's right where one new battalion had occupied. It was too much of a coincidence. By Friday night I was convinced the whole plan had been blown open. I was sure we were compromised."

But RAM held a meeting without Kapunan that night, and agreed to proceed. Go-ahead signals were sent to many of the units right then, while others would await clearance until a last meeting on Saturday morning.

That is where Red Kapunan finally rejoined RAM. The squat, thick-muscled colonel is a formidable-looking man at any time, but at 9 a.m. on Saturday, February 22, 1986, his eyes were dark slits. "The plan is compromised," he informed his inner circle of classmates. "Somebody sold us out!" There was remarkably little panic. The group agreed to hold off on the final signals until Red took another look at the Malacañang compound. When he got there, even more troops were arriving from the provinces. There was no longer any doubt that Marcos and Ver knew what was coming.

Surprise had been a prime factor in the coup plot. With that gone, and the manpower buildup at the Palace, the rebels had no chance. "Our original estimate was for a 95-per-cent chance of success," says Gringo Honasan. "After what Red told us, it was just the opposite. Now the odds were about one-in-twenty to survive. Right then, there didn't seem much chance of winning." Prospects were so bleak that Kapunan phoned a confederate at his "safehouse" and ordered him to destroy the scale-model Palace and detailed plans. If they somehow got out of this alive, it would be best not to see those toy soldiers and tanks at their treason trial.

As Enrile's security chief, Honasan had already taken special precautions. "The minister was at home," says the colonel, "but he was adequately secured. His house, you know, isn't like the airport tarmac. You can't just walk up and blow a hole in his head. There were about sixty men with him."

Bristling with Uzis and anti-tank weapons?

"Not really. The essence of an effective security system is actually information. Guns are just, you know, for cosmetics. Marcos and Ver failed in one very crucial aspect right then. Their information was too shallow. They were tipped that we were coming, but they didn't know exactly who we were, or *where* we were. They couldn't risk an attack and expose their flanks and their rear. So if they tried to arrest the minister, they didn't know what the reaction would be."

A few minutes after noon on that fateful Saturday, the Palace sent a probe to the rebels. Colonel Rolando Abadilla, whose brutality during the martial-law era was legendary, arrived at the Defense Ministry in Camp Aguinaldo with an old-boys'-network message for Honasan. "Greg," he said, "General Ver is asking you not to attack the Palace. After all, you and Irwin [Ver's son] are good friends, and your father and the general are also good friends. Let's not have any bloodshed. . . ."

"Don't worry," Honasan told Abadilla. "We have no such intentions." That was true, but had only been true for about an hour.

Honasan and Kapunan didn't trust the telephone to contact Defense Minister Enrile. They drove without speaking over the ten miles to his house in a prosperous suburb, and went glumly inside. "I'm sorry, sir," Kapunan told his boss. "Something has happened. We're blown wide open." They went to a map in the minister's study and discussed the options. Only two made any sense: disperse to the hills and use guerrilla tactics or make a stand at Camp Aguinaldo. In the midst of their discussions, Enrile's aide-de-camp, Major Noe Wong, arrived to report that even their political plans had been compromised. "Marcos doesn't just know about the tactical operations," said Wong. "He knows all about the ruling council, too."

Enrile pondered for no more than ten seconds. "Okay," he said. "Let's go fight."

Kapunan went outside to his car and yanked the VHF radio from its hook. "Joggers, joggers!" he yelled. "I repeat: joggers, joggers!" It was the codeword to mobilize Aguinaldo and put a freeze on the attack plan. "That didn't cancel the attack," explains Kapunan. "But it put everything on hold. There was no way to go ahead then, because it would kill all of us. But we wanted our people in the provinces to stand by and be ready."

Simultaneously, the order sent a team of volunteers scurrying to evacuate and hide RAM families all across Manila. The rebels had enough on their hands without worrying about whether General Ver was rounding up their wives and children.

Lt.-Gen. Fidel Ramos was in his living room at the time, surrounded by two dozen women bedecked in yellow T-shirts and headbands. The contingent of Cory's Crusaders had come to wave "Ramos resign!" picket signs outside his modest suburban bungalow in Alabang and denounce him as a coward for siding with the government in the election dispute. Typically, the soft-spoken "Eddie" Ramos invited them in for a drink and a chat. In contrast to Defense Minister Enrile, the General had minimal security at his home. Ramos was not involved in the planning of the coup and had no "official" knowledge of it. But his men kept him in touch. As late as Thursday night he had patted one RAM colonel on the shoulder and smiled: "Just don't make it too bloody."

The Ramos phone rang about 2:30 p.m. as a maid was serving cookies. "Eddie," said Enrile. "We're in this bad condition. We're about to be rounded up. Will you come in with us?"

"Sir, it's best not to use this phone," answered Ramos. "It is not secure." Then, almost as an afterthought, he added: "Of course, I'm with you all the way."

"Good. Let's meet at Camp Aguinaldo."

Enrile rushed to the camp with his security escort. Ramos, in his usual unhurried fashion, lit a cigar and spent two more hours chatting with the female Crusaders. The pivotal press conference was slated for

6 p.m. but was delayed a half-hour as the General puttered around the house, taking his own sweet time to get there.

Captain Ricardo Morales never got the freeze order. He had received his final go-ahead Friday night, and attended Saturday morning business classes as usual at the management institute. Then he went directly to Malacañang, trying his best to appear nonchalant. Morales was not scheduled for duty that day, but it was not unusual for security escorts to appear in civilian clothes on their days off. Just to avoid suspicion, he left his gun at home.

"I was sitting in the military aide's office on the ground floor of Malacañang, and I was having a very decent conversation with a classmate," recalls Morales. "And then suddenly Colonel Rex Ver – the other Ver son – comes running into the room with one of those clutch bags. You know, the ones they carry around with a gun inside. He had his open. He looked around and dashed out again. I was surprised. This guy doesn't usually hurry. That was my first inkling that something was wrong. Then he came back later and said, 'Irwin wants to talk to you.' I said, 'Okay, fine, I'll wait.' That was really suspicious, because how did he even know I was there? I don't report to him. And secondly, why would he want to see me? But if I tried to escape, they might shoot me. So I decided to bluff my way out. I sat there and tried to be as calm as possible. There was nowhere to go. I assumed they'd already blocked the exits."

Colonel Irwin Ver entered the room minutes later, also attempting to sound casual.

"So, Dick, what's the news? What's happening?"

"Well, I'm going to school. I've got some tough exams coming up in two weeks, and . . ."

"You know, Dick, the reason I wanted to see you . . . uh . . . We've received some very disturbing information about officers getting involved in politics. Especially with the opposition."

"Really?"

"Yeah. And, you know, *you* figure very prominently in this report."

Morales tried every conceivable bluff. He argued that he had everything to lose by such involvement, and nothing to gain. The First Lady had been wonderful to him. He'd been promoted. He'd been sent to school. . . .

"Yeah," replied Irwin Ver. "It's all true. That's why we were so surprised at you. Why would you do something like this? We have very reliable information from an unimpeachable source that you are part of this plot."

Morales was arrested and taken from the Palace across the river to the intelligence office in the Malacañang Park compound. There, an interrogating officer laid out the whole RAM plot in detail; he claimed that Honasan and Kapunan had already made confessions, then demanded one from the captain. "I was really shocked," says Morales. "They gave me the times, landing spots, the number of men. And everything was right. They seemed only to know about the Palace attack, not the rest of our plans. But everything they knew was right on."

For five hours Morales argued with his interrogators and refused to sign various confessions. "If they didn't shoot me, I'd have to defend myself in court. So I refused to sign. Then, just when I figured they'd send in tough guys to beat me up, someone came and took me back across the river."

Morales was marched in handcuffs back into the Palace and led down a long corridor. He emerged to find himself in an ornate sitting room, face to face with Ferdinand Marcos. The President was pasty-faced and upset, but did not appear worried.

"I'm surprised," said Marcos. "I didn't know they were going to do this."

"Who, sir?" asked Morales.

"Enrile and Ramos. How could they do this to me?"

Morales was confused. He had no idea that the Defense Minister and the Deputy Chief of Staff were involved. It was now 10 p.m., nearly four hours since word of their breakaway had been flashed around the world. But Morales had been sweating under interrogation lights while the rest of the country listened transfixed to the rebel press conference on Radio Veritas. Strangely, the room where he met Marcos was also flooded with bright light. A military aide explained they were TV lights: Morales would have to videotape his confession.

"I thought we were just taping it for the records," he smiles now. "I had no idea it was live television going all over the country. It seemed a little strange that Marcos himself was there to introduce me, especially if they had captured Honasan and Kapunan. . . . But, well, the President got my name wrong. I think he called me Edgardo, but somebody corrected him. It was terrible. The TV business was the worst part of all; I'd rather face guns than that."

Morales sat at a table with three other arrested conspirators: Lt.-Col. Jake Malajacan, Major Saulito Arumin, and Major Ricardo Brillantes. To the millions of Filipinos who watched them on television that night, they appeared ashen-faced and motionless, but they were actually whispering among themselves. "We kept asking, 'Who squealed? Who squealed?' " says Morales. "We were very bitter about losing. Also, we figured we were dead."

President Marcos adopted the air of a weary schoolmaster during the late-night TV broadcast. He announced that an assassination plot against the First Family had been uncovered by his son, Ferdinand Marcos II, and by Colonel Irwin Ver – a blatant falsehood that did much to discredit the true story. The defection of Enrile and Ramos, he said, "was a pre-emptive move to cover up their participation in the plot. We did not know they could reach this height of treason and rebellion."

Mournfully, Marcos confessed that he was particularly saddened because "one of them is even a relative of mine." The President and General Ramos are cousins, related through their grandparents, but have never been notably close. "I call on the Minister of Defense and the Vice Chief of Staff to stop this stupidity and surrender so that we may negotiate exactly what should be done with them and their men. . . . They should now realize that we are in complete control of the situation."

The President declared he had the power to "liquidate, eliminate this force that is surrounding the ministry. I would rather that instead of wiping out this corner of Camp Aguinaldo with hostile fire – because it can be easily wiped out with simple artillery and tank fire, without any of our personnel being involved in the fighting – I would prefer that we talk about how they should be treated if they surrender."

(Those remarks are powerfully ironic in restrospect. Marcos *did* have the power to do exactly as he threatened at that point, but he dithered and hesitated until it slipped away from him.)

Colonel Arturo Aruiza, a close presidential aide, approached Captain Morales right after the broadcast and gripped his arm. "Dick," he hissed, "do you realize what you've *done* to the First Lady? She has been trembling like a leaf since she first found out that you're the one involved in this thing. She likes you, Dick. She remembers you. Now you'd better go over there and apologize to her."

"Why should I apologize?" he protested. "This is political. This is serious."

"Anyway," said Aruiza, "at least go and tell her you weren't going to assassinate her."

So Morales, surrounded by his PSC guards, shuffled over to Imelda Marcos and blurted out an impromptu speech: "Ma'am, I'd like to make one thing clear. Obviously some people have been telling you that we were going to kill you, but that's not true. I was just going to capture you and the President."

Despite the cool elegance of her swept-up coiffure and expensive evening dress, the Philippine First Lady was too shaken to answer. She swallowed and nodded her head, then patted Morales on the shoulder in a gesture of absolution. Imelda then tripped off with a half-dozen aides, dabbing at her eyes with a handkerchief.

Camp Aguinaldo is a sprawling metropolis unto itself near the Manila suburb of Cubao. On a normal day, the visitor is astonished to find soldiers vastly outnumbered by housewives and school kids – military dependants who play tag alongside helicopters or dodge drives on the golf-course fairways. Area residents who stream through the gates are ignored by the armed guards, and the maze of residential streets has the look of a working-class suburb. The camp's walls are ten feet high and thick, but its perimeter is miles long and totally indefensible.

Saturday, February 22, 1986, was not a usual day there. As reporters arrived for the 6 p.m. press conference, Defense Minister Enrile's transport helicopter was the centre of activity. Reformist officers pulled sacks of rifles through the door and ran with them to the back of the ministry headquarters. These were, in fact, the weapons of the Cagayan Hundred, ferried over from Villamor Air Base at the last instant. But, at the time, none of us in the press knew that. Why all the guns? we wondered. Why the guys in camouflage fatigues guarding the stairwells with Armalites and Galils? Why, above all, the press conference at dinnertime on a balmy Saturday evening? The mystery deepened when we arrived at the spacious third-floor reception hall to find Enrile sweating inside a suit of body armor, the sort usually worn by police SWAT teams. The minister was ghostly pale and fidgety, wiping his brow and obviously anxious to get started. The holdup was General Ramos. Thirty minutes late, he came strolling casually into the room with an unlit Tabacalera 1881 cigar dangling from one end of a broad smile. He was in a casual grey jacket and pants, looking cool and friendly. He went and sat with Enrile behind a bank of microphones, leaned back, and clasped his hands over a trim stomach.

"Good evening," chorused the newsmen at the front.

"Thank you," replied the Defense Minister. "I don't know if this will be such a good evening. But anyway, we are ready to answer your questions."

What unfolded over the next hour was more than a journalist's dream: it seemed like drug-induced fantasy. Dozens of questions were asked, and every answer crackled like a news-flash thunderbolt from above. On a normal day, nearly every reply would have made a front-page story. This night, the revelations toppled over each other in dizzying succession as the world press frantically scribbled down wondrous lead paragraphs – only to discard them seconds later when something even better came along.

Enrile started the proceedings with a lie. "Information reached us that there was supposed to be an effort to arrest all members of the Reform Movement, and this afternoon some of my boys came to my house and asked me to move to Camp Aguinaldo. . . ." It was a purely defensive measure, he assured the press. "If there is going to be any shooting, it is not going to start from us here. If we have to die, we die here."

The minister called on President Marcos to respect the people's will, and said he believed Cory Aquino had won the election. "As of now, I cannot in conscience recognize the President as the commander-in-chief of the armed forces. . . . In my own region, I know we cheated the election to the extent of 350,000 votes." And that revelation was just for openers. Enrile went on to admit what most Filipinos had long suspected: that a 1972 assassination attempt against him was faked to provide Marcos with an excuse to declare martial law. And that the killing of Benigno Aquino "could not be undertaken by anyone without an order from above".

Did that mean the President?

"I believe so."

And General Ver, too?

"No one else can do it except those people."

General Ramos had his own bombshells to drop. He seemed remote from Enrile during the early moments of the press briefing, as if suspicious of the minister's motives. But when Enrile admitted his own duplicity and renounced all political ambitions, the General led a small army of military skeletons out of the closet. Many top-ranking officers had become "practically the servants of powerful political figures . . . and they have responded to the commands not from us who are in the chain of command, but to the instructions of these powerful politicians." Regional warlords, he revealed, had actually "received firearms from these military officers for utilization in furthering their political and business interests." And Ramos named names: Eduardo Cojuangco, the brewing magnate and presidential crony with a reputed 3,000-man private army; Imelda's brother, Benjamin Romualdez; the southern warlord Ali Dimaporo, and others. Ramos himself had been kept in a high position "as a deodorant for the government", he smiled.

Amid all the shocking frankness, however, the breakaway leaders were strangely reticent on two crucial issues. Their call for popular support was perfunctory, even defensive, as if they were preparing for rejection. Asked about the street demonstrators who had long plagued the government, Enrile just shrugged and said: "I do not know if they will support us. But even if we are not supported by the people, we have taken a stand, and so be it. After all, life is God's gift. It's only Him who will take it."

And Cory Aquino?

"We have not had any contact with Mrs. Aquino," said Enrile.

Was he willing to accept her authority as president?

"I am not making any conclusion. Whoever is considered by the Filipino people to be the representative of their will must be respected."

Would he seek Mrs. Aquino's support?

"Well . . ." with a what-the-heck shrug "I suppose at this point that anyone who would support us is welcome."

Would he serve under Mrs. Aquino?

"No," came Enrile's unequivocal reply. "I will not serve under Mrs. Aquino, even if she is installed as president. . . . I am not interested in power, or position, in the government. I am not doing this because I want glory, wealth, or power."

The object of these assurances, however, was not buying them. Corazon Aquino had taken her civil-disobedience crusade to the Visayan metropolis, Cebu, the day before. And while her advisors reacted to the rebellion with a dozen conflicting strategies, the yellow-clad housewife adopted two prudent measures: she immediately hid in a convent, and she asked the helpful nuns to get Cardinal Jaime Sin on the telephone.

"Cardinal," she told her long-time mentor, "we've got a big problem. There is a third force now. The military is going to take it away from us."

"No," answered the Archbishop of Manila, plain-spoken as always. "I don't think so. I think this might be the miracle I promised you. This is the answer to our prayers. Without this, you could go on protesting and boycotting forever, but you would still not be president. Marcos would never give up. Maybe this is the only way."

Within a few minutes, phones were ringing everywhere. Mrs. Aquino called Enrile, but their conversation was cool and unproductive. The presidential candidate wished the minister good luck and asked if there was anything she could do. "Just pray for us," he answered. Enrile would recount the call with a dismissive shrug at a 3 a.m. press conference: "What else can a woman do but pray?"

The minister had better luck with other calls he made – and especially did *not* make – in the course of that night. Loyalist generals at the Palace were frantic for information, and had a dozen spies roaming the rebel camp with radios. "We monitored them right from the beginning," says Colonel Kapunan, "and we could have intercepted them. But we learned a lot more just by listening. They were very concerned to spot us all and make sure we were *there* in the camp. Obviously they were worried that some were still outside, ready to attack them. It was me, in fact, that they couldn't locate. And that helped us a lot, because it kept them uncertain."

Marcos repeatedly sent emissaries to Enrile, urging him to call the Palace and open a dialogue. At the time, the minister's steadfast refusals were interpreted as a sign of uncertainty, a virtual admission that Marcos might talk him into surrendering.

"No, no, no, no," Enrile explained months later. "That wasn't it at all. I just wanted to keep him guessing. I didn't want him to find out our condition, whether we felt defensive or euphoric. You know, he has a way of assessing people. I have worked for him for a long time. To Marcos, that is the greatest problem: if there are unknowns. I think it paid off. He hesitated, at the moment of our greatest weakness. All we were hoping right then was just to get through the night."

At that moment, the rebels numbered about three hundred men, with others trickling in from around Manila. They were well equipped with Enrile's personal gun supply, plus the shipment from Cagayan and the normal stockpile at the camp. But they had only four bazooka-like recoilless rifles and virtually nothing heavy enough to threaten tanks or Marcos's fleet of Sikorsky gunships. The two helicopters that formed the rebel "air force" were the personal transport choppers of Enrile and Ramos, and they were unarmed.

The other side had at least ten thousand heavily armed troops in the capital and its suburbs, with plenty of tanks, armored personnel carriers, light armored transport, and howitzer artillery pieces, and an array of gunships and F-5 fighter bombers. Marcos had not exaggerated when he talked of "easily" wiping out the small Reformist redoubt at the ministry.

But the lopsided odds created overconfidence among the Loyalists. That, combined with General Ver's conservatism and the element of doubt, led to a gigantic blunder:

"Sir, we are surprised about this turn of events," was Ver's first comment when Enrile finally agreed to talk to him – but not to Marcos – on the telephone at 9 p.m.

"Well," said the minister, "I was informed that you were trying to have us all arrested."

"No. That's not true. There is no such plan, no such order. We never had any intention to harm your group, and we can't understand why you reacted this way."

Enrile would later describe his response as "Well, the die is cast. We have broken the shell of the egg. The only thing now is to stir it." But that wasn't what he said to Ver. Instead, the minister offered a proposal to hold off all hostilities until morning:

"Look, Fabian, we're already in this condition. All I would ask, if you want to dialogue with us, is not to initiate an attack against us tonight. Let's talk about it in the morning and see if we can find a solution. We've established a perimeter here, and we're willing to die to defend it. So I'd suggest you don't send anyone into this area, and then we can avoid any incidents."

General Ver's reply was astonishingly inept. Despite his total military superiority, he eagerly agreed to the standoff, then sued, in effect, for peaceful parity: "All right. But you must also ask your men not to attack the Palace. You must also commit to that."

Enrile could hardly contain his surprise and delight. Goliath was afraid of *David*. "Certainly," the minister said gravely. "You have my solemn word that we will not attack the Palace. We'll stay in the camp until dawn, and then we can talk."

6 THE CALL TO PEOPLE POWER

AT THIS POINT on Saturday night, God, or Cardinal Jaime Sin, or the Catholic Church, changed the course of the revolution. To understand how this came about, it is essential to appreciate the power of religion in the country's daily life.

You can be weaving down España Street in the midst of a typhoon, fourteen people packed into a smoking twelve-person "jeepney" with its opaque curtains drawn on the sides, when suddenly the entire jeepload – every pert secretary, street tough, and school kid – makes the sign of the cross. In absolute unison. How do they *know* we are passing a church? In a country that sells Jesus Christ watches (like the Mickey Mouse watch, but with Christ's face in the centre and the names of his twelve disciples, including Judas, as hour markers), the crossing motion is apparently an instinctive reflex, part of the ride. As a non-Catholic outsider, I have sometimes been intrigued enough to venture a few questions on the subject.

"Church, was there a church back there?" replied one neatly dressed man of about forty.

"Well, sir, you did cross yourself."

"Did I? Oh, yes. I guess there *is* a church there."

Many foreigners seize upon the colorful jeepney as a symbol of the Philippines. But no jeep would be complete without the country's *real* trademark: a plastic-wrapped statuette of the Santo Niño, flanked on the dashboard by flashing red lights. This regal version of the Christ-child, which first arrived with explorer Ferdinand Magellan in 1521, wears a golden crown and scarlet robes, its hair falling in waves to the waist. The Santo Niño is a virtual Filipino industry, depicted in millions of statues, pendants, rings, pencil boxes, ashtrays, pins, paintings, postcards, pennants, and air-fresheners. Hundreds of boys make a living by selling fresh sampaguita garlands in the middle of the street – to passing jeepney drivers, who drape them over the dashboard icon.

The Philippines has been Catholic for four centuries, since the

Spanish conquerors set about saving the souls of tribal natives – in utter contempt of the highly literate culture, animistic beliefs, and political chieftains already in place. The colonizers uprooted traditional religious practices and used assembly-line baptism to give everyone a name they could pronounce: "O" names in one town, "P" names in the next, and so on. Even today, Bicol residents assume that anyone named Ortega or Ocampo probably comes from a little town named Oas. The Spanish friars exhibited the racist arrogance typical of sixteenth-century Europeans among "heathens", and many intelligent Filipinos still hold them responsible for the country's ills. But the hybrid Catholicism they fostered is among the world's most powerful faiths.

Every Easter, for example, international newspapers carry dramatic photos of religious fanatics being nailed to a cross. If you read the accompanying cutlines, you will discover that virtually all of the incidents take place in small Philippine towns. On any given day, there is usually a five-foot version of the Niño being hauled through city streets on a wagon, while scores of devotees form a procession on all sides. Philippine piety does not stop horn-honking at the resulting traffic jams, but it does hold down the curses to a tolerable volume.

Those who marry a Filipina have few worries about a meddling mother-in-law, since any worthy lady above the age of forty spends her entire day trooping back and forth to mass. Disgruntled customers in the Ermita district, meanwhile, have only one serious complaint about its legendary bar girls: These lovely ladies are happy to spend the night, but insist on rising at 5 a.m. to catch early mass and seek absolution for the evening's work.

On the fateful night of February 22, therefore, many million sets of eyes and ears were trained on the Villa San Miguel. Juan Ponce Enrile was a largely discredited Marcos hack when he made his break, and Fidel Ramos was a general whose time seemed already to have passed. The pair had gambled their lives on popular support, but knew very well the turnout would hinge upon the Church and its pre-eminent Cardinal.

Cardinal Sin's phone rang for the first time late Saturday afternoon, when Cristina Ponce Enrile called to announce that her husband was holed up in Camp Aguinaldo, and pleaded: "Cardinal, help us!" Nobody really understood her husband's motives, Mrs. Enrile told the prelate, and anyone else who would listen over the next three days. He might seem an ambitious politician, a career Marcos man, but he was actually a devout Catholic who did nothing without first consulting Our Lady of Fatima. "What many people can't believe is Johnny's total devotion to

Our Lady,'' said Cristina. ''Every night before he goes to bed, he prays to her. He tells me: 'She has never let me down.' ''

The next call came from the Fatima fanatic himself. ''Cardinal, I will be dead within one hour,'' Jaime Sin remembers Johnny Enrile telling him. ''He seemed to be trembling, and he added: 'I don't mind to die, but if it is possible, please do something. Call the people to support us. I'd still like to live. I already heard the order to smash us.' '' The Cardinal recalls Enrile as very frightened and ''almost crying''.

This account was later denied by the minister, who repeatedly stressed his great fear and readiness to die during the revolt, but has since become embarrassed by that less-than-macho performance. ''I did not quite say those things,'' he indignantly informed me in a July 1986 interview. ''It's true, I told him we were in a bad condition and I asked for help. I said, 'Kindly help us if you could.' Then he said, 'What can I do?' I said, 'Pray for us, first of all. And then if you could call on the people to help us.' But that I was crying or that I was going to die in the next hour . . . that is not correct.''

A more surprising call came next from General Ramos, a Protestant, who informed the Catholic churchman that he had embraced the image of Our Lady of Fatima and said, 'Dear Lady, I know that you are miraculous.' Ramos, too, pleaded with the Cardinal to call on the people, and stressed that the battle was one of Good vs. Marcosian Evil. Cynics later sneered at this strange ecumenical embrace, but their ranks included none who watched Ramos during the revolt's darkest hours. Among all the devout Catholics on the rebel side, it was the Protestant general who was most often found reading his well-thumbed Bible. And it was he who reached for the battered Good Book before Monday's impending dawn attack, ordered everyone in the war room to bow their heads, and led them through a sombre recitation of Psalm 91. ''He is my refuge and my fortress: my God, in Him will I trust. . . . He shall cover thee with His wings, and under His feathers shalt thou trust; His truth shall be thy shield and buckler.''

Outsiders in the room were surprised to note that many of Ramos's men pulled crumpled pieces of paper out of their pockets and recited along with the General. Only later did I discover that he had had copies printed months before, and had distributed them to many under his command. The idea came from his godsister, newspaper publisher Betty Go Belmonte, who had predicted three years earlier that Ramos would become ''Joshua, the soldier of peace'' in Philippine history. Throughout the revolt, there was a marker in the General's Bible at the book of Joshua.

Four months later, General Ramos told an interviewer that every part of the February Revolution was "God's will, purely and simply. . . . It could not have been the plan of any human being, no matter how brilliant. Because, if you remember, the sequence of events was so accurate, so timely, so exact, that it could only have been designed and directed by a Supreme Commander up there. . . . and I don't mean Douglas MacArthur. Those of us who were fortunate enough to have played a key role in all of this were just the instruments of the Divine Director."

With such evident piety on the rebel side, the Cardinal's own quick decision to back them is usually regarded as automatic. He had long prayed for a miracle and had assured Cory Aquino that God would find a way to install her in Malacañang. And it was only two hours after the Enrile-Ramos press conference that Sin was on Radio Veritas urging the faithful to "leave your homes now. I am calling on our people to support our two good friends at the camp. Go to Aguinaldo and show your solidarity with them in this crucial period. Our two good friends have shown their idealism. Take them food if you wish. Keep them safe. I would be very happy if you help them in any way you can. We must all pray to Our Lady that we solve these problems peacefully, without bloodshed. I am sorry to disturb you at this late hour, but it is precisely at a time like this that we most need your support." The immediate response of his nuns and seminarians left an impression of instant, wholehearted Church involvement.

But it was not that simple. The country's most powerful churchman was plunged into deep indecision by the pleas, with no realistic way to judge the possibility of a civilian bloodbath; he spent ninety minutes wrestling with the harrowing spectre of a million Filipinos caught in a military crossfire. Radio Veritas kept its phone line open to his Villa San Miguel office, expecting an immediate decision. Nothing happened for nearly two hours.

Like Enrile, the Cardinal was also negotiating on the telephone. But he was attempting to contact a rather more exalted Party, whose number is not listed in any directory.

"Prioress," Jaime Sin told the Mother Superior of the Carmelite contemplative nuns. "Right now, get out from your cells and go to the chapel with your arms outstretched before the Blessed Sacrament. Pray without ceasing, and fast until I tell you to stop. If we lose, you will fast until the end of your life. We are in battle. Keep your arms outstretched. I will tell you why later." The same command went out to the other two contemplative orders in Manila, until two hundred of the reclusive sisters were stretched before their altars.

Then the Cardinal got in touch with both of the orphanages under his direction. "The children must sing hymns and ask the Lord to help me," he ordered. "I want them to say, 'Father, Cardinal Sin has a problem. Please guide him.' He may not wish to talk to me, but God cannot refuse the children."

With his various human transceivers in place, Jaime Sin sat in the dark second-floor office of his peaceful hilltop mansion in suburban Manila and waited for the message to come through. Within a few minutes he heard it loud and clear. Then he passed it over the airwaves to the six million devout Catholics in Metro Manila, telling them to "go to Aguinaldo".

Clearly, this action directly contravened that evening's order from a "Vatican representative" ordering the Cardinal to "stay neutral" in the fracas. The message almost certainly came from papal nuncio Torpigliani, since Rome would have little time to react before the radio appeal. But my sources inside the Philippine Church will not be more specific. In view of the Vatican's later endorsement, it has become extremely un-politic to remind the upper hierarchy of its attempts to quash Cardinal Sin right at the outset.

In any case, bureaucratic barriers were the least of the Cardinal's worries. His call to the two hundred contemplative nuns was an act of both inspiration and desperation. When first confronted with Enrile's emotional pleas for support, the prelate definitely did *not* know how to respond. His instinct was to send the Catholic flock to prevent violence, but he was keenly aware that strategy might instead set off an urban holocaust. He had no way of assessing the military situation or its likely outcome. He knew nothing about firepower, or the inclination of Marcos's generals to unleash it on civilians. Yet he was about to risk millions of innocent lives. Their blood, if spilled, would be upon his hands.

"Bloodshed, bloodshed. That idea was foremost in my mind," he told me months later. "I knew that the moment I commit a mistake it would mean there would be terrible violence. I could not allow that to happen, so I sought the counsel of God. I thought: if this is truly His will, then He will not allow that to happen. The first thing was to imitate Moses. You know Moses, in the Old Testament, when there was a battle, he stretches out his arms like this" – here the corpulent Cardinal rises gracefully from his office chair and holds both arms out to heaven – "and he prays. The moment he began stretching his arms out to God, the battle was in their favor. And then, when he became tired, his brother Aaron had to sustain him, help him hold up his arms until they became victorious. Taking that as the premise, I called on the contemplative nuns to do the same, to hold their arms out and not to stop until I told them it was time. I didn't even tell them the reason. So you see, ah? It was very scriptural, ah?''

The Cardinal had never used this technique before, and still did not quite know why it occurred to him on the night of the rebellion. "I am always reading the scriptures," he shrugged. "I don't have any problems of my own, but I always pray for other people's problems. But this time . . . well, this is really a battle, and I am supposed to be the leader. So I said, 'Dear God, please do not allow Your children to die.' "

He adopted a dramatic voice, a booming Moses-on-the-mountaintop voice, to recount all of this. But he suddenly stopped, switched on a little-boy grin, and decided there was nothing so grave about it after all. God had the whole episode planned from the beginning. The Cardinal was merely his tool. Anyway, who could go wrong with weapons such as nuns and orphans to unleash upon a helpless dictator?

"These contemplative nuns," he smiled, "you know, these women are all very beautiful inside. These women have truly given their life to God, so that it is a life of penance. That is all they do: pray and work in their gardens. They are our powerhouse. Every time I have a crucial decision, they are affected. Even if I do not speak to them about it, they are assisting the will of God. They are like the antenna of the Church. When I tell them, 'Get down on your knees,' that is a real sign of danger. Then I call the children in our two orphanages, and I tell them the same: 'Kneel! Go on your knees!' Because, you know, I have learned that God cannot refuse the children. When they start asking God . . . oh, ho! Oh, you will see the effect immediately. When they start praying 'Cardinal Sin has a problem, dear Lord. Please help him' . . . something like this. And then they sing a hymn. Then I call my priests and they do the Holy Sacrament and mass. This was our preparation that night."

One more expressive shrug. "Of course, these are all spiritual aids. Then you have to do something after that. It cannot be just spiritual, our actions in the world have to be physical, too. It was a terrible risk, ah? If they had all died out there at EDSA, I would have been blamed. But I knew I would be victorious. It is God who's inspiring me . . . so it cannot go wrong."

Half a world away, Pope John Paul II and his Church hierarchy held their collective breath as the Philippine revolution unfolded. Highly placed informants later told reporters that the Vatican was "terrified" when it heard Cardinal Sin had gone on Radio Veritas to empty the convents and command a sea of Catholics to stand between the guns. Secretary of State

Casaroli fired off numerous cables to Manila's archbishop, but received no answer. The die was cast. Jaime Cardinal Sin could do little but listen to the radio, fend off Rome, and hope for the best.

"I had all the gadgets," he smiles now. "The radio here on my desk, a television over there, and many long-distance phones. It was very easy. But I didn't like to talk to Rome. We kept getting their cables, but we said, 'Never mind, we'll answer all the questions later.' And then afterwards we went to Rome and explained the situation."

A secular version of the Cardinal's call had already been sounded by Butz Aquino, the impetuous leader of the August Twenty-One Movement (ATOM) which had organized many street demonstrations since his brother Ninoy's 1983 assassination. The ATOM executive met immediately after the Enrile-Ramos press conference, but had reacted with strong skepticism. Protest marches had given them plenty of experience with the military, and a deep mistrust of it, in any form. Most of them thought the whole thing was probably a charade; it was best to wait for Cory Aquino's reaction before getting involved.

But Cory's brother-in-law would have none of it. "I didn't know Enrile," says Butz Aquino, "but I had met General Ramos, and it seemed out of character for him to get involved in a con game. So I said, 'Well, I'm sorry, but I believe we should get out and support them. Anyway, I'm going.' " Aquino hopped into his old black Toyota Crown and raced into the rebel camp past the Aguinaldo sentries, like a general reporting for duty. It is some measure of the security in force that he was allowed to roar right into the ministry parking lot. He ran upstairs to catch the tail-end of a press conference, and noticed a Radio Veritas reporter excitedly filing his story over a pay phone.

"You on the air?" he demanded. When the reporter nodded, Aquino simply commandeered the phone and began to broadcast:

"We need all the volunteers we can get," he announced. "Let's meet at midnight at . . . uh . . . the Isetann Department Store in Cubao. From there we'll march to the camp." The impulsive move was totally in character for Aquino, whose shoot-from-the-mouth style had often caused him problems. And without the Cardinal's later reinforcement, the Isetann march might have been a flop.

"I groaned when I heard Butz sound off his call for volunteers to join him in Cubao," Father Francisco Araneta, a prominent priest, now recalls ruefully. "I thought to myself: 'There goes that fool again.' By the time the Cardinal made his appeal it was good I was fast asleep. Otherwise I would be guilty of thinking my dear superior had lost his mind, too."

Aquino reached the Isetann store at 11 p.m., to find a grand total of six revolutionaries awaiting him. "Oh, Jesus," he thought. "Who am I kidding? After fifteen more minutes of agonizing wait, we were still six, and I felt ridiculous." But then people began to arrive in threes and fours, parking their cars, unloading lanterns, radios, blankets, food, and banners. Other cars circled the store, honking their horns in the "Co-ry! Co-ry!" sequence so familiar during the election. When 200 had gathered, someone went off to fetch the ATOM loudspeaker. When he returned fifteen minutes later, there were 2,000. By 11:45, more than 10,000 angry Filipinos were there, straining to get moving, and Aquino couldn't hold them back until midnight. By the time the group crossed Aurora Boulevard on their way to the camp, Aquino was leading 15,000 vigilantes. People Power had been born – chanting, singing, and shouting slogans.

"We had hoped for 3,000," recalls Butz Aquino. "When we saw the response, we were delirious."

Hundreds would have gone to Aguinaldo that night, even if the Cardinal had expressly forbidden it. But his official seal of approval unleashed the thousands of undecideds – including vast hordes of the non-political faithful who had even ignored Cory Aquino's gigantic election rallies. Butz Aquino's famous call to meet at the Isetann Department Store was heeded by an unlikely gaggle of "revolutionaries" that amazed and baffled the veteran street activist. "I still don't know who they were," he said later. "Only a few were our people; the rest just seemed to come from nowhere. You could tell by the way they acted that it was all new to them. They sure weren't hard-core demonstrators."

Benny Abrio, a university student who had been involved in the election campaign, remembers leaping up to gather provisions as soon as he heard the Cardinal's radio appeal. His sixty-year-old mother took one look at the pile of blankets and food and ordered a halt: "Where do you think you're going?" she demanded. "You're my only son. It will be dangerous out there. You must stay home." But Abrio had the perfect response. "Mommy," he told her. "It is the Cardinal calling us. Even if we are killed, we will join the saints in heaven." Mrs. Abrio threw in a couple of extra blankets, picked up her rosary, and accompanied her boy to the barricades.

At 3 a.m., Juan Ponce Enrile was back on the podium at the Defense Ministry, providing footage for 6 p.m. newscasts a dozen time zones away. He told us that General Ramos had joined his men in Camp Crame, the Philippine Constabulary headquarters just across the street. He also told us that Mrs. Aquino had finally been in touch. Then he asked if anyone had been out to Aguinaldo's gates. "Yessir," a Filipino newsman answered. "There are thousands of people there, supporting you. They are chanting your name." Enrile started to reply, but his voice caught and he stopped in mid-sentence. Tears welled in his eyes as he sat silent for a few moments, trying to regain his composure. "It is all turned around," he finally said. "I am the one who is supposed to protect them. And now . . . after all the years I have been part of the Marcos government. . . . Well, Marcos misread me. He thought I'd be like the men who said yes to him." Enrile wiped away the tears.

Months later, as he attempted to undermine Cory Aquino's young government, the once-and-future Defense Minister would discount his night of tears and fears. Enrile denied having told Cardinal Sin that he was going to die; he said he knew from the outset that his faction would win. And he brushed aside the tearful 3 a.m. press conference with an impatient gesture. "That was just an emotional reaction to a very tense situation," he told me. "I was quite confident that I would survive. I never had any feeling of immediate danger."

The response of priests and nuns to what was indeed immediate danger has, of course, often been told. But even before stopping those Marine tanks at the EDSA showdown, they were the backbone of People Power. I remember wandering out of Enrile's headquarters at about 4 a.m. the first night, determined to explore the camp and see how many defenders he really had. There, under a nearly full moon, on the front lawn of the Defense Ministry, were the first shock troops: five tiny nuns in snow-white habits, a few of the "NAMFREL Marines", had formed a prayer circle on the grass. They held candles and recited the Lord's Prayer as soldiers stood around them in awkward wonder. "I know they're here to help us, and I want to believe they really can," said one army captain with a miniature Uzi submachine gun around his neck. "But right now all I can think of is bullets. I don't think these people can stop bullets . . . except with their bodies."

The various religious orders lent immediate form to the human barricades, turning potential chaos into a well-ordered campground. Taking charge of the sacks of rice, bread, crackers, sardines, and doughnuts that helpful civilians had handed through the gates, they quickly set up food brigades that became the crowd's life-support system, and used their religious robes to gently coerce grocers and merchants. This being the

Philippines, of course, half a dozen churches stood near by, open for use as storage depots and restrooms. When they were not lying under tanks, the nuns served as cooks, dishwashers, first-aid workers, and dispensers of instant courage. "Whenever people were afraid," says Sister Anunciata, "they would come to us and say, 'Sister, Sister, please pray for us. Please give us the courage.' Many times we were frightened too, but you could not show it. Anyway, that is our business. We do know many, many prayers."

But if priests and nuns brought order to the barricades, Felix Bautista insists their own participation was "completely spontaneous. It wasn't organized by the Church at all. They just heard Cardinal Sin's appeal on the radio and, you know, if the Cardinal has credibility with the people, he has twenty times more credibility with the nuns. He has a special relationship with many of them that dates back to martial law. When they heard him say, 'Go out there,' they went. It was that simple. The convents were immediately empty."

Such rapt devotion to the Cardinal, however, does not extend to the Church radicals who spearheaded the anti-Marcos movement. Ask Sister Mary John Mananzan whether she responded to his radio call and the dean of St. Scholastica's College replies with an icy glare. "In the first place," says the Benedictine nun, "I am not a Cardinal Sin fan. I'm an activist, and he's not too fond of activists. I had decided to go [to Aguinaldo] before the Cardinal spoke, and I would not have turned back. For me, it was a great chance to take away Marcos. It was a historical event and I had to participate in it wholeheartedly."

Sister Mary John is a member of the leftist coalition Bayan, an ardent feminist and the chairperson of GABRIELA, an umbrella group of women's organizations. Such organizations had long regarded the Cardinal's "critical collaboration" with the Marcos regime as too light on criticism and far too heavy on collaboration Even the devastating post-election pastoral letter did not impress the sister. "That's fine," she says now. "But where were the Cardinal and the bishops during martial law? Their courage came very late in the day."

The internecine quarrels were set aside that Saturday night as activist heavyweights joined their timid, first-time sisters in gathering food for the Aguinaldo-Crame siege. "We thought we should not go out dressed as nuns to buy food," recalls Sister Mary John, "because we might start a panic buying spree if people saw us stocking up. We knew we'd need a lot, because they always come to us in a crisis, so we went out in civilian dress to get as much as we could. But, of course, there's only one big store in our area, and as soon as we went in, one of the wives of our security guards called out to me: 'Sister!' and everyone's head turned.

"We had to laugh in spite of ourselves. That's how the revolution was: very grave, very serious, and then all these moments that were so terribly funny."

Susan Severino left Aguinaldo in the early hours of Sunday morning. She is a well-to-do activist, a woman with enough leisure to spend her time working for "cause-oriented" reform groups, and she had gone to the scene immediately after Butz Aquino's radio appeal.

"We were on a tremendous high," she recalls. "But then, I don't know why, we decided to drive around the city and see what the mood was like, just to get a feel. We went to Malacañang, Fort Bonifacio, and over past the U.S. Embassy. But everything was so quiet, so isolated, it was eerie. It was like the quiet before the storm. It's strange, but I didn't feel in danger at Aguinaldo. It was only in the quiet of the city that you could sense it. Suddenly I became very concerned. We expected tanks and we saw nothing. But that only made it more ominous."

By dawn, People Power had dwindled to about a thousand stragglers sitting protectively around the camp's metal gates. Enrile stood in blue jeans and his bullet-proof vest, receiving mass on the ministry lawn with a few of his officers. A Sikorsky gunship churned high overhead, taking reconnaissance photos for the Marcos generals at the Palace, about four miles to the west.

Manila was strangely calm. The main commotion early on Sunday was caused by a parade along Roxas Boulevard; thousands of smiling children and half a dozen marching bands waved flags in a celebration arranged weeks before. The leading float, in the shape of a gigantic molar, urged children to brush their teeth in honor of Dental Week.

Inside the camp, the tense mood was summed up by a Reformist captain in a blue jogging suit, who would not reveal his name but was more than willing to speculate on the rebels' chances.

"There's nothing to do now but wait," he said, sitting cross-legged on the ground, fondling his Galil. "Maybe they'll attack and maybe they won't."

Did he think Marcos would step down?

"Hah! Marcos? No way. Never."

So what was the point of it all?

"Well . . . the whole point now is just survival. It wasn't supposed to happen this way."

7 *THE AMERICANS*

IT WASN'T SUPPOSED to happen that way. But it did, because someone in the U.S. Embassy tipped off Ferdinand Marcos. That is what the best intelligence brains in the Philippine armed forces now believe. The Reformist coup plot combined speed and ruthlessness, and had been carefully set up by hardened veterans with help from Palace insiders; kept secret, its success was virtually assured.

But on the Tuesday or Wednesday before the scheduled assault, an American diplomat in Manila contacted General Fabian Ver. The man had hard information that Malacañang was to be attacked in the early hours of Sunday, February 23. And he laid out the plan in detail for the Marcos chief of staff: times, meeting points, assault team leaders, manpower, equipment, even the composition of the "ruling council" that would assume power.

The Embassy will neither confirm nor deny this. "I don't know if a message like that was passed or not, . . ." says its spokesman, Allan Croghan. "Anyone who'd undertake to do that would be exceeding his brief." Both the Americans and RAM, however, concede that the U.S. military had detailed advance knowledge of the coup plot. Just a few weeks before the scheduled attack, the Reformists tried to acquire anti-tank weapons from U.S. deputy military attaché Vic Raphael. The request was turned down, but news of the impending coup was gratefully accepted.

"We treated those requests as information," explained Croghan, six months after the revolt. "But we took no action on them. People would say, 'We need such-and-such,' and we'd say, 'That's not our business.' . . . RAM said they needed things to help them succeed. But we couldn't help them."

For their part, the Reformists are not willing to identify the American snitch – because of the diplomatic row that would ensue, and because they are not 100 per cent sure of his identity. This much is certain: General Ver told his son Irwin that an "asset" in the U.S. Embassy had tipped him about the impending attack. Late Saturday night, when a

Loyalist victory seemed inevitable, Colonel Ver bragged about the American informant to his subordinates in the Presidential Security Command. He was overheard by the arrested coup members being held in his custody.

Reformists such as Enrile's intelligence chief, Red Kapunan, and security chief, Gringo Honasan, have conducted an extensive investigation into the leak that nearly killed them all. They are secretive about the findings, and often allude to the "diplomatic blowup" that might result. But they are too angry with the United States to remain close-mouthed. During interviews for this book, the RAM insiders dropped unmistakable hints about U.S. involvement. Eventually they sketched in a more detailed scenario of American foreknowledge – and apparent duplicity.

"The security leak emanated from outside," Honasan revealed during our first meeting. "It was somebody sort of buying life insurance, making sure they had both sides covered. So that, whoever eventually won, the winner would owe debts to this country."

Did he mean an outside power had tipped off Marcos?

"Yes, basically. We have most of the details now."

Was it knowingly, or unwittingly?

"Well, if you knew which country it was, it is fairly consistent with their overall operating policy. At a certain level they cannot control the information they have. There was horse-trading, buying insurance with this [new] government and the government of President Marcos."

Obviously there was only one country that might have such information and the motive to use it?

"Yes, that's true. If I had my way . . . I would share this information with you. But this is beyond my ability to reveal."

Was this the reason Enrile and the Reformists were outraged at the United States after the revolt?

"Yes. Because, you see, it was a moral issue that was presented to everybody – including the foreign powers that control our destiny. They were not able to resolve that moral issue, obviously. So we had to do it ourselves, without their help."

The Reformist officers became less guarded in later conversations, and identified the United States by name. Colonel Tito Legaspi was the first to put flesh on Honasan's skeleton account:

"We had a leak. We heard it was the U.S.," said Legaspi. "It had to be at the military level, because we didn't tell the politicians. Anyway, the Americans have their own very good intelligence groups and knew of some tactical plans . . . they knew some specifics. From us to the Americans, the leak was unintentional. But from them to General Ver, *that* was intentional. Theirs had to be intentional. What else would be the reason?''

Red Kapunan, the RAM intelligence specialist, eventually explained the remarkably close link between the rebels and the U.S. military. He said his group had visited the giant American aircraft carriers stationed off the Philippine coast during the election, and ''discussed various post-election scenarios – all hypothetical'' with the U.S. commanders. He also explained why coup plotters who required absolute secrecy would reveal their plans to an American military attaché.

''We were very close to Vic Raphael, and we needed the anti-tank weapons very badly. We were preparing to tackle the full force of Marcos and Ver, with nothing to stop their armor,'' says Kapunan. ''So we asked in a casual way about the chances of the Americans' providing them. We presented it [to Raphael] as a possibility and didn't give him precise details. We wouldn't trust him with that information. But, of course, we realized Vic would go looking for it. We just assumed that he was DIA'' – the acronym for the Pentagon's Defense Intelligence Agency. ''We're sure that Vic didn't sell us out. He's a friend of ours. But, of course, his information would go up the hierarchy to [Ambassador Stephen] Bosworth. A lot of people in the Embassy would know about it.

''Our assumption is that General Ver and President Marcos had some Americans on their payroll. With all the millions they were throwing around for intelligence, it only makes sense to spend some of it getting inside that powerful Embassy. We don't want to say exactly who it was . . . the one on Ver's payroll. But one of our people who was arrested did overhear Irwin Ver discussing it. Of course, there's always the possibility it was an intentional leak [by Ver]. But there doesn't seem to be a reason for them to discredit the Americans with us – especially when Ver seemed certain to win. The logical assumption, knowing Irwin Ver, is that he was talking about things he shouldn't have been.''

Embassy spokesman Croghan evinces little concern about Vic Raphael's involvement with the coup plot. Asked if the attaché is a DIA agent, he simply smiles and shrugs: ''That's an assumption. I don't ask and they don't acknowledge.'' A request to interview Raphael is answered with another smile and more certainty: ''No. He wouldn't be available.''

Officially, the U.S. response to RAM's accusations is a blanket refusal to answer ''the many charges that have come out of the revolt''. Privately, one Embassy official explained that the Americans ''just can't afford to get into a pissing match with someone who runs the [Philippine] government. Whatever we say, there's no benefit in it for us. It won't do us any good. The world of diplomacy is not always interested in setting the record straight. It's about maintaining a relationship with the host country."

If an American official did warn Ferdinand Marcos, it would be an appropriate climax to the lopsided 88-year relationship between the two countries. President William McKinley set the tone in 1898 when he pledged to "Christianize" the devoutly Catholic Philippines and noted that "territory sometimes comes to us when we go to war in a holy cause." McKinley also promised a "benevolent assimilation" of the country – a message apparently lost on the troops of General Elwell S. Otis, the American commander in Manila. One of Elwell's men wrote: "no cruelty is too severe for these brainless monkeys. . . . with an enemy like this to fight, it's not surprising that the boys should adopt 'no quarter' as a motto and fill the blacks full of lead before finding out whether they are friends or enemies."

It is not entirely fair to castigate the United States for the endemic racism of that era. But the client-state relationship endured, and even expanded during the final years of the Marcos regime.

McKinley's 1900 *Instruction* was followed by the Philippine Bill of 1902 and the Philippine Autonomy Act of 1916, each attempting a trans-Pacific transplant of Americanism. The Tydings-McDuffie law allowed Filipinos to draw up their own carbon copy of the U.S. constitution in 1935, with White House ratification. The colony still operated under that "brown clone" constitution after its independence was granted in 1946, until Marcos rammed through his own code in 1973 to justify martial law.

But even the nine years of military rule were themselves condoned by the American Embassy. Marcos put his martial-law "contingency plan" on the desk of U.S. Ambassador Henry Byroade weeks before its September 1972 imposition. The President and Byroade even lunched at Malacañang – perhaps for a final handshake – the day the draconian step was formally declared.

America's envoy in Manila has always functioned as a proconsul, inspiring awe and fear even among the Marcos clan. In his book *The Conjugal Dictatorship*, former Marcos press censor Primitivo Mijares revealed that the First Family were terrified of William Sullivan, the U.S. Ambassador during the mid-1970s. Throughout his stay, they had Sullivan tailed by the National Intelligence and Security Agency (NISA) and spied upon by General Ver.

"Even Sullivan's Filipino driver reported to NISA," claimed Mijares, a trusted Palace insider during the period. "Some of Sullivan's clerks in the U.S. Embassy also reported to General Ver's office." There was, unfortunately, no Mijares in 1986 to tell us whether NISA and Ver had penetrated Stephen Bosworth's domain.

Twelve years too early, the Marcoses worried that Sullivan might engineer a coup d'état. "Let's watch out for this white man," Imelda Marcos told Mijares. "Yes, yes, the white datu [leader] . . . because he is the kind of man who will do us no good." Perhaps the First Lady had studied the diplomat's track record. Sullivan was ambassador to Laos during Cambodian Prince Norodom Sihanouk's overthrow – amid rumors of CIA, and Sullivan, involvement. He was also a close aide to Secretary of State Henry Kissinger when Chile's Salvador Allende was dumped.

The overpowering U.S. influence had diminished not a jot by October 1985 when President Ronald Reagan dispatched his close friend (and Nevada senator) Paul Laxalt to Malacañang. The crumbling Philippine economy and rising opposition had increased Marcos's reliance on U.S. support. Laxalt went to Manila to spell out the price he would have to pay. Speaking for Reagan, the Republican senator cast doubts on his host's popular support, questioned his economic program, and castigated the clumsy handling of the guerrilla war. These points had already been raised frequently by Ambassador Bosworth and various State Department visitors. But Marcos dismissed their grumbling as the work of pointy-head intellectuals, out of touch with the conservative Reagan.

"So the President decided to send me as a personal emissary," Laxalt explained in a *Policy Review* article. "I delivered President Marcos a handwritten letter from President Reagan. He read it, and afterwards we discussed each of the concerns at length."

Senator Laxalt found Marcos "very personable, very bright" and the two struck an immediate friendship. "In some ways, he reminds me of Richard Nixon," wrote the Republican, apparently intending a compliment. "He just loves the craftsmanship of politics and political strategy." Laxalt's article also offered an intriguing revelation about the origin of the "snap" Philippine presidential election:

"During my October meetings with President Marcos, we briefly discussed the idea of a snap presidential election earlier than the one planned for 1987. This possibility had previously been broached to him by CIA director William Casey, but during our meetings he didn't entertain it very seriously. He said there was no need for it, since he already had the support of the people."

Manila under Marcos was one of the few world capitals where such CIA brainstorms could still receive a gracious hearing. (Everyone in town knows that U.S. diplomat Norbert Garrett is the "Company" station chief, but no one seems to hold it against him. "He just assumes you know," as one Filipino businessman puts it, "and you just assume he knows you know. Then you can have lunch with him and not even mention it.") Over time, as the Americans kept pushing Casey's pet idea, Marcos gradually warmed to it. He and Laxalt had a telephone conversation in late October to discuss their upcoming appearance on David Brinkley's "This Week" TV show. "President Marcos stated . . . that he had the support of the Philippine people, and that this could be demonstrated," recalls the Senator. "And then he said he was considering . . . calling a snap election, at which point I suggested: 'If you are going to do that, it would be very dramatic for you to make that announcement on the Brinkley show. That would be very effective for American consumption.' And that is precisely what he did."

American consumption? It is astonishing enough, in the Enlightened Eighties, for a U.S. senator to suggest that the leader of a foreign nation call an election on American TV. But for Marcos to go along with the idea was an act of eighteenth-century obeisance, and a true measure of his colonial dependence on Washington.

Still, there was a slippery Marcosian brilliance to the move. The President was under pressure to step down in 1987 and allow someone else (his wife Imelda and Juan Ponce Enrile were among the candidates) to carry the KBL party banner. Now Marcos could grab six more years of power before anyone could stop him. The fractious opposition made a half-hearted attempt to oppose the election on constitutional grounds. When the Supreme Court ruled it legal, the President's opponents remained split, without a viable champion.

Little wonder that Marcos believed he would win easily, and invited the world to watch his victory. He could not possibly predict the bizarre coalition against him of Corazon Aquino, Cardinal Sin, Juan Ponce Enrile, Fidel Ramos, Gringo Honasan, People Power, and Divine intervention. Nor, in his worst nightmares, could the President have imagined the "death by a thousand cuts" that the American press and Congress would deliver as the unsavory campaign unfolded.

The improbable rise of a self-described "housewife" to topple the twenty-year dictatorship was a truly Filipino phenomenon. But it both fed the foreign press and fed *from* it, in absolute symbiosis, while Marcos took his re-election drive into America's living rooms. The Western media simply seized the Philippine election campaign and carried it for days at a time – with the full co-operation of both candidates.

BERKELEY PUBLIC LIBRARY

After his dramatic Brinkley appearance, Marcos became a fixture on American newscasts: the Hermione Gingold of the public affairs circuit. His puffy facial features and thick Ilocano accent were on "Good Morning America" and "Today", "Face the Nation" and "Meet the Press", "Nightline" and "Crossfire", the "MacNeil/Lehrer News Hour" and "One on One", the "CBS Morning News" and National Public Radio's "Morning Edition". One four-week survey charted 180 minutes of Philippine coverage on the major U.S. networks' evening news. That compared to fewer than three stories *per year* during the entire 1972-81 period of martial law.

But while Marcos wooed America, the U.S. print media blitzed Manila. Even before the campaign, wire service reports on the congressional "hidden wealth" investigation led by Representative Stephen Solarz in Washington filled the pages of Manila's opposition press. When Mrs. Aquino was forced onto the defensive by charges of incompetence, she used the daily revelations of Marcos-owned Manhattan office towers to fight back.

In mid-January, most observers still placed her behind Marcos. Then a "congressional intelligence report" on the President's failing health was leaked to the *Washington Post* – introducing *systemic lupus erythematosus* to the vocabulary of four continents. Rumors of the degenerative kidney ailment were old-hat in the Philippines. But the sudden U.S. interest, with a sexy new "intelligence" hook, put it back in the headlines. The 68-year-old President then fanned the flames when he arrived at a rally with bandaged hands and "stumbled" at the podium.

That issue was just fading when a blast from the *New York Times* rocked the campaign again. The paper unveiled U.S. army documents showing that the Philippine president's celebrated Second World War exploits were an "absurd" fiction, and his medals an immense boondoggle. Previously unreleased papers suggested that the much-celebrated Maharlika guerrilla unit was a figment of his imagination. Worse, there were allegations that Marcos had actually sold scrap metal to the occupying Japanese. Suddenly Manila's sidewalks were engulfed in a media war as screaming banners in the small opposition papers ("MARCOS FAKE HERO, US ARMY CONCLUDES") battled denials in the dominant crony press: "Marcos laughs off US slurs!" and "Ex-congressman affirms Marcos record!".

In its final weeks, the Marcos campaign pleaded in desperation for Washington's approval – while at the same time hurling angry charges of Yankee interference. Labor Minister Blas Ople blistered a delegation of American scholars with a harangue against their country's "unwarranted intervention". The United States wanted to impose its "monolithic model of democracy" on the world, the Marcos minister claimed, while the Philippines had evolved a government "which is uniquely our own". Marcos-controlled newspapers pounded the same drum daily, in some of the most inflammatory language ever set in type.

"The blatant intervention by the U.S. government, the U.S. press and by American legislators has become intolerable," fumed columnist Teodoro Valencia in the *Daily Express*. "Americans can't permit an Oriental people to show they know democracy, too." Valencia said his nation had become an American whipping boy, "because they have defeated nobody since World War II. They must do it to us, who have always allowed them to save their ego." A few inches away, another *Express* columnist suggested that all foreign observers, including press, human-rights activists, and visiting politicians, be tested for AIDS.

But U.S. influence had barely hits its stride. Senator Richard Lugar, head of the Senate foreign-relations committee, arrived, leading Washington's 20-member team of high-powered and opinionated election observers. Parliamentarians from around the world also came as part of a 44-man group funded by the American Republican and Democratic parties. The observers had scarcely unpacked their luggage before they plunged into the February 7 presidential poll that would demonstrate Marcosian democracy in action.

The outsiders began their work with motherhood comments about non-involvement and a commitment to freedom. By nightfall, the shocked and enraged foreigners were mixing unabashedly in Philippine internal affairs. Senator Lugar, the picture of diplomacy over breakfast, by midnight was scowling darkly as he accused the Marcos government of delaying its vote count "to assess really how big a problem they have". By the time Linda Kapunan led the computer walkout forty-eight hours later, American observers had dispensed with all niceties. "I think these are the most damning comments I've ever heard," said Democratic senator John Kerry, who rushed to interview the computer workers. "And the most dramatic events I've witnessed."

Most Americans, treated to blanket TV coverage of the extraordinary events, seemed to agree. But the only American who mattered to Marcos decided to stick with his "right arm in Asia" a while longer.

Secretary of State George Shultz briefed Ronald Reagan on the Philippine election just before a February 11 press conference. But the President refused to believe the inside reports. Instead, he told reporters there was no "hard evidence" of fraud, and opined that "it could have been that all of that was occurring on both sides." Worse, Reagan showed no regard for the average Filipino voter, stressing the prime importance in the whole electoral equation of the strategic U.S. bases at Subic Bay and Clark Air Base.

The schism was out in the open. For years, State Department analysts had seen the Philippines as a potential Iran and had warned that Marcos could become "another Shah". Their view ran head-on against a president who had known Marcos ever since Richard Nixon sent California governor Ronald Reagan as his personal emissary to Manila. The White House posture was neatly summed up by Senator Laxalt: "Marcos . . . was a reliable and trusted ally of the United States from day one." He might be a son of a bitch, but he was definitely *our* son of a bitch.

"Everybody in our operation knew there was a split," says a U.S. diplomat who has been posted to Manila. "Our last three ambassadors and all the analysts at State were anti-Marcos. But Reagan and [White House chief of staff Donald] Regan were very much in his corner, along with some of the military and CIA. I'd say ninety per cent of the people in our Embassy were sympathetic to the opposition. But Marcos still had some *very* powerful [U.S.] friends, including the guy at the top."

Enrique Joaquin discovered that, to his cost, just before the election. A prominent businessman and close friend of Cory Aquino, he went to Washington to create a bipartisan Aquino lobby there, and found himself neck-deep in Marcos Country.

"We realized there might be an election standoff, and all the pressure groups in Washington would be pushing the Marcos line," explains Joaquin. "So I went there to get sympathetic people from both parties to join a pro-Aquino group" called American Friends of Philippine Democracy. It would counter a $1-million Marcos campaign run by the conservative Washington lobbying firm Paul Manafort, Stone & Kelly, a campaign helped by Imelda's brother Benjamin Romualdez, the Philippine ambassador to the U.S., with access to nearly limitless funds.

Joaquin managed to line up Democrats immediately, starting with former Maryland senator Joseph Tydings. But he found it impossible to recruit a prominent Republican willing to throw visible support behind Mrs. Aquino. Finally he went to see his friend Henry Kissinger, who had taught him at a 1953 Harvard seminar.

They huddled at the exclusive River Club overlooking New York's East River, with the former Secretary of State in an expansive mood. "I want you to brief me completely about the situation over there," said Kissinger; "I'm very interested." Joaquin described the phenomenal popular support Aquino had generated, and the two discussed election scenarios for nearly two hours. But Kissinger remained deeply skeptical. "She can't win," he reasoned, "and if she did, how could she govern?" He then noted President Marcos's "unflinching record against Communism" and absolute support for the strategic bases. Kissinger couldn't possibly support a pro-Aquino lobby, he told his former student. "It would ruin me politically."

"It was a very depressing experience," says Joaquin, now the Philippine Immigration Commissioner, "to hear such a great thinker talking about my country in simplistic terms. He obviously had no grasp of the subtleties. Worse than that, I felt I was just being used. We talked for two hours, although he was late for another meeting. After a while, I realized he was simply milking me for information. He charges huge fees to advise his customers on international matters, and he knew *nothing*. Now he could go and sell this 'fresh' information. I felt terribly let down."

Ronald Reagan played for time after his "cheating-on-both-sides" blunder, and dispatched emissary Philip Habib on a Manila "fact-finding" mission. This angered Senator Lugar, who was touching down in Washington with a plane-load of facts just as Habib took off. The arrival of Reagan's retired Lebanon trouble-shooter also enraged Cory Aquino, who turned her sarcasm on the White House.

"I would wonder at the motive of a 'friend of democracy' who chose to conspire with Marcos to cheat the Filipino people of their liberation," she jibed, in one hand-written press release. Nor did she back off when a conciliatory Reagan asked her to work for change within a two-party system. Cory reminded the U.S. president that it might be "difficult for leaders who have been and are being killed, to suddenly settle down in a Western-style opposition role in a healthy two-party system. Too many will be dead the moment the world's head is turned."

U.S. Embassy insiders now say that Habib was actually sent to coax Mrs. Aquino into accepting defeat. In the Reagan plan, she was to play an "advisory" role in a compromise government, then run for president six years later. Cory exploded in rage when feelers were sent out by the Embassy, and threatened to snub Habib if he dared make such an offer. So the unfortunate emissary went through the motions of gathering "facts" that the entire world already knew. As a final indignity, he boarded a flight to Washington on Saturday, February 22 – at exactly the moment Juan Ponce Enrile and his colonels made their stand at Camp Aguinaldo.

Ambassador Stephen Bosworth was stunned when he returned from waving goodbye at the airport and received a frantic call from

Enrile. "I'll inform my government" was all he said when the minister informed him of the breakaway. Pressed for some hint of U.S. leanings, Bosworth cut Enrile short; his first priority was to get a bulletin off to Washington, and he would not delay even to pump Enrile for further information.

Enrile was not satisfied by the Ambassador's response. U.S. support was so vital that, even before going to Aguinaldo, the minister had called his close friend Rene Cayetano and ordered him to Bosworth's house. Cayetano, one of Manila's most successful lawyers, was asleep on the couch in his plush Makati office when a secretary burst into the room at 3:20 p.m. "Sir," she said, "I hate to wake you. But the minister wants to speak with you."

"Rene, it's Johnny," said Enrile. "We're going to be arrested. But we're taking a stand at Aguinaldo. Remember what I told you? Okay, now, do it and do it quickly. We need help. I don't know how long we can last."

Cayetano had unknowingly been part of the coup plot for exactly a week. In his role as an assemblyman for Marcos's KBL party, he had approached Enrile in the National Assembly chamber before the President's "victory" was ratified by a show of hands. "I want out," Cayetano told his political godfather. "I want to leave and go home right now. We can't be a party to this charade."

Enrile gripped Cayetano's right arm and gave him a firm shake. "Just trust me," he instructed. "When the voting comes, just raise your arm and don't say anything. Do you think Marcos won?"

"I don't think so. I know he lost in my district."

"Well, I *know* he lost," said Enrile. "Just do what I told you, and very soon we will rectify this grievous error."

Cayetano stayed for the voting, and cast his ballot in favor of the trumped-up canvass. Rejoining Enrile after the session, he noticed that his friend had a bullet-proof vest under his suit coat.

"Nowadays you cannot be too careful," explained the minister. "Come on, let's go to Malacañang and congratulate the President. We must behave as if everything is normal."

Two days later, on Monday, February 17, Enrile came to Cayetano's law office late in the afternoon. The minister is an unofficial member of the Cayetano firm, and maintains a wood-panelled corner office with a three-foot statue of the Blessed Virgin hovering over his desk. Enrile seemed melancholy and depressed, holding his face in his hands, so Cayetano tactfully moved the other law partners away.

"What's the matter, Johnny? I've never seen you look this sad."

"They are really going to kill me," the minister answered. "My boys have gotten new information that they're going to assassinate me and round everyone up" – an apparent reference to Marcos's planned Operation Everlasting.

"Look," said Cayetano. "My testimony will be no good if they do it. The best thing is for you to write it all down and address it to your wife." He gathered up a yellow legal pad, two felt-tipped pens, a brown manila envelope, and some tape to seal the package. Enrile then went into his office and closed the door, to emerge eighty minutes later with his last political will and testament. "It's all here," he said, holding out a neatly wrapped envelope with his initials across the seal. "Guard it with your life."

Cayetano still has the package, and produced it for a curious reporter six months after the revolt. "Rene, in case of my death through assassination," Enrile had written on the back, "please open this in the presence of the media, so that the world and our people will know. Thank you so much. Please help my family for old times' sake." Cayetano has taped the two Flair Ultra Fine Point pens to the envelope, either as souvenirs or as evidence.

Four days later, just hours before the scheduled coup, Enrile gave Cayetano last-minute instructions. In case something happened to him, his law partner should (1) see the U.S. Ambassador immediately; (2) contact the media; (3) try to get in touch with Cardinal Sin; (4) take care of Enrile's family.

"But what do you mean by 'something'?" Cayetano protested. "How will I know when to do it?"

"Just keep your eyes open," replied the minister. "If I have time, I'll call you myself. Or maybe you'll hear it on the radio. Make your own judgement."

Cayetano had his eyes shut the following afternoon when the lid blew off the plot. But he was wide awake after Enrile's call, and knew his instructions by heart. Within minutes he was speeding down Ayala Boulevard towards Bosworth's mansion in North Forbes Park. Cayetano had dined there many times, and felt confident about approaching the Ambassador with a personal plea. He rolled into the driveway at 3:45 p.m. and raced up the front steps.

Philip Kaplan, the Embassy's second-ranking officer, met him at the door.

"Phil," said the Enrile emissary, "I've got to see Steve."

"Why do you want to see him?" demanded Kaplan. "You tell me first."

"The hell I will. This involves my friend's life. I've got to see Steve right away."

Bosworth peered out of a doorway and asked what was going on. He seemed to be in the midst of a consultation and he was not pleased to see Cayetano. "I hardly recognized him," says the Assemblyman. "For the first time in my long association with him, he was stern and unsmiling. I'd been there many times at his house, but he acted like he didn't know me."

"Steve," said Cayetano. "You guys have to do something. Enrile is in trouble. His life is in danger. Please help him."

"I've just talked to him on the phone, and I've contacted Washington . . ." Bosworth answered.

"Is that all you can do? Can't you put out a warning to Marcos? Do *something*, for Christ's sake, before they're all killed."

"Sorry," shrugged the Ambassador. "There's nothing I can do. Do you have any idea what time it is in Washington?"

"What about the American press? Can't you at least contact them?"

Bosworth shook his head. "We have no access to the American press. No access at all. If you want to call them . . . uh . . . I think most of them are in the Manila Hotel."

Cayetano was stunned. He knew very well that the U.S. Embassy kept a list of both visiting and resident media for its own press briefings. On a normal day, a simple request would produce a typed page of phone numbers. What the hell was going on? Cayetano got back in his car and realized that it was too dangerous to go home. He checked into the Manila Garden Hotel under an assumed name and started phoning every reporter he had ever met.

The U.S. Embassy, meanwhile, had switched on the big microwave transmission dish in its backyard and opened a secure line to Washington. It would hum without interruption for the next four days. While oppositionist members such as Butz Aquino's ATOM group tried frantically throughout Saturday to reach Cory Aquino in Cebu, and failed, Bosworth's operatives found her hiding place immediately. The Ambassador offered safe asylum on an American navy ship; Mrs. Aquino refused, politely.

The Reformists got in touch with their friend Vic Raphael, who promised to plead their case with the Pentagon – but held out little hope of military help. "We knew there were some parts of the U.S. government for and against us," explains Colonel Legaspi, "so we asked Raphael to put us in quick touch with the State Department and [Ronald] Reagan. He was able to do that. He was giving the Defense Department first-hand information."

"It was very important to get our side across to them," adds Colonel Gringo Honasan. "We just *had* to stay in touch, or we might have gotten crushed."

"Crushed" is correct. For, like every other aspect of Philippine-American relations, the military balance is outlandishly lopsided; the two American permanent bases alone have enough firepower to destroy the Philippine armed forces. And U.S. logistical support is so crucial that no Filipino unit can fight without it for more than a few hours. By no coincidence, a stream of U.S. battleships and aircraft carriers (including the gigantic USS *Enterprise*) had "visited" the country during the election, and many were still anchored offshore.

"You have to be a military man to appreciate their power," says Lt.-Col. Antonio Romero, a RAM officer who spent the revolt as a "mole" inside Loyalist-held areas. "Even if our entire armed forces were united, the Americans would wallop us. One aircraft carrier could blow us all to hell. Not the personnel, but the jets, the fighters. Even their re-supply was absolutely crucial.

"The revolt was strictly Filipino. But we'd be liars if we didn't admit it: Psychologically, every one of us [soldiers] was waiting to see which way the U.S. would jump. If they backed one faction, the other would have no chance. None."

Most Reformists are tremendously bitter about the first two days of the revolt. They were helpless against the superior Marcos forces, and faced annihilation at any moment. Yet all pleas to their friends at the U.S. Embassy were met with indifference, obfuscation, or promises to "get back to you" soon.

"We owe them nothing. They gave us nothing," stormed Juan Ponce Enrile, on his way in to President Cory Aquino's first cabinet session after the rebellion. And the Defense Minister's disgust was echoed even months later by his close-knit "special operations group".

"We have a term for it in Tagalog," sneered Captain Ricardo Morales in July 1986. "It's called *segurista*: somebody who plays it safe and refuses to do anything. It's a derogatory term, and it describes the Americans perfectly."

"Obviously they just waited to see which way the wind was blowing," says Legaspi. "They wanted to be sure which side would win, and *then* come in with support. When our lives were on the line, we saw very clearly who our friends were. And the worst part was that they tried to take credit for helping us, after it was all over."

One man's duplicity, however, can be another's careful prudence. The Americans were certainly no help to Enrile and Ramos in their hour of greatest need. And the United States may even have "bought insurance" with Marcos, by tipping him off to the impending attack. But the Embassy's job was not to seek justice or to win plaudits for courage. It was there to protect *American* interests, regardless of which side won the EDSA standoff. And Bosworth's crew set about that task with relentless efficiency.

Idealists might have moral objections to that stance, but Embassy spokesman Croghan sees no need to apologize. The United States, he makes clear, followed the strict dictates of *realpolitik*. "Maybe RAM felt they should have got more help than they did at that crucial moment," concedes Croghan. "Those big machines were coming at them and we were talking non-violence. They obviously resented it. But what could we do? Nobody knew who was going to win. Nobody knew what was going to happen. And anyone who thinks about it can see why we couldn't help them. Imagine if they had lost. What kind of situation would we be in with Marcos? In such cases, you have to think a couple of steps down the road."

American spy-in-the-sky satellites may have monitored all radio and telephone conversations over the next seventy-five hours. Certainly that's what Philippine commanders such as air force general Antonio Sotelo – then a colonel – still suspect. "Almost every scrap of 'inside' information I know about the revolt came from my American friends after it was over," he smiles. "They knew everything that was done and said. Every word, every comma."

But the excellent U.S. intelligence had little to do with hi-tech miracles. The Philippine military uses outmoded crystal radios with fewer than a dozen possible frequencies, and the crystals were never changed. So anyone with a decent monitor could hear every order issued from the Palace. For further information, the Embassy immediately placed agents at the airport, outside Malacañang, at Camps Crame and Aguinaldo, and in Loyalist strongholds such as Fort Bonifacio and Villamor Air Base. They also cleverly tapped secondary sources. "We left a phone line open to the U.S. Embassy during the whole revolt," concedes Father James Reuter, head of the influential Catholic Federation of Broadcasters. "The guy on their end was a very dignified black man in the political section named Bruce Thomas. He was constantly interested in what was happening in the world of Juan Ponce Enrile, and that was easy for us, because we had a mobile radio unit in Enrile's war room. So, any time Thomas wanted to know something, we could just ask. I suppose it was only a backup for them. I assume they had direct contacts with Enrile, too."

Nor did the Americans need satellites to steal key telephone conversations. Ambassador Bosworth was on the end of most of the important calls. More than two dozen of his phone exchanges have come to light, indicating he was on the line constantly – probably with Washington listening in. Every White House statement was relayed by Bosworth to Marcos before its release, and the response passed back across the Pacific. The Ambassador offered sanctuary to Mrs. Aquino and Cardinal Sin, and revealed details of the Marcos "roundup" to the Catholic prelate. When the rebels were baffled by false reports of a Marcos departure, they simply phoned Bosworth, who told them: "Sure, Marcos is still here. I just got off the phone with him." Every rumored Loyalist attack was immediately followed by frantic Enrile-to-Bosworth telephone calls. The final Marcos airlift required hours of telephone negotiations throughout Tuesday. And when President Marcos asked to be flown to Ilocos province, the request was channelled to Cory Aquino through . . . yes, the inexhaustible American envoy.

"He didn't get much sleep," concedes Croghan. "Everybody was in touch with everybody in this town. That's one strange thing about the whole episode. Nobody spent much time wondering . . . everything was right out in the open. But I don't know how crucial the Ambassador's calls were. President Marcos thought Bosworth represented the State Department bureaucracy, not President Reagan. So he wouldn't have much persuasive leverage."

Bosworth read Washington's first official statement to Marcos early Sunday morning, and it must have come as a shock. The White House pointedly ignored his coup allegations and concentrated on the claims of Enrile and Ramos. "These statements strongly reinforce our concerns that the recent elections were marred by fraud, perpetrated overwhelmingly by the ruling party, . . ." said the sharply worded note. "Many authoritative voices in the Philippines have been raised in support of non-violence. We support these voices and expect them to be respected."

8 _SUNDAY SHOWDOWN_

ON TELEVISION SCREENS around the world, it was all valor and victory. Nuns stopping tanks with their bare hands. Housewives and children huddled in the path of ugly metal monsters. A display of other-worldly faith that held much of the planet transfixed and, briefly, transformed.

None of that was evident at noon on Sunday, however, as confused crowds surged along Epifanio de los Santos Avenue [EDSA], driven in circles by conflicting rumors. Trucks of combat-ready Marcos soldiers were reported arriving from the north. No, from the south. It was the paramilitary police under General Lim. No, they were army troops under General Oropesa. Helicopter gunships were coming. No, wait. They were tanks. Marines in tanks. Near the Guadalupe Bridge.

Frustrated and frightened, most of us abandoned ourselves to the flow of the crowd. Forty or fifty thousand had jammed the four-lane boulevard between Camp Crame and Camp Aguinaldo. Young men shovelled roadside gravel into bags, and set up pathetic shin-high barriers. Traffic was blocked, and disabled transport trucks guarded the military gates. The scene made a fine impression when TV cameramen mounted the street-lamps and panned over the human barricade. But it took ten minutes, no more, to stroll a half-mile to Ortigas Avenue and discover that the Revolution was virtually naked.

That intersection, soon to be a Philippine legend, was a bleak patch of asphalt surrounded by empty office towers. Buses, cars, and jeepneys still went about their Sunday routine. The few pedestrians were suburbanites on their way to Crame; they had parked cars far from any impending confrontation, and now strolled to war with their kids in "Cory yellow" sun visors, lugging lawn chairs, picnic hampers, water jugs, blankets, Walkman radios, stalks of bananas, plastic bags stuffed with green mangoes, and opposition newspapers bearing the day's banner headline: "MILITARY REBELLION – Enrile, Ramos challenge FM!"

Cheers and whistles rose periodically from the crowd around the camps. But the curious who ran to the scene found only a sand truck arriving with a load of burlap bags. The mixture of fear and euphoria was a potent drug, lending great significance to the most mundane events. Hoist a sandbag in the air and a hundred people cheered. Blow your horn and the crowd would take up the rhythmic chant of "Co-ry! Co-ry!"

But General Artemio Tadiar had a sobering antidote for our intoxication. When he appeared on the EDSA horizon leading nine armored personnel carriers (the tank-like APCs), a dozen jeeps, and two thousand Marines in trucks, it was like an eclipse of the noonday sun.

"They were death coming towards you. It was like meeting death on the road," recalls singer Leah Navarro, who had been up all night with the vigilantes outside Aguinaldo. By Sunday afternoon, she and some friends had organized an impromptu highway patrol: four cars, with two lookouts each. They had barrelled down EDSA to investigate a Radio Veritas report about tanks – and ran smack into Tadiar's armored column. "The rumble of the tanks was so loud you couldn't hear anything else," she recalls. "We sent two cars ahead to warn the people there at the barricades, while the rest of us trailed the tanks. Something had clicked inside of us; we all became very brave."

Two carloads of society matrons turned onto EDSA just as the armored column emerged. Still miles from the rebel barricades, the ladies eased alongside the tanks with nervous smiles and tentative waves. The Marines responded with their battle faces. One leaned towards the ladies' car and flashed an obscene middle finger, while his buddies sniggered.

One car opened its window so the driver in a pale-blue dress could flash the L-sign with the thumb and forefinger of her right hand. "We're all Filipinos!" shouted the woman. "We all want the same thing. Let's not fight among ourselves!" A soldier riding shotgun on the second tank pondered this logic for perhaps ten seconds, then turned and spat out a succinct Tagalog reply: "Mamamatay rin kayong lahat." Translation: "You are all going to die, too."

The sleepy EDSA-Ortigas intersection was suddenly a chaotic "choke point", the spot on the map where People Power and the Marcos forces intersected. Just after 2:30 p.m., General Tadiar had his first moment of decision as he peered through a gunner's slot at the cars, buses, and massed humanity blocking the crossroads. The Marine commander postponed the confrontation, swung his column to the right, and smashed through a concrete wall.

Now it was the civilians' turn to make hard choices, though few of us actually did. The panic and horror hadn't quite settled over the crowd at the barricade before the first hotheads – or heroes – vaulted the wall and ran to surround the APCs. The rest of us followed like lemmings, shouting and waving and scraping our knees on the whitewashed concrete. Courage or insanity – something contagious – was certainly in the air.

Tadiar and his officers were confounded by this turn of events. They stood in an angry knot beside one tank, screened off from the crowd by a ring of young Marines and their Armalites. Civilian leaders tried to shout pleas past the armed guard or force their way through, but the General had his back turned and a radio jammed against his left ear. The frantic entreaties were lost in the rumble of APC engines, while the entire Marine unit adopted the same frozen military glare.

The next move was quintessentially Filipino – or Filipina, actually, since only the women could have managed it. In a country where virtual strangers call each other "older sister", and every female above the age of thirty is lovingly hailed as "auntie", cold hostility cannot last long. The Philippines is arguably the warmest, most affectionate, most matriarchal society on earth, and with the largest family ties. So it was perhaps inevitable that, somewhere in the front lines, a venerable "*tita*" would discover some tenuous kinship with General Tadiar and come bustling forward to show him the error of his ways. In fact, a host of indignant matrons attempted to push through the forest of M-16s and dress the General down. It isn't possible to say who got there first, but the initial wave certainly included Viring Ongkeko, Aida Ciron, Vangie Durian, and her teenage son Jojo.

Vangie had sifted the situation for its social possibilities and had reached a grim conclusion. "It's the Marines," she whispered to her companions, "so it must be General Tadiar. He is known as a real terror. That's why he's called *Tadjak*" – a Tagalog word meaning kick, as in "shit-kicker". But Mrs. Ongkeko wasn't about to be stopped. "Well, at least we know who he is," she reasoned. "So we should be able to talk to him. Let's go up there and dissuade him from whatever orders he has."

This piece of eminently Filipina logic drew immediate approval from the males in the vicinity. "That's right," they chorused. "Go ahead. Go ahead. You women confront them. They will never hurt you because you are women."

It was not easy to reach the General. He was still on the radio, informing army commander General Josephus Ramas (no relation to rebel General Ramos) of the stalemate, and was surrounded four-deep by edgy Marines. So the first female foray was easily repulsed by rifle butts, elbows, and broad shoulders. This did not sit well with the surrounding masses, or with the feisty Mrs. Ongkeko. "Hah!" she huffed at a young

Marine. "Why do you have to push us with your guns? You only have to push us with your hands and we will already fall down."

The outburst had the intended effect. The young Marine's machismo was punctured, and was entirely deflated when the General fixed him with a reproving glare. Tadiar waved his hand in an abrupt take-it-easy gesture, his guards shuffled back a few steps . . . and the ladies rushed in where no male dared to tread. Aida Ciron found a hole in the Marine formation and, like an NFL defensive tackle on a quarterback sack, lunged right at Tadiar and wrapped her matronly arms around him. As it happened, Mrs. Ciron was the wife of Colonel Ruben Ciron, an aide to Juan Ponce Enrile. All she knew about Tadiar were the Filipino essentials – his nickname and his family ties. But that was easily enough to open the assault on his emotions.

"Temmy, Temmy," she pleaded, tears streaming down her cheeks. "You also have a wife and children. Please don't do it."

If he had not been deciding the fate of thousands, Tadiar would have made a comic sight. He is a squat, dark, bulldog-faced man, the very image of a Marine general. And he had turned out in full battle gear, complete with a camouflage cap, ammunition belts, and a bullet-proof vest. Yet there he stood, squirming and ducking out of Mrs. Ciron's grasp like a ten-year-old being kissed by an unfavorite auntie.

His squirming did him no good. Aida Ciron held on until reinforcements could arrive. Within seconds, Vangie Durian had grabbed him by the hand and delivered the social knockout blow. "Temmy," she informed him briskly. "You know me. We were neighbors in Navy Village."

The General could only surrender to the dictates of Filipino politesse. "Is Jess there?" he asked, courteously inquiring whether Vangie's husband – Captain Jesus Durian, another Enrile assistant – was holed up in Camp Aguinaldo. "Yes, and this is my son Jojo." The boy stepped forward smartly to complete the introductions, as if the exchange were taking place around the swimming pool of the Army-Navy Club. "Sir," said Jojo, "I used to go to your house to play with your son."

These pleasantries, of course, were barely audible beyond the ring of Marine bodyguards. The surrounding crowd had swelled quickly, and some vigilantes were near hysteria. Women wailed, men jostled for position, and the entire mass pressed closer around Tadiar. One Marine guard was knocked off his feet, and his buddies reacted predictably, jabbing the crowd with M-16 barrels and roughly shoving people back.

The masses were still leaderless, but employed a form of instinctive "psy-war" against the soldiers. Nuns, children, and housewives gravitated to the front. So the hapless Marines were hamstrung; it is one thing to bash out the brains of a New People's Army guerrilla, quite another to slam your rifle butt into the serene visage of a Good Shepherd nun. Women began hollering questions at the General. Perhaps softened by his contacts with the Navy Village clan, Tadiar now responded. "We are not going to harm any civilians," he shouted above the din. "Our orders are only to confront Enrile and Ramos." As if to underscore his good intentions, Tadiar began unbuckling his flak jacket with some help from his men. The gesture may have had primordial military significance, like a gladiator doffing his armor, but the civilians took no notice. "What are you going to do to them?" they demanded. "Are you going to kill Enrile and Ramos?"

"Look," lied Tadiar, "we just want to talk to them." The human barricade took one glance at the machine-gun turrets on his tanks and replied with derisive hoots and howls.

"How can you say you're just going to talk?" yelled a middle-aged man. "How can you say you won't hurt civilians? Once they see you, they will surely get nervous and fight back. There will be an exchange of gunfire and many people will be killed."

The tanks had been motionless for twenty minutes by this time, and the human barricade had tripled or quadrupled. Pairs of young men had taken up posts along the retaining wall as human elevators, boosting nuns, children, and the aged into the compound. Those at the back had missed Tadiar's comments and began repeating the same questions.

But the latecomers were far less spontaneous than the first wave. They included Gerry Esguerra and his band from the SMK, the "urban armed warriors". That group alone – a descendant of the notorious Light-A-Fire movement that torched many tourist hotels – included three hundred armed men with a quaint variety of weapons: Smith & Wesson .45 revolvers, pistolized M-1 carbines, sawed-off shotguns, plastic bombs, and 288 grenades, all stashed in sporty-looking duffle bags. "Obviously, we'd have been outmatched by the Marines' firepower," concedes Esguerra, now security chief at the Manila International Airport. "But we were there to provide some measure of self-defense. If they had fired, our job was to fire back. Our instructions were not to start anything, but to do what we could to defend the crowd if the army opened up on them. We didn't want it to be a slaughter of helpless people. We wanted to make the soldiers pay a price."

Here and there in the crowd – unarmed – were the militant groups that sprang up after the Aquino assassination in 1983 and led hundreds of anti-Marcos rallies. Groups such as ATOM and Bandila arrived with their banners and immediately assigned their members to positions in front of each tank. The nuns, of course, were placed in the vanguard, for maximum emotional impact upon Marine tank commanders.

People fanned out across the vacant lot, to make impassioned appeals to the soldiers lounging atop the dirty grey APCs. One such encounter is recalled by singer Leah Navarro, who linked hands with two friends and slowly approached one tank crew:

"My heart was pounding and I had to fight down this great desire to cry. I was really scared. There were 50-mm machine guns staring at us. I said to a soldier in a tank: 'Boss, wouldn't you like to come down here? It must be hot in there.' But he said: 'No, ma'am, we have air-con here.' Other people had joined us and were talking to the troops. Somebody had thought of bringing a cassette and was playing the [Radio Veritas] appeal of General Ramos. One very brave lady climbed up the lead tank and sat down on top of it. The soldiers begged her to go down, but she only asked them to light her cigarette. Then she called to the people on the ground to give the soldiers food. We were asking the troops to join us, to listen to Ramos, and we offered to tie yellow ribbons to their tanks. But they kept their mouths shut."

While the soldiers remained aloof, parts of the crowd grew hostile. There is a Tagalog term for the type of tough guy who inhabits every barrio: *halang ang bituka*. It translates as "criss-crossed guts" but refers to men who simply don't give a damn if they live or die. Some are criminals, others are former policemen or soldiers. All carry knives or guns, and most would be glad to kill you for ten U.S. dollars. Now their male bravado was offended by the hard-faced silence of the Marines, bristling with youth and guns. So, once the APC engines had stopped rumbling, the tough guys began plotting adventures, bragging what they would do if they could only take over a turret-mounted machine gun, and urging the crowd to mount an attack.

"There are so many of us. Let's charge them," hollered one group near the whitewashed fence. Shock waves rippled through the crowd. A single idiot on either side could touch off a massacre, and here was a whole section of idiots trying to put a torch to the fuse. Tagalog obscenities flew as men ran to the belligerents and made menacing gestures with their clutch bags. For a tense moment it seemed that the Marines might have to separate warring civilians, but the peaceful faction won out. "Hands against machine guns?" they demanded, with convincing logic. "Even General Ramos could not win such a fight."

Hundreds stood atop buses at the intersection for a bird's-eye view of the scene. Spontaneously, they set up a familiar chant that gripped the area for five minutes and seemed almost to shake the tanks: "CO-RY! CO-RY! CO-RY!" When it died down, people took turns yelling questions and pleas to Tadiar and his men: "Why do you support that son-of-a-whore dictator Marcos?" Or, more to the point: "We are all Filipinos. Please do not kill us."

A light-haired man who had been conferring with Tadiar then clambered onto a tank and motioned for silence. "I am just an ordinary citizen," he announced. "The decision is not mine, but for all of us. General Tadiar is requesting that his orders are only to confront Enrile and Ramos. He doesn't want to hurt us, and he'll let us accompany them. We can follow along." He switched to Tagalog to pose the question: "Papayagan ba natin sila?" ("Will we let them through?")

The crowd took no time to ponder the request. "Hindi!" they screamed back. "Hindi puede! No. No. No."

Strangely, Juan Ponce Enrile slept through most of this. It was a cool afternoon by Philippine standards, perhaps 75 degrees (24°C) and drizzly, and the rebel Defense Minister and General Ramos had been up most of the night. Once, while studying plans, the pair had fallen asleep side by side. Ramos was startled awake by a man's face snoring beside his own. It was Enrile, still cradling a baby Uzi and wearing his bullet-proof vest.

After 2 p.m. on Sunday, the minister was napping behind his desk in Camp Aguinaldo, unaware of the tanks about half a mile away. In his exhaustion, his dreams and reality had intertwined, and he recalls that moment as a hazy respite from the tension. "I was assessing the situation [before dozing off]; I could not believe that we were in this kind of condition. It had a feeling of unreality, as if it was a dream . . . a bad dream. Anyway, I guess one would go into this kind of situation when you are faced with danger. . . . But I was serene in my thoughts."

He was nudged awake by his security chief, Gringo Honasan, who had been monitoring EDSA. "Sir," he told Enrile, "we must prepare to move out." Enrile leapt to his feet, certain that the camp was under attack. But Honasan's decision was strictly tactical. "It is better for us to abandon this camp, and move across to Camp Crame to consolidate our forces with General Ramos," he explained. "We cannot defend both camps."

Inexplicably, the exodus of Enrile's forces from Aguinaldo became an emotional drama. Everyone involved, from the nuns in the crowd to Enrile and Honasan themselves, now speaks of it with moist or averted eyes. Nothing of great outward significance took place. A few hundred soldiers, led by the minister and Honasan, pushed out of the gate in disciplined formation at about 2:30 p.m. and slowly made the 500-yard trip to Camp Crame through a crush of humanity. Somehow, two civilians hoisted a four-foot statue of the Blessed Virgin above Enrile's head, and kept it teetering there throughout the crossing. Thousands of people reached out to touch him or shake his hand. Honasan's men kept opening pathways through the crowd, but they were immediately filled with tearful supporters who refused to be shoved aside. The scene was almost biblical, like the parting of a human sea.

"I was nearly crying myself," recalls Colonel Red Kapunan. "It was the first time we realized how much the civilians supported us. They were wiping the sweat from our brows, handing us food and rosaries. That's when I began to believe we could win."

The ubiquitous Butz Aquino materialized at Enrile's elbow and whispered in his ear. The procession slowed, and changed direction, and the minister made his way to a makeshift stage.

"All I said was, 'Johnny, talk to them,' " Aquino recalls. "I told him to thank the people for being there, and maybe they'd stay longer with us. So that's what he did. He got up a couple steps on the platform and started to speak, but the people drowned him out. They were chanting 'John-ny! John-ny!'. Everyone was crying and grabbing. He looked like he might start crying, too. But, you know, he's a politician, and with a reception like that . . . well, he climbs a couple more steps to show himself some more. Meanwhile, Honasan and the security people go wild. They can't protect him up there. Anyway, by the end he's all the way up on the platform and his three-minute thank-you speech goes on for at least ten minutes."

The 320 rebel soldiers were bristling with attack rifles, grenades, ammunition, and perhaps twenty jeeps and cars. But that was all. The hardware impressed military neophytes in the crowd, who oohed and aahed among themselves. More sophisticated observers had the opposite reaction: *"That's all there is? We're betting our lives on two companies with rifles?"* In all, the combined rebel force now stood at 750 men, including General Ramos's constabulary officers and the Cagayan Hundred. One nun nearly swooned when she saw "all those soldiers with all those guns", and she remembers them as "hard-faced, staring straight ahead; they wouldn't answer our questions." Yet a lawyer who watched the soldiers from the same spot was struck by their fear and uncertainty. "Some were nearly crying," he says. "They were very moved by the crowd's reaction."

Certainly the civilian embrace was as much spiritual as physical.

The madonnas, rosaries, and crucifixes were powerful symbols of a prodigal's return. For many in the crowd had hated the military for years, despising them as the brutal cutting edge of the Marcos dictatorship. The President's power had too often reached Filipinos at the muzzle or the butt end of an Armalite, and few could look at a military uniform without seeing the sickening image of Ninoy Aquino's blood-soaked body. Thousands had more personal reasons for their loathing: raped daughters, stolen property, indiscriminate beatings, tear-gassing at rallies.

"In the years of Marcos . . . I had developed a deep contempt for people in his government and especially for those in the armed forces who made his regime possible," says Antonio Mapa, a shipping executive who welcomed the soldiers that Sunday. "But, as Enrile crossed over to Crame, we shook the hands of his troops, wished them well, and told them we were praying for them. Many soldiers wept and hugged us. Perhaps they realized . . . that they were finally fighting for the right cause when they saw the huge throng that waited outside the gates and greeted them already as heroes."

Enrile's own reaction was less romantic. "My men had to surround me for security reasons," he recalls. "With a crowd like that, somebody can stick a knife in your belly or back; that's it."

Safely inside Camp Crame, the minister joined General Ramos on a fourth-floor terrace that offers a panoramic view of EDSA. The crowd had swollen to several hundred thousand, and would eventually exceed one million. When they caught sight of the rebel leaders on the balcony, they set up a rolling thunder of whoops and cheers. Enrile and Ramos waved and flashed Cory's L-sign. It was the Defense Minister's first look at People Power, and it struck him nearly dumb. He smiled at Ramos, shook his head in disbelief, and said: "Oh, my God."

Things were not so encouraging inside, where pins on the war-room map showed a nearly hopeless strategic situation. Not only were Tadiar's Marine APCs massed at Ortigas, but intelligence had picked up another tank unit in Cubao, on the opposite side of the camp. It was a classic pincer move, and the rebels had nothing to stop it except gasoline bombs and massed flesh.

Colonel Honasan and his RAM pals were toiling elsewhere in the building, desperately seeking a way to stop Tadiar's armor. "From our point of view," he recalls, "the situation wasn't good. We knew Tadiar was fiercely loyal to General Ver, so we expected the worst. We figured he'd try to push through. But, as to combat experience, that was different. We felt he might make some mistakes. He had come in from a diplomatic post in London, where he'd been for more than fifteen years. Also,

Marcos and Ver were dilly-dallying over the kind of information they had. They were still not willing to expose their flanks."

The rebels decided to exploit the APC's main weakness: poor peripheral vision. "The tanks cannot operate properly when they're buttoned up," explains Honasan. "There has to be someone who exposes himself, like the tank commander, or the gunner or driver. They can see from inside, but the vision is very limited. Ideally, tanks should operate with infantry support, to cover their vulnerable areas. Tadiar simply forgot all about that. They thought tanks could be sent in just like that." Honasan's men had produced Molotov cocktails, made from San Miguel beer bottles and stacked in stubby brown piles, ready for use when the Marines opened the tank hatches to peer out.

"We also had one surprise for them. We had made provisions to cut power lines and use the whole tanks as conductors for 15,000 volts. It might have been very uncomfortable," he grins, "for the men inside."

Enrile, meanwhile, was conducting a war of words. The instant he heard about the twin tank movements, the minister called Ambassador Bosworth. He explained the strategic set-up in detail (a waste of time, since the Americans almost certainly knew more about it than he did) and used the hundreds of foreign newsmen as a bargaining chip with Washington. "Look," he told the U.S. envoy, "there are many people in this building. If they shell it, there are many people who would die. Among them are hundreds of media men from foreign lands. And among them are a number of Americans."

But the phone call was more devious than it seemed. Enrile was already aware of the American strategy, which the Embassy deemed "even-handedness" and the rebels viewed as self-seeking duplicity. Either way, the minister was certain that anything he told Bosworth would soon be relayed to President Reagan's "good friend of democracy" in Malacañang Palace.

"My purpose [in calling Bosworth] was possibly to inform the Palace of the condition of the target they intended to attack," Enrile later revealed. "At the same time, I was hoping that he would inform his government, so the White House would at least caution the Palace to take a more prudent course."

The next step was more direct. Enrile phoned General Ver and proceeded to insult Marcos's chief henchman. There was no profanity. The minister merely called Ver a butcher and warned that he was about to become a mass murderer.

"General, I know your columns are coming towards us," he said.

"I want you to know that this building is full of civilians. Not only former officers who served you and who served the President but, more than that, there are many foreign correspondents with us. And if you are going to kill us, you and the President will go down in history as butchers of your own officers and men. You'll go down in history as butchers of the Filipino people and foreign media men. I'm warning you: you will be hitting civilians first, and that will be a terrible blow to your superiors.

"Kindly tell your tank commanders not to proceed."

Ver was oddly conciliatory in the face of this outburst. He grunted a few apologies into the phone, called Enrile "sir", and made a vague commitment to avoid bloodshed: "Well, sir, I will tell them not to push the civilians."

Only a military expert can fairly analyze Ver's tactics, but there is strong consensus today that he bungled the situation. The Enrile-Ramos position consisted primarily of a massive bluff. They had little hope of stopping the tanks, and no defense against the pinpoint artillery available to Ver, which they knew could take apart every building in Camp Crame, office by office, if necessary. Even the human barricades, although charming a world satellite TV audience, could be dispersed with minimum bloodshed by the highly disciplined Marines. That, at least, is the view of a Marine colonel on the Loyalist side, who will eventually add his own chilling perspective to the EDSA showdown.

Obviously Ver should have cut all communication to Crame, and stopped the satellite feeds of the showdown that held Western audiences and governments enthralled. Such orders were issued, but they were never carried out, and the lame excuses sent back to Ver's headquarters were accepted with little objection. Even Enrile, a lawyer by training, was shocked that Marcos held his top general in Malacañang Park, and attempted to dictate strategy. "Just imagine!" says the minister. "A president allowing his generals to operate in the Palace, where there are no maps, no communication lines. Ver had forces available to him. Over at Fort Bonifacio, he could have called a meeting of his generals, convened a war council, and decided what to do. But Marcos wanted control. They ran the whole thing from his bedroom. It's very difficult to be a king and commander of the troops at the same time. Only Alexander the Great was able to do it."

But the command situation on the Marcos side was worse than that. While the world's attention was focused on EDSA, General Ver was on a public relations mission at Villamor Air Base. He had been informed of morale problems at the base, where some pilots had expressed open disbelief at the RAM coup plot. Ver had the solution. He rounded up three of the captive "confessors" and ran them over to the air base for a tête-à-tête with the wavering pilots. Ver went with them, just to show the flag and let the young officers rub elbows with the chief of staff. So, while General Tadiar desperately tried to bluff his way past a million civilians, the "brains" of the Loyalist operation was having his picture taken on the tarmac, leading the confessors past a line of skeptical fly-boys. Ver didn't know it, but most of those pilots had already opted for the rebels; they were only awaiting orders on when and how to defect.

Army commander General Josephus Ramas was left to oversee the EDSA operation from Fort Bonifacio, a few miles due south of Camp Crame. His reaction to the standoff owed nothing to subtlety: "Ram through," he told Tadiar over the radio. "Ram through the crowds, regardless of casualties." The Marine general automatically said "Yessir!", then realized that he could not possibly carry out the order. "I don't want to hurt these people," he told his boss. "I am also human."

Minutes later, the crowd was terrified to see a black Sikorsky gunship come roaring out of the south and land behind the stalled tanks. Marines rushed to form a circle around it, brandishing their Armalites to hold back the masses. Two officers poked their heads out the window, and Tadiar jogged over to confer with them. All three were seen to be poring over documents, before the Marine general finally disappeared through the helicopter door.

"It's Ver!" the crowd told each other. "Or maybe it's someone sent by Ver. Tadiar must be getting his orders."

Most journalists reported it that way, and even now the Sikorsky's arrival is viewed as a turning point in the EDSA stalemate. It seemed logical that Ver or an emissary had arrived for an on-site inspection; in reality, the chopper's occupants were General Angel Kanapi and Colonel Lisandro Abadia, who had arrived with exactly *nothing* in the way of instructions. The trio sat with their hands in their pockets, perusing aerial photographs already two hours old, and looking wise. A series of "Well, what do you think?" conversations led nowhere. Then, rather than appear to be doing nothing, the three officers decided to go aloft and reconnoitre the area. The view from above did little to inspire new strategy. A solid wall of flesh – it seemed bright yellow from 1,500 feet, with all those Cory T-shirts – now stretched the half-mile from the intersection to Camp Crame.

Back on the ground, it was Kanapi who finally offered the semblance of a game plan. Why not swing away from the civilians down a road to the right, and try to outrun the crowd to the back gate of Camp Aguinaldo? "Great," thought Tadiar. "Now all I've got to do is get the tanks out of here without crushing a thousand nuns, and race a million people down a sideroad." As they departed, he exchanged salutes with the helpful men from headquarters, and rejected their brainstorm as unworkable.

"Tadiar didn't get much help from the top," says a high-ranking officer among the Marcos forces that day, who prefers not to be identified. "Nobody wanted to take the blame for a massacre of civilians, so they kept giving him more and more ambiguous instructions. Basically, they kept stressing results instead of methods. They kept ordering him to attack Crame, but they didn't come up with any workable plans for doing it. After a while, Tadiar figured out that he was left dangling in the wind."

That view is supported by subsequent events. Only an hour after Enrile talked to General Ver, he received an unexpected emissary from Tadiar. The two messages were *not* coordinated. Tadiar's man made clear his general was under orders to attack Crame. His plea was vintage "psy-war", mixing threat and olive branch. Tadiar would obey the attack order, civilians or no civilians. But before making a hostile move, he wanted a one-on-one meeting with the Defense Minister.

Enrile pondered the offer, and responded with guile. He stalled for time, sending word that he was in conference with the media and would soon be in touch with the Marine leader. That, of course, was the last Tadiar heard from Enrile.

Back at the vacant lot near EDSA, the frustrated General Tadiar grasped at another straw and prepared to dispatch yet another messenger. Two representatives from the Cory Aquino campaign, her sister-in-law Tingting Cojuangco and advisor Teofisto Guingona, were huddled with the General beside a tank. They passed word to the crowd: the pair would go to Crame, this time to meet General Ramos. But the encouraging news was accompanied by a stern warning. They had just thirty minutes to return with an answer. After that, no quarter would be given. The Marines would attack Crame, and the civilians would be caught in the crossfire.

Hundreds of thousands of Filipinos simultaneously checked their watches and made the calculation. It was now 4:20 p.m.; Armageddon would begin at ten minutes to five.

Radio Veritas had a man high atop a nearby broadcast tower, reporting the standoff to the country in a blow-by-blow staccato. Tadiar's ultimatum immediately flashed across the airwaves. The response, slightly insane, was by now predictable. All across Manila, people who had stayed home now began leaping into their cars and driving furiously towards EDSA. Far from creating nervous flight among the human barricade, the General's ultimatum seemed to provide a welcome rallying point. Finally it was all set. Tanks vs. Nuns, 4:50 p.m., corner of EDSA and Ortigas. An exact time for the Superbowl Showdown had been announced, and nobody wanted to miss it.

In the crowd, the nuns and priests began praying the Joyful Mysteries as thousands joined in. Then they switched to the Sorrowful Mysteries. Even for a lapsed Canadian Protestant, it was like being suspended between heaven and hell. Beautiful voices were being raised in the very shadow of death, represented by the greasy grey personnel carriers. Everywhere the same eerie juxtaposition: guns above rosaries, bullets beside plastic statues of the Santo Niño.

Butz Aquino arrived from a confrontation on the far side of Camp Crame. General Alfredo Lim, the other half of the Marcos pincer movement, had arrived with about four hundred soldiers. He and Butz had huddled in an antique shop and eaten Chinese *siopao* buns, until Aquino persuaded Lim to call General Ramos on the phone. The short conversation was completely one-sided. "All Lim said was, 'Yes, sir. Yes, sir. Yes, sir,' " recalls Aquino. "Then, after a whole bunch of yessirs, he put down the phone. I looked at him and said, 'So, what happened?' He shrugged and said: 'Well, he asked me to stay put. So I'm going to stay put.' "

That crisis solved, Aquino joined his ATOM mates at Ortigas, arriving in time to hear Tadiar issue his deadline. The General was standing on a tank, along with a priest and a series of photographers who kept getting turfed off by soldiers. A PA system had somehow been installed, and Tadiar tried to monopolize the microphone. As always, Butz Aquino simply bulled into the middle of things; he ripped the rear end out of his pants on his way up the tank, but he ended up with the microphone.

"Somebody was talking on top of the tank, and I guess a lot of people weren't satisfied with his manner of persuasion," he recalls. "Anyway, they recognized me and started shouting, 'We want Butz.' So, you know me . . . here comes John Wayne to the rescue. They lifted me up on top of the tank and I just started talking. I don't really remember what I said. . . ."

Fortunately, Aquino's short address is in my notebook. It wasn't quite in a class with Mark Antony's speech, but, in the circumstances, it was almost as effective. "I guess everybody knows who General Tadiar is taking orders from," Aquino told the assembled masses, in a remarkably laconic tone. "He's getting them from you-know-who, the guy in Mala-cañang. And you people . . . well, I'd like you to tell the General who *you're* taking *your* orders from."

That set off a chant of "Co-ry! Co-ry! Co-ry!" that nearly shook Butz and Tadiar off the tank. In fact, the General retreated from his metallic centre stage, while Aquino pulled an old street-demonstrator's trick. He told everyone to sit down and "let them see how many you are. Let them know how many they're going to have to run over." Gradually his advice made its way across the vacant lot, over the wall, to the thousands barricading the intersection, and far, far beyond. People began sitting in confused little knots, and ordered their neighbors to do likewise.

Just then, the tank engines roared to life, one after the other, kicking out belches of smoke and a deafening rumble. I looked at my watch: 4:53 p.m. General Tadiar was right on time.

Once again the crowd ran *towards* trouble instead of away from it. People scrambled to get closer to the tanks, scrunching together to cram their bodies right under the metal tracks. Aquino, with his ripped pants now flapping in the breeze, leapt off a tank and found himself crouched in front of it.

"I didn't realize how big tanks are," he says now. "When you're there, it is as big as a house. It is so immense. But I was thinking: 'They probably won't do anything. They're just trying to scare us.' Then they shifted the gears and the thing started to inch forward. The sound alone is enough to kill you. It's more than quadrasonic, with all of that steel moving forward. You can literally hear the clanking of the steel. My fear was . . . well, it lasted longer than a few seconds.

"I looked around at the nuns to my left and my right. They didn't seem like budging, so I would have been too embarrassed to move out. Of course, I was trying to think up an excuse. Could I tell them I have an appointment somewhere else? I remember, I was looking at the bottom of the tank to see if the opening was big enough. If I would lay down, would it go over me? So I suggested this to the guy beside me, and he said, 'Sure, what if it turns?' I just shut up and waited. People were praying, singing, crying, all at the same time. It was some chaos."

The scene was almost incomprehensible. Aside from the tension, few of us had seen a million people in one place before – not at a carnival, a football game, or a political convention. To find them here, clad in Cory yellow, packing EDSA to the horizon and waiting peaceably for their own massacre . . .

It set my own head ringing as if I'd been clubbed. I should have taken notes, and should have pursued the small knots of priests and political negotiators hurrying onto the scene. Instead, I stood immobile beside one tank and stared at the crowd. Perhaps I was afraid for myself, or for them; the distinction was irrelevant at the time, and doesn't matter now. I know that I kept glancing at my watch to keep track of Tadiar's deadline, but I cannot recall whether the time passed slowly or quickly.

There was, however, an important difference between my own reaction and that of the human barricade. This was not my country or my fight. Much as I adore the Philippines, I was not about to lie down under the tracks of the Marine tanks. If firing had begun, I would certainly have run for cover. Marcos was not my dictator. Dying was not my patriotic duty.

So it seems wise to abandon the foreign journalist's perspective at this point, and to observe the next few minutes through the eyes of a Filipino. Screenwriter Amado Lacuesta, Jr., a former businessmen who is not a political activist, arrived on the scene just before Butz Aquino did, after spending the day with his wife Lolly outside Crame. He wandered into EDSA more out of curiosity than from revolutionary fervor, but the diary he recorded is an eloquent account of one man's decision to die for his country. Mr. Lacuesta has kindly allowed me to quote at length from his private journal:

> My curiosity leads me on. Soon I am on Ortigas, looking at my first APC, although I initially think it is a tank. Its engine is off as it squats there, surrounded by the people. . . . The vacant lot is crowded with what must be tanks, although only their tops and red pennants are visible. It reminds me vaguely of a war movie. My heart starts to beat a little harder.
>
> I squeeze through the crowd on the traffic island and suddenly I am standing on the edge of a sea of kneeling people. They are praying. A pious-faced matron in white is leading the Rosary, face lifted to heaven, praying in a loud, pleading tone. Around her, the crowd on its knees is mostly men and some young women. An Afro-haired mestizo is holding his rosary up before his chest, near a middle-aged man who looks like a long-suffering government clerk. A young woman is weeping as she prays. Someone is holding up a small statue of the Blessed Virgin, similar to dozens I have seen today along EDSA.
>
> My attention is drawn to a tight knot of civilians and camouflage-suited soldiers standing between the kneeling people and the APC,

which looks even larger and more menacing. A man breaks away from the group and I recognize him – it is Teofisto Guingona, one of Cory's wise men.

Then someone, a civilian, is grudgingly given a hand by some grim-faced soldiers as he joins them atop the APC. He looks familiar – probably an ex-Atenean I saw during the mass . . . at the Ateneo [University] campus. He looks very serious, very concerned. Someone calls for a megaphone. . . . The soldiers on the APC look tough and deadly, ammunition strung around their bodies. People in the crowd talk to them with almost desperate kindness, toss packs of cigarettes to them. But they show no response. They survey the crowd with hard eyes from time to time, but avoid eye contact. They seem even more tense than the people before them. Their discipline is frightening.

Someone says these are Marines just in from Davao and somehow, I feel a disquieting sense of kinship. I want to say that I too am from Davao, but I don't. The desperate Rosary pauses as the ex-Atenean starts to address us.

He and Guingona have been negotiating with Gen. Tadiar of the Marines. While awaiting Guingona, who has gone to Ramos with a message from Tadiar, he informs us that Tadiar wants the crowd to let his armor through. The crowd turns ugly, boos, mutters angrily. He pleads for attention. Now, the General climbs up beside him, helped by his unsmiling Marines.

The General looks short, slightly stocky but, like his men, is brown and tough-looking. . . . He takes the megaphone to address the crowd, fixing them with a baleful look when they hiss. I help quiet the crowd, afraid of trying this man's patience.

"I have my orders," he says. He explains (in the tone of one who is not used to having to explain what he wants) that he only wants to move his unit behind Aguinaldo, a simple request. He does not wish to harm anyone. The ex-Atenean tells him, and us, that it is our decision. He reminds us that we are here because we want to prevent a bloody confrontation. If the General's men and the armor reach the back of Aguinaldo, they will come face-to-face with Enrile's and Ramos's men. Who knows what might ensue then?

The prospect wrenches angry, urgent "No's" from the crowd. Suddenly, I am no longer just curious. I, too, shout "No!"

From atop distant buses and the whitewashed walls, the people begin to chant defiantly: "Co-ree!" Tadiar grimaces. The soldiers atop and before the APC hold their Armalites at the ready. I wonder if the safeties are off. "I have my orders!" This time it's a threat. Darkness is less than an hour away, the General says. Who knows what might happen when darkness falls? Let us now pass in safety.

Butz Aquino . . . clambers up unbidden, and takes the megaphone away. Tadiar looks piqued. Aquino plays to the crowd. He repeats what people power is all about – to prevent bloodshed. We are asked again whether we will let the Marines through. The response is unanimous, loud, defiant: "No!"

The General shrugs, says something to his soldiers. The soldiers prod Aquino, the ex-Atenean and an intrepid Japanese journalist off the APC. Suddenly, the APC's engine coughs to life, spews black smoke. Cries of surprise, of anguish. The Rosary starts again, more urgently this time. Panic sweeps over us all. Unthinking, I drop to my knees.

The APC's engine revs up again, spews black smoke again. In the back of my mind I think of Lolly and our children. . . . Tears rush to my eyes, unbidden; my chest heaves mightily, unbidden; a sob wrenches out of my throat, unbidden. Looking up, I see only the General and his Marines, disciplined, hard-eyed.

I am angry. I am hurt. I am desperate, not knowing exactly why. I only know these men in combat gear are Filipinos. I only know this should not be happening. But there is nothing else now, not here in the path of this huge mountain of ugly metal looming over us.

I shout and raise my hands, daring them: "Go on, kill us!" I am only dimly aware of angry booing and hissing, from the thousands on the streets, walls and buses; of cameras clicking, motor-winders whirring furiously.

The metal mountain jerks forward. Defiant, nervous shouts all around. The praying voices raise another key. I wonder what it is like to be crushed under tons of metal. The metal mountain jerks forward again. But no one stirs except the excited journalists jockeying for better angles. Then the engine stops. There is an astounding split second of silence. The crowd erupts into wild cheers and applause.

Gen. Tadiar looks at us, turns and shakes his head. He disappears somewhere to the rear. His soldiers look around uneasily, unwilling still to concede eye contact.

But the ordeal of Amado Lacuesta, of the many thousand Lacuestas, was not over.

9 ONE HOUR TO SUNSET

IT WAS NOW ABOUT 5:30 P.M., well past Tadiar's deadline, and the exasperated Marine commander had merely paused to consider the situation. His men began pleading with the nuns to "for God's sake get out of the way before you are crushed." Their choice of that phrase was an irony not lost on the Sisters.

This is the part most of the world watched on television. The frail, tiny nuns had pressed so close to the tanks they could actually reach out and touch them, seeming almost to hold them back. They were kneeling, praying, and appeared so serene that I fought an impulse to shake them by the shoulder and shout: "Wake up, Sister. These people aren't fooling around. They are going to kill you."

These were not the activist nuns who had battled Marcos for weeks as key figures in Cory Aquino's campaign. People such as Sister Anunciata – a Good Shepherd nun who attended every rally and investigated human-rights abuses for the Task Force on Detainees – came late to the EDSA showdown, rushing from other duties. She was as astounded as everyone else to see the political neophytes in starched white habits holding off Tadiar's war machines.

"I didn't get there until after four o'clock," she recalls, "because we were working on the food brigade at Aguinaldo, and actually we just abandoned our post and said, 'Come on, let's find out what's happening.' It's a long walk for an older person like me, but, going to the tanks, it was a festive mood, like a real Filipino fiesta. I kept stopping to talk to people, because I go to all the rallies and we know each other.

"But as we got closer to the tanks, I realized it was no longer so jovial. That big black helicopter came down and deep inside me I was scared. I've never really admitted it. I have never told anyone how afraid I really was.

"Then I was so surprised. All the nuns I saw in front of the tanks were nuns I'd never seen before. Not anywhere. They came from different congregations. They did not go to the rallies. Many of them, I could not even recognize their habits. I guess they had come in response to the Cardinal's plea on Veritas. It was their first time as activists, and they were not really as calm as they looked on foreign television.

"In fact, I was with a Sister of Charity, also from the food brigade, and we had to get back to our job. But when we were leaving, one of the other nuns rushed up and pleaded: 'Sisters, please stay. Don't you know you are needed here?' And my fellow Sister just shook her head in wonder. 'Look at her,' she said. 'It's her first time here. Doesn't she realize we all have our duties to perform?'

"Then I looked out over that field, with the tanks rumbling there and those soldiers all so fierce, and I had only one question in my mind: If all these people die, how can Marcos bury us all? He cannot have the heart. He cannot be so cruel."

The agonizing hiatus stretched on for nearly an hour. The Marines were tense and edgy, ready to attack at any moment. The terrifying APC engines would be silent for a while, then would suddenly rumble into life, emitting a black exhaust that one woman later recalled as "the breath of an evil dragon". Politicians from the Aquino camp and high-ranking bishops seemed to arrive on the scene every few minutes, huddling with supporters, huddling with Tadiar, huddling with newsmen, and then hurrying away.

Hundreds of people were carrying portable radios, so snatches of the Radio Veritas coverage wove into the general hubbub. Shortly after the first tank assault had fizzled, an announcer's voice shouted a message right to the heart of the EDSA standoff: "We have an appeal to General Tadiar! General, are you listening?" There was a brief pause before a deeper, older voice came on the air: "Artemio? This is your Uncle Fred speaking. Your Aunt Florence and I and all your cousins are here inside Camp Crame. Now, boy, please listen to me. . . ." Uncle Fred was not some bumpkin from the provinces. He was Regional Trial Court Judge Alfredo Tadiar, who sternly instructed his nephew to "make the right decision on the basis of the evidence and your intellect." Under normal circumstances, we might all have chuckled at a tough Marine general being addressed as "boy". But the only reaction in the crowd was to crank up the volume and turn all the radios in Tadiar's direction. We never discovered whether he heard "Uncle Fred" 's plea.

The scene was a journalist's dream, and nightmare. Every inch of the vacant lot was covered with dramatic stories, but it was impossible to be everywhere at once. I looked at the stone-faced Marines standing on guard around the perimeter, and decided to ask the only question that mattered: Are you going to shoot these people? Are you going to shoot these people? Are you going to shoot these people?

The first respondent was a young private who seemed to regard me as some foreign officer – perhaps a U.S. Navy captain – on a guest inspection. He kept saying ''Sir'', and seemed to be fighting the urge to salute. ''Sir, I am not permitted to speak, sir.'' But surely he could just say yes or no? ''No, sir.'' What did that mean? No, he wouldn't shoot? Or no, he won't talk? ''Sir, I cannot speak, sir.''

The next one looked even tougher, a killer with a teenager's face. Eyes frozen on the horizon, M-16 thrust rigidly towards the crowd on the retaining wall. His whole body was criss-crossed with bandoliers of bullets. When I approached, he looked mean enough to run the gun through my chest, so I adopted the manner of a bored census-taker asking the same question for the millionth time. Say, Jim, how do you like this cool weather? And, by the way, are you gonna shoot these people?

''No, sir.''

The answer came with a speed and a certainty that stunned us both. We looked at each other in surprise, and I glanced down to make a note of his name badge. He instinctively clasped his hand over it, then grinned in embarrassment. But the eye was quicker than the hand. The badge said PFC D. G. Nucum. I asked Private First Class Nucum what he would do if ordered to shoot. He just shook his head and grinned nervously. I asked why he was fighting for Marcos, and he replied very quietly: ''I don't know, sir. You should ask the officers.''

Perhaps feeling guilty at having said too much, PFC Nucum then launched into a TV commercial for the Philippine Marines. He said his was ''a very, very good unit'' with a great deal of pride. He said the Marines were the best fighting force in the entire country, and were very loyal.

But who are you loyal to, PFC Nucum? Are you loyal to Marcos?

''Myself, sir? No, sir.''

I moved along the line of Marines, repeating the question and trying to penetrate the stony glares. Most said nothing, some averted their eyes, and a few shook their heads in a subtle signal that they were not willing to blast their fellow countrymen. Glancing back, I noticed a young seminarian in a full-length white robe who was also going from Marine to Marine. He would put his arm around their necks and whisper in each ear for a minute or two; then he would hand out crackers and sandwiches from a wicker picnic basket strapped to his back. The soldiers would nod, take the offering, and set it down on the grass behind them, before resuming their gun-pointing posture.

The priest was about the same age as the young Marines, and his face was white with tension. "What do you think?" I asked him. "Are you getting any response?" He shrugged and looked noncommittal. "It is so hard to tell," he said. "But we *must* get through to them. If there is shooting, a lot of people will die. There will be so much bloodshed."

By this time a nun had collared PFC Nucum and was whispering sternly in his ear. He kept nodding and staring straight ahead, but did not lower his gun for an instant. What had she told him? "She said God loves the Marines," he reported, with the now-familiar embarrassed smile. "She said not to obey illegal orders, not to obey the dictator, but listen to the orders of God." Anything else? "Uh . . . yes. She said she would pray for me, no matter what I decide to do this afternoon."

That would be a heavy injunction for a twenty-year-old to handle in any society. But in the Philippines, where Roman Catholicism hangs in the air like humidity, and where the dictates of an "older sister" are virtual law, PFC Nucum had just been hit with a double whammy. There was no way this man would shoot anybody now. I happily jotted all this down in my notebook and moved away, beaming with optimism. My reaction turned out to be absurdly naive, but it was perhaps necessary at the time.

Journalists were scrambling over one another and shoving microphones in someone's face near one tank. The celebrity was Bishop Federico Escaler, yet another of the would-be peacemakers. His own anxiety was palpable, and he had nothing encouraging to report from his talks with Tadiar. We kept asking about possible solutions, but the poor bishop could only speak in hopeful generalities. "There is still some human warmth here," he said. "Just the fact of so many thousands standing in the way of the military . . . I think that might lead others to question their own loyalties. It's still a hopeful situation. We Filipinos are not Nazis. We are still thinking human beings with a sense of morality."

Just then, former senator Ernesto Maceda arrived with more urgent messages for Tadiar, and the media abandoned the bishop. I stayed behind, to find out who was organizing the priests and nuns. "They have just responded to the Cardinal's call," said the bishop, with a wan smile. "It isn't a concerted drive. These priests and nuns have taken the initiative on their own. They're trying to soften up the soldiers. I'd say their message is very simple: Consider your conscience, and question whether your orders are legal. We speak of God, of course. But there is also the question of whether Marcos is really the duly-elected president. Does he have any right to give orders? We are trying to put this doubt in the minds of the Marines."

A great roar suddenly drowned out the bishop. The tank engines had growled to life once again. The air was putrid with exhaust smoke; the ground trembled.

Amado Lacuesta was about to face another test. This is how he remembers it:

> One of the Marines atop the APC seems especially belligerent. When someone tosses a pack of cigarettes up to him, a peace offering, he stares balefully at the person. He is booed and hissed. He gathers himself up to his full height, deliberately turns his back on the crowd, and viciously jabs his hand into the air in an obscene gesture. He heads for one of the far hatches, opens it, takes out an Armalite, pointedly lays it on top of the hatch. The gesture is not lost on the crowd. I am afraid of what might come next.

> My fear is well-founded.

> The soldier now walks back to the near edge of the APC. Arrogantly, he turns his back on us, signals to the invisible driver. The engine comes to life again, coughing black smoke.

> "Sit down! Sit down!" we cry out to each other, following our own urging quickly.

> A woman in white raises her praying voice again, as do those around her. I link arms with the men on either side of me. Some of us are weeping. Some are also cursing. Perhaps, this time, they will not stop. Perhaps it will be bloody after all. And all this for one man's impulse to hold on to power. The thought stirs me again and I do not care what happens next.

> The APC jerks forward. Men brace themselves against the advancing metal wall, trying to hold it back. Behind them, the nuns stay on their knees, praying. I am several people behind the nuns, but the APC is so huge it seems to loom even over me.

> The soldier continues to signal the APC on. I wonder how many will be crushed before they realize we mean to stay, or before the pile of bodies makes it impossible for the APC to continue.

> All around us, the horde of people that stretches far back to the intersection a block away begins to chant angrily: "Co-ree!

Co-ree!" as if the name alone and the *Laban* sign had the power to
stop arrogant men and metal.

We who kneel in the APC's path alternate between defying it with
prayers and imploring the taunting crowds to stop, lest they goad
the soldiers to anger. Let them kill us unprovoked, in cold blood.
Let them hear the crunch of bones.

Just as I am ready to hear the first shriek of agony, a miracle –
the APC stops, its engine winds down. Cheers and wild applause.
We have won again. The soldiers glare down at us. Again, the
thousands gathered chant Cory's name.

The tanks may have been stopped by pity, conscience, tactical considerations, warnings from Washington, the courage of a million Filipinos,
the cool-headedness of General Tadiar, the clever psychological ploys of
the Enrile-Ramos camp, the intelligence reports from the Sikorskys up
above . . .

Then again the tanks might have been stopped by the Blessed
Virgin Mary. Not metaphorically, but in actual fact. She may have
descended from heaven to place Her own hand against the war machines,
and touch the hearts of the Marines. That is what Cardinal Jaime Sin and
many thousands of other Filipinos now believe. The religious leader
speaks slowly and carefully as he tells the story, very much aware of how
it will sound to the skeptical outside world. The Roman Catholic Church
is not in the business of fostering apparitions, he assures me. The Church
is always the very last to believe in such things. And he himself did not
actually see the Blessed Virgin.

"Still," he smiles, "I think you must write this in your book. The
soldiers who told it to me sat right there, in that chair beside you, and they
cried and cried. And I personally believe it is true."

Here, then, is the authentic story of how the tanks were stopped at
EDSA, in the words of Cardinal Sin:

"The tanks were trying to penetrate the crowd. And then the nuns
were pushing and people were trying to show their Rosary and pray. That
is when, according to these soldiers, they saw up in the clouds the form of
the cross. These were the Marines who were riding on top of the tanks,
the so-called Loyalists. The many Sisters had tried to stop them, but [the
soldiers] told me they had already decided to obey instructions and push
through. It is now just a question of ten minutes or so. You push the
trigger and there you are – everybody will be dead.

"Then a beautiful lady appeared to them. I don't know if she appeared in the sky or was standing down on the ground. So beautiful she was, and her eyes were sparkling. And the beautiful lady spoke to them like this: 'Dear soldiers, stop. Don't proceed. Do not harm my children. I am the queen of this land.' And then, when they heard that, they put down everything. They came down from the tanks and they joined the people. So, that was the end of the Loyalists.

"I don't know who these soldiers are. All I know is that they came here crying to me. They did not tell me that it was the Virgin. They told me only that it was a beautiful Sister. But you know" – he laughs heartily – "I have seen all the Sisters in Manila and there are no beautiful ones. It must be the Virgin. They are not telling me that, but I am already thinking that it was Mary. My heart was telling me: This is Mary. And since they obeyed this woman who appeared to them, then Marcos had nobody any more. So he had to flee away. That was the end of him."

The Cardinal's claim must be taken strictly on faith. The Church will not produce the soldiers for interviews, because it does not wish "to make them a curiosity, or foster belief in apparitions". There were no reports at the time of any soldiers joining the crowd. And Marine commanders loyal to the Aquino regime, who have no reason to hide it now, deny that any such defections took place.

Still, Cardinal Sin would not invent such a scenario. It is certain that some soldiers have tearfully told him of their supernatural vision on Sunday afternoon. Perhaps they embellished it with an account of climbing down to join the masses. Or maybe the Cardinal misunderstood that part.

Whatever the case, there is widespread belief among Filipinos that God played a direct role in halting the armored personnel carriers. Many in the crowd closest to the tanks now claim they saw a "Blue Nun" appear from nowhere and place her hands upon the machines. People looked for her after the excitement had died down, but she was no longer to be found.

"She does not appear in any of the photographs," concedes Mrs. Marites Tolentino, a bank employee who crouched in front of the tanks. "But that is perhaps because she cannot be photographed. Still, many of us know we saw her. We do not know exactly who she was. We do not know if she was Mary. All we know is that she was dressed in blue. That's why we call her the Blue Nun."

If heaven stopped the tanks that Sunday afternoon, the celestial powers got a large assist from devious humans. At a moment when General

Tadiar desperately needed a reason, any reason, to hold his fire, former senator Ernesto Maceda simply produced one, like a rabbit from a hat. The chunky, officious Maceda pushed his way to Tadiar just after the tank engines died, and informed him gravely of new peace talks "at the very highest levels". The politician claimed he had been sent by Cory Aquino to prevent violence while they negotiated a solution. "Please, General," he pleaded. "This is our best chance. Don't do anything now that would endanger the talks."

There is no telling whether Tadiar actually believed this message, or simply seized upon it as a face-saving device. Whatever his motive, Tadiar the kick-ass Marine bulldog suddenly became Tadiar the concerned statesman. He nodded thoughtfully, motioned the officers atop the tanks to relax, and shook Maceda's hand like a man reprieved from the gallows.

By now, the human crush around Maceda was greater than that surrounding the tanks. Television cameramen climbed one another's backs to get a shot, kids crawled on hands and knees through the pile, even priests and nuns were throwing elbows. What did he *say*? What did Tadiar say? Are the tanks stopped for good? Maceda's answer was vague, but impressive. "At this point," he intoned, deepening his senatorial voice an octave for the microphones, "I am more and more confident that we'll weather this crisis without violence. I have just informed the General that very important negotiations have begun at the highest levels, and . . ." Blah, blah, blah.

The message, of course, was a complete charade – what Filipinos call a *zarzuela*. The so-called "talks" amounted to a few phone calls, mostly acrimonious and abortive, between the principals on each side. It was a desperate ploy, plucked from a beginner's "psy-war" manual, but it was in everyone's interest to make it work. Maceda may have used her name, but Cory Aquino had been in touch with no one apart from her own entourage and Ambassador Bosworth. She had recently arrived from Cebu, and was holed up at her sister's house in nearby Mandaluyong.

The only "highest level" contact made all day was a phone conversation between Ferdinand Marcos and Juan Ponce Enrile. And that brief conversation hardly qualified as a peace talk.

Enrile had dodged Marcos for nearly twenty-four hours, refusing to meet him or take his repeated calls. An emissary from the President had phoned Camp Aguinaldo three times on Sunday morning, and again when the minister arrived in Crame. Enrile's answer: No, no, no, no. The blackout had become a fundamental rebel strategy, a tactic to keep Marcos in the dark. "We wanted to keep Crame as mysterious as possible,"

Gringo Honasan later explained. "They started miscalculating about us right from the beginning, and the idea was to keep it that way."

Then came a visit from Alfonso Reyno and Rodolfo Albano, a pair of ruling party MPs who were close to both Marcos and Enrile. They had come as personal emissaries from Malacañang, and their logic was impeccable. "You know you two will have to talk some time," Reyno argued. "If you don't discuss it, the only alternative is violence. What other choice is there?"

Enrile was tempted, but wary. "What's the use of it?" he wondered. "I can't negotiate and I can't surrender. We're totally committed now and there's no way to change it. What does Marcos want?" Reyno did not know, but said he believed it was urgent. With the tanks set to steamroll a million people, that seemed something of an understatement. "It was a time when Tadiar and his tanks were approaching," recalls the Defense Minister. "So I said, maybe it's an ideal time to finally talk to Marcos – to find out what really was his state of mind, the state of his emotions. So I told them to go ahead and call me. . . . I understand that when he heard I was on the line, he almost jumped from his chair and ran to the phone."

But his former political patron was not interested in discussing tanks. Instead, Marcos tried a gambit that would not have fooled a supply sergeant, much less the smooth, Harvard-trained minister. After brief pleasantries, Marcos offered Enrile a way to climb off the mountain. "Well," he said, "I have no intention, really, to punish your men. All I want is for Honasan's group [RAM] to go through a pro forma trial in order to show the public we can enforce the law. And I assure you that they will be pardoned."

A show trial, in other words, like the one that had recently cleared General Ver and two dozen military henchmen of guilt in the Ninoy Aquino assassination. That outrageous perversion of justice had been cited by Enrile and Ramos only the previous night as a prime reason for abandoning Marcos. But the Philippine strong man has never been noted for his keen sense of irony.

Enrile's choice was not terribly difficult. He knew Marcos better than most Filipinos, but his deepest belief was no different from that of every street-sweeper and newsboy: the President was a congenital liar. This, after all, was the man who had just been clobbered in a presidential election but had somehow emerged with fifty-five per cent of the vote. He could go into a turnstile behind you and come out in front. For the moment, Marcos would say anything to lure the rebels from Crame. Later, he would do what he pleased.

"I'm sorry, sir," the minister replied. "But I cannot make any commitment about what the men want to do. They haven't committed a crime, so why should they surrender? Anyway, I will convoke with them and discuss the matter. Then I'll call you back. It will take a few minutes, because we've agreed to operate on a one-man, one-vote basis. I'll have to find out their feelings." The discussion ended that way, in cold formality without a hint of compromise on either side. Enrile knew his men would never agree to surrender, and he had no intention of "convoking" with them. Marcos probably knew that, too.

But the call was a huge morale boost for Enrile, who glowed with excitement while recounting it months later. "He was *pleading* to find a solution to the problem," said the minister. "And so I knew that, psychologically, he was in deep trouble. That was the first time I had talked to him, and it was a surprise." In Enrile's memory, at least, the conversation was completely one-sided, with himself in the driver's seat. He says he dreamed up that "one-man, one-vote" angle on the spot, as a way of pressing his advantage. "It was not quite correct," he smiled. "I was just making up that story in order to give him some more pressure, psychological pressure."

Enrile was so excited that he completely forgot to inform Marcos of the rebels' basic demand. Fortunately, Marcos's go-between, Reyno, was still at Crame, and was immediately dispatched to Malacañang with a punchy postscript to the phone conversation: "I told [Reyno] to tell the President that our demand was for him to step down, resign, to prevent further conflict. I sent the message that, in our honest belief, he no longer had the people's mandate." Then the minister strode into a press conference and told the world the same thing. Marcos must quit. That was the "non-negotiable" bottom line of the revolt.

Reyno and Albano were dumbfounded. They had arrived thinking of Enrile as a cat up a tree, and themselves as helpful firemen. Now they had to return to Marcos with word of a full-blown revolution. They knew the President would hit the roof – and he did not disappoint them. The Ilocano "Apo" flew into a towering rage, spraying curses and knocking over the big strategic map near his desk. Loyalist insiders say the President was "so furious that he didn't know what to do. He was ranting, saying he would demolish the rebels." Where the hell was the artillery? he demanded. Where were the gunships? General Ver assured him that there was no reason to worry. Already, artillery emplacements were within easy target range, at the University of Life in nearby Greenhills. The air force was loyal. Tanks could be moved into firing distance at any time. And though the growing crowds were an annoyance, they could be dispersed with tear gas.

Marcos was only partly mollified. He instructed Information Minister Gregorio Cendaña to prepare a fire-and-brimstone television speech. When Marcos delivered it a few hours later, it was accompanied by much fist-banging on the presidential desk and was punctuated at regular intervals by the verb "annihilate".

Readers of the Toronto *Globe and Mail* awoke the next morning to a heart-warming saga of nuns, tanks, and PFC Nucum. The story told how the average Philippine soldier refused to slaughter his fellow citizens on behalf of President Marcos. It revealed how young warriors such as Private Nucum had obeyed the Church and the people, not General Tadiar. It was a masterful piece of journalism which neatly foreshadowed the end of the Marcos era.

Unfortunately, it didn't happen to be true.

"That is a very good scenario, and I am sorry to ruin it," Colonel Braulio Balbas told me four months later. "But, you know, these Marines were very certainly prepared to shoot. In fact, our problem was keeping the hot-heads under control. They are more accustomed to battle conditions. They are very much in the habit of firing their guns. I was afraid all the day that one of them might just start shooting."

That spine-tingling piece of information comes from an impeccable source. Aside from Tadiar himself – now in military eclipse, and inaccessible – Colonel Balbas was the highest-ranking Marine officer that Sunday, and is now deputy commander of the corps. He was in charge of 960 men, one of two brigades that faced the human blockade. By his own description, he passed those hours in a near-transcendental state of anxiety.

"We spent so much time talking to the civilians," the fifty-year-old commander recalls. "They were charging towards us desperately, offering flowers and candies. Many were pleading for the safety of their husbands and civilians at Camp Aguinaldo and Crame. At one point . . . you know, I saw a woman who looked the same as my wife. I had to look twice. Then I saw her son, and he also looked just like *my* son. I was so touched and saddened. I was able to picture in my own mind this exact same scene, with my own family in their roles and me in Camp Crame. It was like a vision. At that time I almost could not tell which scenario was more real. I cried. My tears rolled down.

"No, that's not true. I am a Marine officer. There were no tears rolling down my face. It's just . . . your eyes get wet."

The Colonel stresses, however, that his own emotional state was not typical of the men he commanded. Further, he insists that the Marines were not nearly as helpless against the civilian barricade as they appeared. It is widely assumed that Tadiar faced just two options: either commit a massacre, or back down. That was the press and TV portrayal, and it has since been regurgitated by many Filipino books on the rebellion. But it is not how the Marine commander viewed the situation. Colonel Balbas met with Tadiar periodically throughout the afternoon, reviewing intelligence reports and considering options. This was the surprising view of the standoff from the other end of the machine gun:

"Very often we heard the crowd talking about tear gas, yelling instructions about what they should do if we used it," recalls Balbas, allowing himself a faint smile at the memory. "I guess they did not realize we were a combat unit. We did not carry any tear gas that day . . . only the guns we normally use against the NPA [Communist New People's Army] guerrillas. We're not an anti-riot squad. But when you view it from a strictly military perspective, we had many options to disperse the crowd. It would not have been too difficult.

"I should stress there were many moral pressures on us. This was not a normal situation. So many millions of Filipinos were deeply angry with President Marcos. Speaking personally, I was trying to weigh between following orders, doing my job, or following the dictates of my heart – to support the people. I was torn between the two. But, you know, as professional soldiers, we are able to size up situations in a strictly tactical manner. We did that during the afternoon and, tactically . . . no, it was not so difficult.

"With our cannons and firepower, the terror factor was enormously in our favor. If we had been willing to kill even just a few, the crowd would have been dispersed immediately. I know everyone says they were prepared to die, prepared to sit right there. But we are combat Marines, we know what happens under fire. Nobody is ever ready to be killed. Even the most battle-hardened soldier will instinctively look for cover. It is natural, the most basic instinct for self-preservation. If it happens to us, how much more would it be with the civilians?

"Probably the best, the most effective, dispersal tactic at that time would be simply to fire in the air. I assure you, the people would have run. There would have been a panic. But even then, we didn't know how many people might be killed in the stampede. There were nuns kneeling, and small children. And maybe there would be some bad soldiers, people who would shoot right at the crowd. There are always a few bad soldiers in a group that large."

That last remark is even more ominous than it sounds, and was probably a deciding factor in General Tadiar's retreat. The Loyalist problem did not, as everyone believes, lie in getting the Marines to shoot people. Quite the opposite. They simply could not trust their high-strung troops to *refrain* from shooting during a chaotic dispersal.

Obviously soldiers such as PFC Nucum had decided to heed the nuns and hold their fire. But Colonel Balbas was certain that the majority would obey any order, and feared that the small minority of "hardheads" might take things into their own hands.

"That's what I felt at the time," says the Colonel. "And it proved true just a short while later. The Marines are very disciplined, very well organized. They will do whatever their officers tell them. But later, when I had some men marching on foot, we ran into a blockade of civilians. Some of the hard-heads immediately cocked their rifles and were ready to shoot. I had to run in front of them and hold out my arms to avoid a massacre right there.

"I can tell you before God . . . these men were ready to shoot."

Manila eases almost instantly from broad daylight into early evening, its famous sunsets blazing and dying in just twenty-five minutes. So General Tadiar had barely begun to organize his retreat before the vacant lot was plunged into darkness. The crowd mixed nervous relief with wary optimism. They pressed against the tanks on all sides, forming an escort as the stinking machines swung slowly around and exited one by one. In the deepening gloom, the vigilantes wanted to be sure that none would crash through and make a sudden dash for Camp Crame.

Soldiers lounged atop their APCs, or huddled in the backs of canvas-covered jeep trucks. One drew wild cheering when he emerged from a tank hatch clutching a *Philippine Daily Inquirer*, and unfurled the opposition paper's headline: "Enrile, Ramos: We'll fight to the death!" Another Marine drew more cheers when he flashed the L-sign.

Civilians clustered behind each jeep before it moved off, offering handfuls of cigarettes and seeking assurance that the soldiers would really return to Fort Bonifacio. A Benedictine nun named Sister Aida went from soldier to soldier, armed with a beatific smile that nearly shone in the dark. "We want peace, hah?" she urged. "No shooting." I tagged along and asked what she had been telling the soldiers all afternoon. "There is only one message," she shrugged. "We are all Filipinos. We should not be killing each other. I tell them we are praying for their families, praying that they will make the right decision."

The response? "So far," smiled Sister Aida, "I think God is winning."

The crowds behind the Marine jeeps were less certain. I drifted from one to the other as the soldiers pulled out, trying to gauge the response. Their mixed replies should have made me suspicious.

"They are with the people; they don't believe there will be blood-shed," reported one knot of vigilantes. "They said they are also using their conscience. They believe in the will of the people. We pay the taxes, so we have the right to choose the government," said another.

But the next contingent was in shock after their talk with the Marines. "We gave them cigarettes and told them we were all for Cory," said one young man. "But they . . . well, they were not for Cory. Maybe they will still change their minds."

What exactly had they said?

"They advised us to pray very hard."

That was excellent advice. The happy crowd began to disperse, and I went back to the Midtown Hotel to write my upbeat account of the showdown. Meanwhile, nearly a thousand of the heavily armed Marines embarked on a circuitous journey designed to shake off their civilian escort. They were not returning to Fort Bonifacio at all.

10 *THE MARINES RETURN*

THE JUBILANT CROWD at EDSA was oh-so-careful on Sunday night. They surrounded the defeated tanks and escorted them back a mile towards Fort Bonifacio, flashing Laban signs and cheering the Marines. Those left at the Ortigas intersection sank to their knees in relief and exultation. "I wasn't afraid," one shaking college girl told her friends. "But now – I can hardly stand up." Her classmates hugged her and waved yellow "CORY!" banners, then they staggered off in search of their car and a hot meal. Someone hollered that the danger wasn't over, that the Marines would surely come back. "We'll be back, too," said one of the human barricade. "We'll see you later."

But Colonel Braulio Balbas and his brigade of 960 heavily armed men would not wait for later. In all the concern over tanks and jeeps, his foot-soldiers were hardly noticed. They marched briefly towards Bonifacio, giving the impression of retreat, but went only a few hundred yards before swinging left down a convenient side street. Their orders were to "inject" themselves into Camp Aguinaldo, and set up mortars to shell the rebel headquarters at Camp Crame, just across the street. The plan was to circle away from the major thoroughfares jammed with People Power and cut through the almost-vacant back streets. A Sikorsky reconaissance flight had spotted an apparent weak spot in the Aguinaldo defense – a side gate in an area known as Libis. That was the Marine target.

At first, says Colonel Balbas, "it wasn't really difficult at all. If you go on foot, you can just mingle with the people. We were in uniform, organized, very heavily armed and . . . you know, there was nothing the people could really do against us. They were surprised when we suddenly came upon them [in the streets], but they didn't put up any resistance. Everyone was concentrating on the vehicles. All the reports on the radio were, 'The tanks are moving here,' or 'Armored vehicles are there.' But no one reported on us."

It took about ninety minutes for Balbas's brigade to wind through a maze of streets and get close to the gate. The commander was in the middle of his troops at about 8 p.m. when they skirted a gasoline station, entered a narrow street bounded by high walls – and ran headfirst into a human barricade.

There was a brief hesitation, and then a chilling metallic "click-click-click-click" as the Marines in front instinctively cocked their M-16s and machine pistols. The unit had been flown in from the Mindanao battle zones only hours before, and had reached a hair-trigger level of frustration during the EDSA showdown. Now they were scowling and cursing, and many had their guns pointed right at the civilians.

Balbas sprinted to the front of his column and threw both arms wide. "Don't shoot!" he yelled in Tagalog. "Unload your weapons!" A shiver ran down his neck as he realized how close his young charges had come to firing. One shot would have touched off a volley, and a bloodbath. "This unit had some real hard-heads," he said later. "They are great to command in battle . . . but here there were no enemies, only the friendly faces of other Filipinos. I was so afraid of some atrocities. A massacre might have been committed."

The Colonel sized up the strategic situation. He was trapped in a tight corridor with high walls on each side and an immovable mass of humanity in front of him. Either intelligence from the air was wrong, or the situation had changed. There was no weak spot in the Aguinaldo barricades. He told his men to retreat. He halted them after they had gone about two miles, and they sat along the side of the road, a fully armed Marine brigade, bristling with bazookas and mortars, like a Grade 3 class waiting for the school bus. Fort Bonifacio had been informed, and had promised to send transportation. But it took nearly five hours to arrive.

"We didn't really hide," says Balbas. "But we tried not to attract any attention. Several people came up to us and asked what we were doing. We told them we were waiting for orders. Of course, they were suspicious, but what could they do? There was enough firepower sitting there to capture Crame. And they were unarmed. How could they stop us? They just stood and looked at us. We looked back."

At General Fabian Ver's headquarters in Malacañang Park, meanwhile, the strategic wheels were turning. Ver was on the phone to General Felix Brawner, the deputy operations chief who also commanded the First Scout Rangers. They considered, and rejected, a Marine air drop. It was dangerous at night, and perhaps even more so at dawn, when the helicopters could be blasted before landing. In fact, the rebels had nothing except four recoilless rifles to threaten them, but, as usual, Ver greatly overestimated his opponents. He and Brawner finally decided to send the same Marines back to Aguinaldo, but now with armored vehicles – and with heavy artillery.

"But this time," Ver reasoned, "we must disperse the crowds first. Do we have anyone who can do it?"

"Yes, sir."

"Okay, let's make sure. Get the people out of the way, and *then* use the Marines."

Balbas and his men would get no sleep that night. They were finally picked up at 2 a.m. and returned to Bonifacio. By 4:15 a.m. they were again on the road to Aguinaldo, this time following two CDC (Crowd Dispersal and Control, commonly known as "anti-riot" squads) units and accompanied by many gallons of tear gas.

Ferdinand Marcos was still outraged by the presumptuous rebel demand for his resignation. Late Sunday night he finally gave full vent to that fury before the entire Philippine nation. His televised press conference began about midnight as I was filing a story in the Associated Press bureau office on bay-front Roxas Boulevard. The place was crammed with reporters and photographers, all absorbed in their work and paying scant attention to the President. The speech was being taped, and we could check later for anything important.

It took less than two minutes, however, for Marcos to capture the newsroom's undivided attention. The man was not simply angry, he was *wild* with rage. He started reading from a prepared text, but veered off into a fist-shaking rant that had us squirming in our chairs. This was no longer a gifted politician, the master manipulator of the Filipino psyche; it was a raving and desperate tyrant, who appeared capable of anything. His eyes bulged, his chin quivered, his hands were balled into fists.

The rebels, he bragged, were now "forced into a small corner of Camp Crame . . . pushed into a small room." They had "raised openly the flag of insurrection, the flag of rebellion, and we will deal with them as such." Then Marcos stiffened with indignation as he cited rumors that he was too sick to handle the situation. "If they think that I am sick," he shouted, almost rising from his chair, "I may even want to lead the troops to wipe out this Enrile-Ramos group. I can tell you that I am as strong as ever. I am just like an old warhorse, smelling powder and getting stronger. But I am certainly shamed and humiliated that two former comrades, Enrile and Ramos, can stoop down to the depths of this ignominy, trying to grab power by coercion and intimidation. . . . I am ashamed that they are Filipinos.

"Some of their own people are saying that the President is incapable of enforcing the law. They repeat that once more and I'll sic the tanks and artillery on them!"

He then turned with a sneer to the subject of Cardinal Sin, "who is spouting all kinds of inciting to rebellion, inciting to sedition". Marcos made a sharp motion of dismissal and glared into the camera: "We'll attend to that later on."

In fact, the President was not merely threatening future calamity; he was unveiling his true hidden agenda. Generals Ver and Brawner were at that moment attempting to "sic" their tanks and artillery on Crame. The Cardinal's life, meanwhile, was hanging by a thread at his quiet hilltop mansion in nearby Mandaluyong. He received a phone call early Monday morning, just hours after the Marcos speech, from U.S. Ambassador Bosworth. The Americans had received intelligence that the Cardinal was to be killed, and Bosworth advised him to leave Villa San Miguel immediately. Sanctuary at the Embassy was implicitly offered, as Bosworth invited Sin to drop by the U.S. compound and await developments "if you have nowhere else to go".

(The Archbishop of Manila took the threat seriously and did prepare to evacuate. "Because, you know, I don't also like to die, ah? But if God does not allow you to die . . . you do not. By the time I was about to leave, I heard that the military situation had changed. Marcos was then losing, so I let *him* leave, instead.")

The scripted portion of the midnight speech was a clever attempt to divide the opposition and convince Filipinos that Juan Ponce Enrile was seizing power for himself. That was by no means a farfetched scenario, given the minister's involvement in the RAM plot and his inclusion on its planned ruling "council". But the President's credibility had dipped below zero, and his fuming "warhorse" threats did little to enhance it. Marcos blinks habitually when telling lies – which, during the election campaign, had been most of the time. No one seemed to notice that he was not blinking on Sunday night, but stared straight into the camera. Marcos was the little boy crying "Wolf!" once too often. Having snorted derisively at his revelations of the aborted coup, Filipinos simply dismissed his conspiracy charges as the absurd invention of a fevered mind.

"Now it is very obvious that Juan Ponce Enrile wants to run the country," fumed the dictator. "They are not doing this for Cory Aquino. They are insistent that I step down and that a junta or council will take over. Now, who is the chairman of that council? It's Juan Ponce Enrile. . . . In short, this is a new power group trying to grab power from both the [ruling] KBL [party] and the opposition. I am surprised that the opposition does not smell this. . . . They are blinded about the new power group."

Perhaps, after twenty-one years together, Marcos and Enrile had begun to think alike. Or maybe the President's comments stung his former minister into action. Whatever the reason, Enrile decided at about this time to create an alternative civilian government for the Philippines. He met with opposition leaders Homobono Adaza and Luis Villafuerte, and strongly suggested that the Aquino-Laurel team be sworn in as the country's duly elected chief executives. That would provide another rallying point for People Power; more important in a long military siege, it would also allow Cory and Salvador Laurel to lobby foreign powers for diplomatic recognition.

"I asked these people to form a civilian government," Enrile said later. "In order to show . . . that we must earnestly try to restore a democratic government . . . and also to relieve us of some political work while attending to the military component of the effort." He dictated his own terms to the oppositionists: Ramos and he would be the new government's chief of staff and defense minister; Cory could appoint whomever she wished to the other cabinet posts.

Significantly, Enrile remembers this meeting taking place just before the Marcos broadcast, around midnight Sunday. The other participants seem to recall it happening well after the President made his accusations, possibly as late as 3 p.m. Monday afternoon. (Months later, as the Defense Minister publicly criticized the new government, he would argue that he could not be fired because he had never been appointed. The Aquino government, he claimed, was a "coalition" of equal partners. To dismiss him would be to dissolve the government itself.)

Rebel commander General Fidel Ramos missed the President's televised rampage. He chose that moment to tap his cigar on a table, smile at reporters and aides in his Camp Crame office, and say: "Let's take a look around." A fitness fanatic who walks at a near-jogging pace, he was almost immediately out of the Camp's gate and into the crowd – with a gaggle of notebook-toters and six armed men struggling to keep up.

The slight, neatly groomed general fits no one's stereotype of a Third World jungle fighter. He is a bookish aristocrat whose father Narciso Ramos was a Philippine foreign minister, and his passion at West Point was for editing literary journals and yearbooks. At fifty-seven, Ramos is a veteran of both the Korean and the Vietnam wars, and a specialist in guerrilla "psy-warfare". He is an early riser who sleeps four hours a night, and likes to jog before dawn and get his paperwork out of the way before breakfast. As a military strategist, the General is noted for his low-key style and for a penchant for keeping the opposition off balance.

"Ra-mos! Ra-mos!" cheered the vigilantes when the living symbol of military defiance came jogging in their midst. The General was on a morale-building mission, shaking hands and beaming confidently at the crowd, but his own morale seemed the most boosted. "This is the greatest thing I've ever done in my life," he told reporters, after a few minutes of basking in the midnight limelight. "I feel that just being a part of it has more than fulfilled my wildest dreams." Then he began to count off the latest armed forces defectors: they included Philippine Constabulary commanders in all seventy-four provinces, and a few officers of the Presidential Security Command.

Ramos spent a full hour on his walking tour, breaking into a trot in the last few minutes and weaving playfully through the crowd to shake off reporters. A few astonished members of the human barricade were nearly bowled over by their commander-in-chief.

All that boyish exuberance, however, was strictly for public consumption. Back in his office, the legendary Ramos calm returned, as he lit up a "Sumatra" cigar and studied reports under the unwavering gaze of a statue of the Virgin Mary. The news was not good. He huddled with his officers and then told reporters to expect an attack at 2 a.m. "It'll probably be artillery," he said. "There are shovels for anyone who wants to dig a foxhole on the lawn." For once, the General's acerbic wit fell flat; nobody cracked a smile.

A particular oddity of the Philippine uprising was its near-total lack of secrecy. Troop movements were noticed immediately by rebel intelligence, or by the civilian ham radio operators, or by Father Reuter's army of informants, or by the more sophisticated operatives of the U.S. Embassy. Thus, before they had cleared the gates at Fort Bonifacio, a Loyalist tank crew could, and actually would, listen to its arrival announced on the Catholic Radio Veritas or on Radio Bandido, the new channel that mysteriously sprang up in support of the rebels. Indeed, all movements were charted far in advance by RAM officers glued to three different radio monitors.

So everyone knew for five long hours that the Marines would attack. About 3:30 a.m., three tanks were reportedly sighted in Santolan, near Camp Aguinaldo; worse, a huge commando team was moving along Horseshoe Boulevard and two battalions with mortar emplacements were at Annapolis in Greenhills. The news screeched through the civilian ranks in the high-pitched tones of "General" June Keithley as thousands of radios outside Crame tuned in to her Radio Bandido pirate station, which she had turned into an information centre for the rebels. Ramos himself went on the air in the middle of the night to tell Filipinos that "it is Mr. Marcos who is massing troops, not us. This is the blood of our people on his hands. We pray he will not do this. . . . Do not obey illegal orders," he told the Loyalist soldiers. "Please do not commit crimes against your own people. Do not violate your military oath."

That impassioned plea was replayed constantly. Whatever effect it had on the troops, it certainly did little to reassure the human barricade. There was, however, one scrap of good news: the three "tanks" turned out to be garbage trucks.

But by 4:30 a.m. there was no more doubt. Colonel Balbas's brigade was on its way to Aguinaldo with full armor and an anti-riot escort. General Ramos looked unaccustomedly grim when he heard the report, and turned to Enrile with a what-do-you-think? shrug. "There are tanks outside," answered the Defense Minister. "If you want to capture them, you'd better start now." A colonel burst into the room with confirmation that the enemy would attack at five. Ramos glanced at his watch, and discovered it was already 5:10 a.m. Balbas had been delayed by People Power, but he was creeping inexorably towards his target.

"Well," said Ramos, who now had two large sweat patches under the arms of his blue Lacoste polo shirt, "this could be it." He turned to the civilians: "You may stay or not. It's your individual decision now. If there are any foreigners here, please inform your embassies right away. Are you willing to stay with us all the way?" The press, burrowed right inside the world's best news story, nodded and stayed put.

Two Ramos aides struggled in with an orange "shrapnel sheet" and began laying it over the largest table they could find. The idea was for us all to lie beneath the table during an artillery barrage, so that the sheet could deflect flying pieces of metal and concrete. "The thing I remember most about it," says Rene Cayetano, the Enrile emissary who had joined his friend at Crame, "was that it didn't even cover the table. Anyway, there wasn't room for even half of us under there. I wondered how they would choose who survived."

Ramos was back on Radio Bandido again, issuing another telephone plea "to all Filipino soldiers out there . . . Don't inflict harm on people who have no arms. The blood spilled today will be on Marcos's hands. We offer you friendship. I advise you to turn around and join us.

We offer nothing but friendship. Mr. Marcos has assembled an over-whelming force against us. . . . We are ready, but please tell the world it is Mr. Marcos who is about to inflict violence and terror, not us.''

It seemed a hopeless appeal. What were the chances of Balbas and his men listening to Radio Bandido? But this was the Philippines, and a distinctly Filipino revolution. Balbas, sitting atop a V-150 commando vehicle, actually *was* tuned in ''. . . and I recalled that General Ramos had always been good to me. I felt saddened.''

After his radio address, Ramos became acutely aware of imminent mortality. He turned to address reporters as if dictating his final memoirs. ''If they don't respond to our friendly overtures, then we will fight. We have to defend this movement in order to survive, in order to keep this movement going. It is obviously an overwhelming force, and we don't have the forces to counter them.'' A colonel suggested it might be a good time to read a passage from the Bible, and Ramos reached for the battered copy he keeps on his desk. There was already a tab marking Psalm 91, the ''soldier's prayer''. One officer told reporters that a British unit had recited it every morning during the Second World War and had suffered not a single casualty. His listeners just nodded and smiled nervously.

Enrile, who had been so shaky and emotional in the first hours of the revolt, was now making an elaborate show of coolness. While Ramos talked on the radio, the Defense Minister languidly crossed and uncrossed his legs from deep within a stuffed leatherette chair. Someone handed him a rosary and another aide told him Ambassador Bosworth was on the phone. ''This is a good cause,'' he announced, getting to his feet and smiling. ''We will gladly die for it.''

Perhaps the phone connection was noisy, or the minister was nervous. In any case, his exchange with Bosworth took place at top volume, and everyone in the room could hear. ''Just for the record,'' he declared, ''we would like to inform you that Marcos's troops will attack us at any moment. We're going to make our stand here. We're ready to fight to the last man, to save freedom in this country.'' He handed the phone to a lieutenant and told the room that ''Ambassador Bosworth says he will inform his government right away.'' In fact, the Pentagon was probably listening to the call, on the line the U.S. Embassy kept open to Washington on its secure microwave transmission system throughout the revolt.

Secretary George Shultz was the only State Department official on the ''crisis management'' team quickly formed in the American capital. Other members included Defense Secretary Caspar Weinberger, National

Security Advisor Admiral John Poindexter, White House chief Donald Regan, and, eventually, the jet-lagged trouble-shooter Philip Habib. All except Shultz had been pro-Marcos "hawks", but the fast-breaking events were soon to scuttle any hopes of saving him. "By the time they saw the nuns stopping tanks on TV," says one diplomatic insider, "even the crisis team realized the connections were fried. Marcos didn't have the Church, he didn't have the army, and he didn't have the people."

But he still had guns, and the Americans feared that he would use them. The crisis team met at 10:30 a.m. Sunday morning, in Shultz's suburban Washington home. That was just before midnight in Manila, so the Reagan advisors could review the day's events on videotape over their coffee. They were terrified by what they saw, and by the latest message from the Manila Embassy: a strong rumor of another attack. The team took only minutes to reach a consensus and phone President Reagan at Camp David. Marcos had to be reined in, they told him. Reagan must send a personal warning against the use of force.

The note was relayed to Malacañang early Monday morning, Manila time. Reagan threatened to cut off all military aid if Marcos used heavy weapons against the rebels. Hours later, a formal version was released to the media: "The U.S. provides military assistance to the Philippines . . . in order to strengthen its ability to protect the security of the Philippines. . . . We cannot continue our existing military assistance if the Government uses that aid against other elements of the military which enjoy substantial popular backing."

Colonel Luis San Andres, the spokesman for and close friend of Ramos, led his squad from the office and down a flight of stairs on a "personal" mission. He went from room to room in search of a chaplain, and finally shook a priest from a deep sleep. San Andres and his men knelt right there beside the chaplain's bed to receive general absolution. There was not enough time for individual confession, and "we didn't want to die with any sins on our conscience."

The Ramos operations chief, Colonel Alexander Aguirre, put in a call to the "safehouse" where his family was hiding, and talked to his son, Aleksei. "I gave him last-minute fatherly advice. I told him, 'Be always a good boy, be responsible like a man, be strong and take care of your Mommy and your sisters.' He was crying. I told him the attack may come any moment. We will stand our ground, but if overwhelmed, I will be either dead or else in the mountains. . . . I didn't talk to my wife any more. I didn't want her to cry. 'Aleksei can explain anyway,' I thought."

Businessman Roger Cleofe had arrived at Crame thirty-six hours before, just to pick up a friend. But he stayed and joined the food brigade when he realized what was happening. Now Cleofe wrote his name on a half-dozen scraps of paper and began stuffing them into his shoes, pockets, belt buckle, anywhere he imagined they might be found. "I had this image of lying there dead, and nobody would know who I was," he recalled later. "It didn't seem to matter so much that we were going to get killed, but . . . well, it seemed important that somebody should know about it."

It was 5:30 a.m. The soldiers in General Ramos's office were ready to move out, but their boss kept receiving phone calls from radio and TV stations around the world. "We are about to be attacked . . ." he was hollering at a morning newscaster somewhere in Australia. "Yes, they have two battalions. . . . There are thousands of unarmed civilians between us, and many foreign correspondents here . . . Swiss, Japanese, Canadian, American, and many others . . . They are all willing to stay. . . . Yes, we'll fight back. Of *course* we'll have to fight." The General was apparently annoyed by the line of questioning. His men stood around impatiently, adjusting ammunition belts and toying with their guns. Some used the rifles as a crutch, distractedly leaning against them. "It is Mr. Marcos who is massing troops. . . . Mrs. Aquino is safe and she is joining us very soon. The regional commanders have promised to stay behind us. . . . No! This is not what we want! This is what Marcos and Ver want! . . . Look, I cannot answer any more of your questions. We are about to be attacked. . . ."

Ramos slammed down the phone. "That son of a bitch is on Marcos's side," he scowled.

The General tried to exit with his men, but was met by a crush of reporters and another volley of stale questions. His patience had reached its limit. The media war was about to become a shooting war, and he was trapped in a crowd of foreigners who wouldn't know an M-16 from an M-60. "Look," shouted the exasperated leader of men, "can't you see we're about to be attacked here? We are going out on an operation, and you people are still asking questions."

II FIREPOWER

TIME FOR A TRADE SECRET, a shame-faced confession: there is hardly a foreign correspondent anywhere who will pass up the chance to inject an M-16 assault rifle, a Sikorsky gunship, or an Uzi submachine gun into a news dispatch. Uplifting as it is to file a 1,200-word economic profile of the Philippine sugar industry, such stories have a nasty habit of being buried at the bottom of page 62. Not so with smoking guns and whistling bullets – which spin an entrancing web of danger over the bored deskmen back home. Young Corporal Cruz has a chance of making the front page whenever he says something interesting. But the corporal's odds increase dramatically if he happens to be menacing a crowd of nuns with an Israeli-made Galil rifle.

The kicker to this rule, of course, is that few Western journalists know much about military fighting gear. If a soldier carries anything bigger than a handgun, it automatically becomes an M-16 in the *Daily Gleaner* – unless, of course, it is an abrupt, ugly killing tool riddled with holes. In that case the intrepid reporter from Cleveland or Sydney nudges his Canadian counterpart and asks: "That an Uzi?" I shrug and we both jot down "Ponce Enrile . . . Uzi hangs menacingly from neck" in our notebooks.

Many Filipinos are more sophisticated about guns. Indeed, a large segment of the male population feels absolutely naked when not in possession of a "clutch bag" bulging with cold steel. Before the 1972 declaration of martial law, Jesse James would have felt perfectly at home in most of the country. Prime entertainment on a Saturday night was to stick a Colt .45 in your belt, belly up to the nearest bar, and blow the brains out of anyone who gave you crap. In those days, Philippine Airlines used to make a polite pre-flight announcement requesting everyone to kindly unload their firearms before takeoff. Up and down the aisles there was a satisfying "click-click-click-click" as customers complied.

The crowds who thronged EDSA on that unforgettable Sunday included plenty of gun-toting street toughs, and even a 300-man urban guerrilla army lugging Adidas sport bags full of plastic bombs, grenades, and M-1 carbines. But the vast majority of people there could not tell a Molotov cocktail from a dry martini. The nuns, housewives, and children just gaped and shivered as the rebel soldiers pushed across the street from Camp Aguinaldo to Camp Crame – wrapped to the armpits in grenade belts and trying gamely not to conk anyone's granny with an Armalite assault rifle.

"That's when I really got scared," says Sister Anunciata, the Good Shepherd nun who was guarding the gates when Enrile's contingent crossed over to join General Ramos. "The soldiers looked so fierce, you know. I thought it was war already. It seemed like there would be shooting any minute. I don't ever see guns, and there were so many. I called out desperately: 'What's happening? Where are you going?' But nobody would answer. They just passed with their guns. Only later I realized they were in a very bad situation."

That awestruck innocence did not last long. Even by Sunday night the crowd's ignorance of modern-day weaponry was matched by its studied indifference. It was, we discovered, impossible to appear brave while gasping open-mouthed at an armored personnel carrier. So the mood quickly shifted to the other extreme. The idea was to look as if you had been around tanks all your life – as if, perhaps, your dad had picked one up second-hand when you were a kid, and Mom used it for shopping.

By the second day, even the *colegialas*, those shy, skinny girls from strict Catholic private schools, were napping in the shade of 50-mm machine guns. I and the other reporters vied among ourselves to appear absolutely blasé, casually nudging Armalites aside with our elbows to keep both hands free for note-taking. (That word Armalite, by the way, is another journalistic trick. It is only an M-16 by a different name, but you get twice the mileage from it by switching terms.)

Our exaggerated nonchalance was partly a façade, but partly caused by that quirk of human nature which reduces anything extraordinary to the mundane in about thirty minutes. "I'm terrified of guns," says Susan Severino, the food-brigade volunteer who served breakfast to hundreds of soldiers. "It's such big, unkind, unfriendly-looking stuff, and I was like a timid schoolgirl in the beginning. You go to pick up someone's plate, and there's an M-16 sticking in your face. 'Excuse me, sir. Could you please move your gun?' I was practically shaking. But, you know, after the first half-hour I didn't even think about it any more. They had guns. So what?"

Similar treatment was accorded the sleek F-5 fighters that drew smoke patterns across Manila's sky. When asked about them, even the rebels inside Crame would shrug and make one of those "Geez-I-dunno-but-I-hope-to-hell-they're-on-our-side" faces. Few civilians had any notion what kind of planes they were, why the vultures were gliding above us, or which side had sent them aloft. So we just dubbed them "the fighters", and came to regard them as a mildly ominous force of nature – like a dark cloud or a full moon.

The veneer would occasionally crack and crumble, as on Monday morning in front of Crame's main gate, when a premature victory celebration was cut short by the sudden appearance of Ferdinand Marcos on television. The President glared menacingly from the screen, threatening instant annihilation and warning all civilians to "get out of the line of fire, right now". A girl of about sixteen, standing next to me, looked up at the two F-5s and trembled so violently in the tropical heat that her teeth chattered audibly. I was completely absorbed in the story at the time, concerned only with getting the Marcos quotes, checking out a rumor of attacks on the government TV station, and finding a telephone. So my response was a plastic smile of reassurance and a deep-seated sense of superiority.

As it turned out, the young girl's terror was the sane, even prescient, response to that situation. My own thoughtless bravado was built on total naivety. Later, I was to discover that a battery of 105-mm howitzers was at that moment trained on the exact spot where we stood. The Philippine army's commanding general was screaming over a walkie-talkie at a Marine colonel: "Fire on the target and report compliance. The President himself is waiting for confirmation." Thanks to an unsung hero of the revolution, Colonel Braulio Balbas, those guns were not fired. The girl's fear passed, my story got into my paper, and the world swallowed another fairy tale about the remarkably bloodless revolt and humanitarian "reluctance" of President Marcos to use force.

Colonel Balbas is now deputy commander of the Marines, a hardened military man whose assessment of the carnage if he had fired at Camp Crame is delivered in the dispassionate tones of a civil engineer sizing up a bridge-building project. "The effect would have been devastating," he says. "The building would have been totally destroyed and the civilians . . . well, a massacre, a slaughter. I was willing to obey all legal orders, but I did not believe I could commit an atrocity."

Few of us surrounding Crame that Monday morning had more than a vague idea of what a 105-mm howitzer would do to its target. Fortunately, such calculations are second nature to the Colonel. In the end, that technological "overkill" was what stayed his hand and saved thousands of lives.

"The howitzer is very heavy stuff," explained an army captain, while guiding me around a now-peaceful Camp Aguinaldo. The precision artillery piece can be fired accurately to about seven miles, blasting a door-sized hole in most walls. Even a modest barrage of 105-mm shells will collapse a building in seconds. When lobbed into a crowd of human beings, the effect is nearly apocalyptic. "It would create complete havoc," says the captain. "Especially if it was adjusted for the maximum killing range."

Ah, yes, those exciting "adjustments". The modern weapon bears little resemblance to that clumsy Second World War stuff that everyone has seen in the movies for four decades. Today's weapons are a marvel of sophisticated flexibility, able to knock down buildings or splatter civilians with equal efficacy. Yet most of those huddled under the tanks along EDSA were trapped in our cinematic time warp. When Marcos sent a Sikorsky over the camp on Sunday morning, we all gazed skyward, gulping in astonishment: What the hell was *that*? It did not sit out there on the horizon for five minutes, churning the air like an upturned eggbeater, checking out the rush-hour traffic. Its shark-like nose simply appeared from nowhere, then shot out of sight. It was a whirlybird jet, a sinister black missile. And that "persuasion sortie" had its intended psychological effect upon the human barricade.

Still, I approached this book with scant interest in the implements of modern warfare. This is the story of a nearly bloodless revolution, so it seemed irrelevant that both sides were armed to the eyebrows. Only after repeated research trips to Aguinaldo, Crame, and the Villamor and Sangley air bases did the chilling truth begin to dawn. The Philippine revolt was "peaceful" only because the near-maniacal orders from Malacañang Palace were disobeyed. And that mutiny grew in large part from the sheer, sickening killing power of the weapons available.

Colonel Balbas was fully prepared to obey the orders of his commander-in-chief. He was willing to fire *something* at Camp Crame. The hitch came when he was ordered to create a holocaust with that ghastly howitzer.

Its artillery shells – more than four inches in diameter – are not just giant firecrackers that go bang when they hit something. They are selected from a range of "designer weapons", programmed to reduce people and places to bones and rubble. The howitzer's explosion can be delayed until it is imbedded deep inside a target, vastly increasing the destructive wallop. It can be touched off on impact. Or it can be transformed into a terminator of human beings by setting its detonation fuse to the "minimum pressure" mode.

"Normally, a 105-mm round has a lethal area of about 35 metres," explains the captain, "because of the fragmentation effect." Meaning anyone within field-goal range is dead when the thing blows up. "But when you set it on minimum pressure, that changes everything. It means that almost anything will set it off: a leaf, a tree branch, even a bird. It only needs to graze an object. So, basically, you want it to explode in the air, before it hits the ground. That gives you a much wider dispersal and it would . . . uh, obviously kill an awful lot of people. If they had sent even one like that over the crowd at EDSA, there would have been wholesale panic, absolute terror. No one would stay after something like that. Nobody is that courageous."

And the howitzer, of course, is just one weapon in the mighty military arsenal. The Marines who trained their guns on Crame that Monday morning also set up nine 81-mm mortars: the "firing tubes" you see in so many films, tilted up at a sharp angle to bury the enemy under a barrage of falling bombs. Individual mortars are not quite as deadly as howitzers, but, considering that hundreds of shells could be lobbed into the crowd in just a few minutes, they would have had equal destructive power.

The potential impact on the rebellion of those F-5 fighter jets cruising overhead can be gauged by their standard payload: a selection of bombs, rockets, and 20-mm cannons, augmented by lethal air-to-ground or air-to-air missiles. If they had ever followed the orders to "strafe" Crame, the rebel base and its human defensive wall would have been incinerated. Aside from moral suasion, the camp was defenseless against such an attack. The rebels had just four bazooka-like recoilless rifles that *might* have knocked out a tank or a chopper. Otherwise, they were powerless to stop the phalanx of Sikorsky gunships awaiting orders at Villamor Air Base just four minutes – as the Sikorsky flies – away from the rebel headquarters.

When aides told Marcos and Ver that navy warships were sitting in Manila Bay, their huge five-inch guns trained on the Palace, there was much consternation. It was absolutely true, but utterly meaningless – and thus provides a revealing insight into the military prowess of the President's hand-picked high command. "The ships and guns were really out there, all right," smiles navy captain Felix Turingan, a prime organizer of the RAM group. "And our guns really were pointed towards the Palace. But anyone with any military sense would have known right away that we couldn't possibly hit it. Navy guns shoot straight. They can't lob shells in an arc over buildings and obstructions. They're designed for sea battles, and you may have noticed there are no buildings at sea. Ver should have known that, but apparently he didn't. The reports we got said they were all terribly upset when they heard we were out there. Actually, we were just blockading the bay so they couldn't make a run for it in one of their speedboats. If we'd tried to fire, we'd have knocked down half of Manila before we could hit the Palace."

The Philippines is one of the world's great gossip capitals at any time, and the rumor mills went wild during the three-day revolt. The presence of the warships was somehow known immediately on Monday, quickly followed by stories of a civilian "suicide squad" that had been armed and trained to stop Loyalist advances around the city. Bizarre as it sounds, that rumor too had more than a grain of truth.

There were actually two "suicide squads", though neither would use that term to describe themselves. One was the highly organized SMK (a Tagalog acronym for Urban Armed Warriors), which included Charlie Avila and Gerry Esguerra, a pair of armed outlaws during the Marcos regime who received high-profile positions under the Cory Aquino government. Avila became officer-in-charge of sequestered "crony" newspapers and hotels; Esguerra is security chief at the Manila International Airport. There is no doubt about the authenticity of their urban guerrilla band.

"The world saw a drama of spiritual power and peace," says Avila, "but that's all in retrospect. Worried people such as us knew that it could explode into violence at any time. We had seen, many times, soldiers shooting into crowds. It had happened here, and I was in Thailand in 1976 when a million students were dispersed in ten minutes. People were determined to stay, and ready to die . . . but, well, when they shoot, you run. Our strategy was to resist dispersal at all costs. If the soldiers fired, we'd shoot back. We had a lot of guns, just like Marcos always accused us of having."

The SMK had deployed a force of 200 armed men and women inside Manila, and intended to build it to 1,000 during the scheduled 1987 presidential election. They were caught short by the "snap election" call, and fielded only 300 for the February 7 poll. But all had been trained in the countryside, and their arsenal included boxes of grenades ("the smooth ones, not the pineapple type"), plastic explosives, handguns, carbines, submachine pistols, sawed-off shotguns, and a sophisticated array of communications gear. In heavy crowds like that which stopped the tanks on Sunday afternoon, they moved in groups of five – unarmed, but trailed closely by a strong-armed confederate carrying their weapons in a bulky sports bag.

Some may doubt the sanity of opposing 2,000 battle-hard Marines, not to mention a fleet of tanks, with a motley crew of semi-trained civilians. If they had been spotted with their guns, the SMK might even have touched off the conflagration they were trying to prevent. But Avila sees the strategy in a different light. "If the military started shooting," he says, "we believed that only a few would actually be firing, with the majority holding back. If we had returned the fire, maybe we could have stopped them. Obviously, people would have been killed, including some of us. But perhaps there would only be one hundred dead instead of ten thousand. Would we have that kind of capacity? I don't honestly know. But we were certainly going to try."

Less is known about the other civilian army, set up on the spot with the backing of Jose "Peping" Cojuangco, a powerful businessman and, by no coincidence, the brother of Cory Aquino. Their branch of the family had quietly formed a so-called "Yellow Army" to combat the 3,000-man private force controlled by their cousin Eduardo "Danding" Cojuangco in Tarlac province. Danding's army, always at the disposal of President Marcos, was responsible for much terrorism during the election and had destroyed the Radio Veritas transmitter in Malolos right at the outset of the Enrile-Ramos revolt.

According to insiders, Peping Cojuangco assumed that his cousin would send men to sabotage the civilian barricades, and quickly created his own counter-force. Organizers in the various Manila neighborhoods were each ordered to gather twenty volunteers on Sunday morning and report to various suburban schoolyards. There they were issued firearms and put through a crash course in guerrilla warfare, with special emphasis on using grenades and Molotov cocktails to disable armored vehicles. "It all happened pretty fast," says one informant who was involved in the scheme, "so it's hard to say if we really could have done anything. But the hardware was certainly available and the recruiters did a good job of recruiting. These guys were really eager to kill soldiers."

Gerry Esguerra, who was involved with the Aquino presidential campaign, says Peping Cojuangco's plan was an outgrowth of election security measures. "He always wanted to create a militia force, and he had that idea of twenty-man groups even then," says Esguerra. There is no reliable estimate of the numbers involved. "He had an arsenal," shrugs Esguerra, "but I don't think that at that point he could approximate Danding's force."

Amazingly, these two groups of gun-wielding civilians played no part in any of the sixteen deaths attributed to the almost bloodless revolt. The killings were all done by soldiers, Loyalist thugs, and one gang of drug-crazed policemen. Four men died in military fire fights at two television stations – including a civilian whose heart gave out in the excitement. One man was shot by guards at the Palace barricades, another was stabbed with an ice pick inside. By far the largest number, nine, were gunned down in an insane shoot-out at a police station in a Manila suburb.

A sergeant named Esteban Bandai entered the Makati station Tuesday afternoon with eight to ten other cops, disarmed six men, and announced that he was taking over in the name of Cory Aquino. There ensued a three-hour standoff, during which an Aquino spokesman denied any connection and described Bandai as a "known scalawag". The sergeant was finally persuaded to leave, but, during the evacuation, he suddenly grabbed a policewoman and tried to take her hostage. She was shot in the scuffle, and the ensuing hail of bullets killed eight more policemen and wounded nine, including civilian bystanders. "Bandai was a drug dealer, and the whole bunch of them were high," a Makati policeman later told me. "That shooting should never have been included in the revolution's death-toll. It was cops vs. drug dealers, not tanks vs. nuns."

The celebrated showdown at EDSA and Ortigas, of course, made the nuns international heroes. It also made the Marine tanks the most famous of the revolution's unused guns. Most were not tanks at all, but armored personnel carriers, mud-splattered and greasy and pockmarked with bullet scars from the insurgency battles around the country. The Philippine army has a number of British Scorpion tanks with big 90-mm cannons. Those, however, were supposed to shell Camp Crame from miles away, not to push through crowds. The rumbling APCs that approached the nuns were not equipped to blast down walls. Their hardware was ideal for spraying human beings with bullets.

"It's easy to see why civilians would call them tanks," says the captain who instructed me on weaponry. "They're about the same size and they run on tracks. But their armor is lighter, they carry more men inside, and they've got that machine gun up top instead of the heavy cannon." The gun fires 50-caliber bullets, wicked metal missiles a half-inch in diameter. And the captain has a graphic way of translating their impact into civilian terms. "They make really big holes," he smiles. "If you lined up ten people back to back, it would go right through all of them."

Identical guns were also mounted on something called the Commando V-150, an armored car on wheels that is cleverly outfitted with dual machine-gun turrets. They can swivel a complete 360 degrees without getting in each other's way, and therefore spit out death in all directions at once – a quality much appreciated by the military.

Other Marines, meanwhile, roamed Manila's streets in their LVTs, an acronym that stands for "landing vehicle, tracked". These are amphibious units more suited to swamps and jungles, and they come equipped with the aforementioned howitzers. The ones brought in from Bicol were badly scarred with bullets, their windshields cracked and pitted, and they had a stirring psychological effect as they rumbled between the city's ubiquitous pizza parlors and girlie bars. I actually watched one park in front of Shakey's, and saw a fatigues-clad sergeant stroll over to the take-out window. He came back with two large specials and a tray of drinks. I still have the entry in my notebook: "one orange, 3 colas . . . can't tell if they went for the double cheese".

Last on the deadly hit parade came the bewildering assortment of long and short arms carried by both soldiers and civilians. Armalites and Galils, Garands, Fals, M-1s and Manlichers, bazookas and M-60s, baby Uzis and their parents, shotguns with laser telescopic sights, Brownings, Magnums, Smith & Wessons, Lugers, Colts, and "Cebu .38s" – the Philippine-made pistol that fires about every third time you pull the trigger.

Forget all that cinematic stuff about recoil and powder burns. The modern attack weapon has built-in compensators to virtually eliminate the old-fashioned kick. It just burps a bit when fired, an affectionate nudge on the shoulder to let you know it is working. Powerful as they are, modern guns do not even make much noise; when an M-16 or Galil goes off, there is just a neat series of "thunk-thunk-thunk" sounds, and a lot of people fall over dead. Such weapons are deadly accurate up to approximately a quarter of a mile. They will kill anything they hit up to almost a mile away, but that is apparently a dicey proposition. "You can't control it that far without a telescopic sight and maybe a tripod," says Captain Ricardo Morales, the infamous coup plotter and one-shot TV star. "So mostly you just have to keep firing and hope you hit something."

You may think all of this would be a fool's paradise for a soldier. But no, there are myriad headaches and drawbacks attached. It is impossible, for instance, to operate a big M-60 machine gun all by yourself. Somebody has to trail you around with about fifty pounds of bullets strapped to his body and "feed" the gun as it fires. The M-60 bullets are about the size of a big man's middle finger, and the belts are each three or four feet long. They are not exactly easy to hide.

Then, too, there is the mathematical imperative of today's weapons: this boils down to a formula as simple as 30 divided by 1500/60. The answer works out to 1.2, which is about how many seconds it takes to empty the mini-Uzi machine gun.

"The problem," explains Captain Morales, "is that modern weapons fire very fast but don't contain very much ammunition. That's where the training comes in . . . the ability to conserve your ammunition." The baby Uzi, for example, would fire 1500 bullets a minute if you could feed it that many. But the standard clip contains only 30, so it is dangerous to drill too many holes in one target. Even the regulation Armalite rifle becomes a kind of machine gun when placed on automatic setting, and its 30 bullets last less than three seconds. The idea is to master the delicate art of the three-bullet burst. "But in the heat of battle it's very common for soldiers to squeeze too long and end up with an empty gun," says Morales. "If you do that in an insurgency situation, you are probably dead."

Filipino officers are endlessly fascinated with their guns. Most, indeed, manage to aquire a personal collection by "confiscating" illegal arms or by capturing them from the well-equipped New People's Army (NPA) guerrillas. One of the more bizarre aspects of the revolution was the steady stream of rebels sneaking home from Camp Crame to their suburban bungalows – not out of cowardice or for personal comfort, but simply to grab a favorite rifle or scoop up an armload of choice grenades.

Brig.-Gen. Rene R. Cruz, for instance, was already in Aguinaldo when the rebellion erupted on Saturday night, but he drove thirty miles back and forth to a suburb called Alabang so he could pick up his guns. Why was that, sir? Didn't you have any guns at the office? "Well, sure, there were guns at the camp," he responds, a bit testily. "But the ones at home are *my* guns. I feel comfortable with them. I've got my own Armalite and a machine pistol. If you're going to make a last stand, you have to do it with guns you can rely on."

Colonel Braulio Balbas had just the opposite problem as he rolled towards Camp Aguinaldo before dawn on Monday: far too much firepower for the job at hand. Aside from his armored vehicles, howitzers, turret-mounted machine guns, and nearly 1,000 Marines, he had 400 of the army's anti-riot troopers with their face masks, helmets, and Plexiglas shields.

Sister Anunciata had lost her voice by the time the Marines approached. She was the only one among the band of vigilantes who knew the rosary in Tagalog, and the people from the nearby slums did not understand the English version. "So I had to repeat it, over and over, all night," she recalls. "It was so funny. We were saying the rosary and there was another group not far away with a tape player and disco music. They were dancing in the streets, and we were praying. It was so Filipino."

Everyone in the area had been told of the impending attack, and they all knew there would be tear gas. Citizens' brigades came around with buckets of *calamansi* – tiny local limes – to fight off the stinging gases. "We were ready for the tear gas," says the Good Shepherd nun, who goes by the nickname Sister Ciats. "We had a big tub of water in the middle, and people were coming from the other groups to dip their towels in it, to cover their noses. But you need the calamansi, too. You squeeze it into the towel, and it really works. Some people rub the juice all over their faces. We'd been gassed before at rallies in Quiapo and Lawton Plaza. It worked fine. We'd already tested it."

The human barricade could not see the Marines coming, but they heard all about them on the radio. Announcer June Keithley on Radio Bandido was nearly frantic by now, her voice cracking with fear and desperation. She added her own pleas to those of General Ramos, and yelled over the air for everyone in the Camp Aguinaldo neighborhood to switch on their lights, open their windows, and turn their radios up to top volume. It was like a scene from the film *Network*, when New Yorkers yelled into the night: "I'm mad as hell, and I'm not going to take it any more!" But this was real, and the people were *scared* as hell. Hundreds did go to their windows, and the Marines reached the attack site bathed in light and sound. It was just before dawn, with only a slight purple on the horizon. Keithley put the Philippine national anthem on Radio Bandido's turntable, and kept it there. If the Marines were going to kill Filipinos in cold blood, then, God damn them, they would have to do it with their own anthem ringing in their ears.

Many myths have been repeated about the Monday tear-gas attack, and some have become accepted as fact. Most Filipinos believe that the assault was against Crame, and that it was repulsed by indefatigable nuns who once again refused to budge. There is even a much-repeated apocryphal story that the wind suddenly shifted and blew the gas back in the Marines' faces – another of the EDSA miracles.

It did not happen that way. The Marines sat back in their armored vehicles while the army's anti-riot squad attacked the Santolan gate of Camp Aguinaldo. The plan was not to storm Crame, but to use the neighboring camp as a base from which to shell the rebel headquarters. Participants on both sides now agree that the defenders were scattered almost immediately, and ran, terrified, from in front of the gate. "We just sat there and waited for them to clear the area," says Colonel Balbas. "It was not our duty. We were inside the vehicles and we saw them [the crowd] running away. They were easily dispersed, in about ten to fifteen minutes. They started scampering around and the anti-riot people were running after them. The story about the wind . . . no, that didn't happen."

The event appeared somewhat less routine from Sister Ciats' perspective.

"The anti-riot squad hit just after 5:30," she recalls, "and it was a very big squad. We'd piled our boxes of food along the walls [beside the gate], so the tanks wouldn't crush them. We didn't know what we were going to do. But I told the sisters, 'If the worst comes to the worst, just run for your lives.' We were ready to die, but . . . you also try to save your life. We were all confused. Nobody knew what would happen.

"The squad came . . . and these two young girls near us were trembling with fear. They cried out to us: 'Sisters, we are afraid. We cannot run. We cannot go with you.' We had already begun to run, but when we heard them cry we turned back. The Loyalist soldiers saw us and they whispered: 'Sisters, just hide behind the boxes and keep still. You'll be all right.' So there we were, all crouched down between the boxes and the wall. And I told the men there, 'If you even peek out I'm going to knock your heads.' I think perhaps the soldiers were touched by our kindness, because we had been feeding them all. We never asked which side they were on, we just fed them. Also, I think they were confused, too. They didn't know exactly what was happening."

That observation was confirmed by reporters who arrived later and asked some of the riot squad – outfitted with shields, helmets, Plexiglas face guards, and truncheons – what they were doing. "I don't know anything," shrugged one. "We are just following orders."

From behind her barrier of boxes, Sister Ciats could hear the clash of shields and the cries of people shouting and running. "I was very, very afraid at that point," she says. "We have had very bad experiences with these anti-riot squads before. They had been very cruel. Finally they lined up in front of the gate, and a few of the people who were left started to pray. We called out to them: 'We are also Filipinos. We are doing this also for your sake.' Some of the soldiers sat down, exhausted. The people were quiet, too. Then somebody said, 'Everyone is hungry. We must serve them breakfast.' But I just said, 'You do it. I don't want to.' "

By now, Colonel Balbas's troops had moved in with their armor and were pushing away the transport trailers, sand trucks, and buses that barricaded the gate. There was no resistance from the people as three big V-150 armor-plated commando vehicles went about their work. The nuns and people sat alongside, praying, while the riot squad pulled off their helmets and sprawled, sweating, on the curb.

Suddenly there was a scream of engines overhead, and everyone looked up at once. Five Sikorskys were zinging towards Crame, not one hundred yards off the ground, their rocket launchers poised for attack. Three more helicopters were coming over the horizon. "Oh, Jesus," said Sister Ciats. "What on God's earth are they?"

12 *"SIR, YOUR AIR FORCE IS HERE"*

NOTHING YOU HAVE SEEN of normal helicopters is any preparation for the arrival of the first true-life gunship. It does not "chop" through the air, as its nickname suggests. Instead, there is a deadly whir of propellers and the almost instant appearance of that sinister snub nose. Sikorskys are theoretically capable of hovering in place, but that is too humdrum a manoeuvre for the air force fly-boys who scream them across the sky as if they'd been fired from a slingshot. They arrive and disappear in seconds, leaving only a shiver in their wake.

Pilots can hardly contain themselves when comparing Sikorskys to the plodding Hueys they have largely replaced. They are faster, more mobile, and a perfect tool for jungle warfare. But there are a few peevish plaints about the newer plane's versatility. It will carry either 7.62 machine guns or rockets, but not both at once. "You have to choose between them," one Philippine general complained to me. "And you can't put one on one side and one on the other, because it unbalances the ship. The Huey is slower, but it carries a lot more."

These malignant whirlybirds have made a distinct impression on the world, although few Westerners have seen one in real life. Most viewers of the film *Apocalypse Now* were dazzled by the scene in which the choppers strafe a Vietnamese village at dawn, spewing classical music and bullets. (A sequence that was filmed, ironically enough, in the Philippines.) Certainly the Sikorsky has become a huge favorite in the Third World, where no self-respecting junta would miss the thrill of chasing guerrillas through the underbrush. They were particularly popular with Marcos and Ver, who had amassed a fleet both for their personal transport and for the ongoing insurgency war.

Now it seemed that their rockets, which can punch large holes in thick walls, were about to be employed against Camp Crame, or their machine guns used on Sister Anunciata and the rest of the crowd cowering below.

• • •

The first of those menacing gunships was flown by Colonel Antonio Sotelo, who was grinning from ear to ear and feeling "free as a bird. If there is a heaven," he would say later, "this must be it." But to understand the colonel's dawn euphoria, we must flash back to the first few hours of the revolt.

Sotelo was sitting at home in his neat bungalow that Saturday evening, cradling a San Miguel beer and listening in stunned silence to the Enrile-Ramos press conference on Radio Veritas. His phone rang right in the midst of the revelations about Marcos's cheating, just after 7 p.m. The colonel picked it up, listened, and stood straight up from the sofa. When he finally spoke, the conversation sounded strange indeed to the rest of the Sotelo family. Their father said, "Yes," and then "Yes" once more. He hung up, stared into space, and "suddenly realized that I might soon be facing a firing squad."

Air force colonel Hector Tarrazona had called from the rebel headquarters to find out Sotelo's sympathies. It was a gamble, a long shot, because Sotelo had never been a RAM sympathizer and was completely outside the Reformist network. But he commanded the 15th Strike Wing, one of only two air combat units in the Manila area. He was in charge of the lethal Sikorskys at Villamor Air Base and another squad of aged T-28 fighter-bombers a few miles south at Sangley Point. Although no fan of Gringo Honasan and his gang, the colonel was known to dislike General Ver. He admired Enrile and considered General Ramos the most professional soldier in the Philippine armed forces. All of that might just be enough to swing him towards treason.

The conversation was a simple one. Colonel Tarrazona had been on the phone since mid-afternoon, trying to entice a long list of commanders onto the rebel side. By the time he reached Sotelo, he had dispensed with any preliminaries.

"I'm calling on behalf of Minister Enrile and General Ramos," Tarrazona said crisply. "Are you willing to help them?"

"Yes," answered Sotelo.

"Can I tell them this?"

"Yes."

"Thank you. We'll be in touch. Goodbye."

Even the rebels were surprised by such immediate, unequivocal support. They had been working on other plans to snare the 15th Strike Wing – all of which called for the neutralization of Colonel Sotelo. And if they had been able to peek inside his head over the next few minutes, they might have opted for an alternative scheme.

"I will admit," he says ruefully, "that I wavered right then. I suddenly realized that . . . one slip-up and I'd be dead. But if you understand the situation in our military at that time, you'll see why I really had no choice. I wasn't a Reformist, but I knew with all my heart that reform had to come somehow. I guess the best way to describe it is just 'fed up'. I had thirty-two years in the service. I was there before Marcos, and I saw what he and Ver had done to us. Perhaps I even know a few of their secrets. These are the most evil and sinister people I have known in my whole life. If you get people like this at the top, without any sense of morality, they can never really lead. That is my basic conviction . . . and I had watched it being violated by Marcos and Ver many, many times."

The colonel's sentiments are instructive, for they were to be echoed by scores of veteran officers over the following days. These men were never involved in the RAM coup plot, and might well have turned in the traitors themselves if they had uncovered it. But now it was a different question. The siege of Camp Crame was a reality, and the choice was clear-cut: they could stick with Ver, or they could back Ramos. With few exceptions, those middle-level officers opted overwhelmingly for the squeaky-clean West Pointer, Lt.-Gen. Fidel V. Ramos.

Colonel Sotelo sat with his wife, Lilian, for two hours, reviewing their life together. He was fifty-two, with four grown children and two grandchildren. "I said to my wife: 'Are you scared to die?' because the rebel cause looked almost hopeless at that point. I just wanted to feel her out. But together we realized that we had already experienced most of the pleasures of the world. We had seen and done enough. So, at that point, everything changed for me. I harmonized myself with the situation and admitted that my country must come first – over my family, life, and everything else. After that, I had peace of mind all the way. There was no more fear. I just went about my business."

The colonel conferred immediately with his helicopter squadron commander, Major Charles Hotchkiss, and came away believing that he had won him over. The truth is that Hotchkiss – described by a fellow officer as "the toughest guy in the air force" – was a secret RAM supporter who spent that evening watching Sotelo closely. Was the colonel *really* on side, or was he a Loyalist trying to penetrate the rebel camp? Hotchkiss had to know, and would have "eliminated" his boss at the first sign of treachery. The Sikorskys were absolutely pivotal, the single element that could ensure Camp Crame's survival. By peaceful agreement or by blood on the tarmac, RAM had to get control of them.

Sotelo's next stop was Sangley Point. He drove the twenty miles with Radio Veritas on the car radio, listening to the endless appeals for People Power to surround the defectors. He checked out the fighter-bombers, and also drew three Armalite rifles and all the ammunition he could carry from a supply depot. Sotelo drove back home "happily . . . and armed to the teeth".

Rebel strategy at this point was coolly sophisticated. They might have panicked and ordered Sotelo to bring as many Sikorskys as he could hijack to Crame. But General Ramos was playing a far more subtle game. The idea was to give the colonel time to assess his pilots' loyalties and then bring the whole batch of attack gunships in together. Meanwhile, the 15th Strike Wing would do everything Malacañang ordered – short of actually killing anyone – thereby dispelling suspicions and giving the Marcos-Ver team false confidence.

The plan worked to perfection. Colonel Sotelo was on the flight line at Villamor before dawn on Sunday, the very picture of a crisp Loyalist officer awaiting his orders. The first command was to prepare two gun-ships to strafe Crame and destroy the two lone helicopters (personal transport planes of Enrile and Ramos) that constituted the meagre rebel "air force". Sotelo saluted, assembled his pilots, and asked for volunteers. None stepped forward. The colonel smiled inwardly . . . and wondered what in heaven had given him such an idea.

"That's never how we operate," he explains. "The normal thing is just to schedule the people to go ahead. But no. This time, perhaps in God's wisdom, it suddenly came into my mind to ask for volunteers. And that's how I knew they were with me. I don't see how I could have found out, otherwise. I'm not a mind-reader, and you can't just ask 'Which of you want to betray Marcos?' "

Again, however, the situation was not quite what it seemed to the colonel. Major Hotchkiss had been busy asking his young pilots about their sympathies, and he had made sure there were none on the flight line who were willing to attack the rebel fortress. Marcos and Ver may have been rubbing their hands at the prospect of unleashing jungle gunships against Crame, but RAM already had the 15th Strike Wing tied up from every conceivable angle.

That was clearly illustrated in the afternoon, when Sotelo went back to Sangley Point to sound out his closest officers. There is a famous incident involving his deputy that was first revealed in a Rotary Club speech after the Revolution, and has often been cited since in the Philippine press as evidence of the rebels' uncanny good luck. "I needed to know how my No. 2 man felt," Sotelo told the Rotarians, "so I could let him supervise the Sangley operation if he was with me. . . . With God's help, I found out what I wanted to know. My No. 2 man and myself were sitting in the maintenance shed. We heard Maj.-Gen. Delfin Castro on radio saying that the President is the duly elected authority and therefore he would obey his instructions. My No. 2 man suddenly said: 'Ayun ang tama' (That's the truth). I knew then that he'd be out of the plan.''

It is a terrific story, another of the small miracles at EDSA, except for one detail. Sotelo's No. 2 man, Colonel Jose Commendador, happened to be firmly among the Enrile-Ramos supporters at the time. Their Sunday-afternoon shadow-boxing session in the maintenance shed involved two committed rebel sympathizers, each pretending to be a staunch Loyalist. They fooled each other completely.

''I talked to Commendador that morning,'' says Colonel Pedro Juachon, posted at Ramos headquarters throughout the revolt. ''And we agreed that Sotelo was very loyal to [air force chief] General [Vicente] Piccio. We figured Piccio had placed him there as wing commander precisely because of that loyalty. I remember saying to Commendador: 'Are you supporting Crame?'

'' 'Yes.'

'' 'What about the pilots?'

'' 'Yes. We have control of them.'

'' 'What about your commander, Sotelo?'

'' 'I'm not sure,' said Commendador. 'I think he's a Piccio man. We'll have to move carefully.' ''

So the careful Commendador leapt at the first chance to put Sotelo at ease, with that exaggerated show of faithfulness. His boss nodded, too – conclusive evidence that he was indeed a ''Piccio man''.

Such elaborate deceptions would all have been blown apart on Sunday afternoon if Marcos had ordered the Camp Crame assault. The 15th Strike Wing was merely going through the motions, and everything would have been forced into the open if the unit had disobeyed a direct attack command. Instead, Marcos apparently yielded to U.S. warnings against using heavy weapons, and scrubbed the mission at 1 p.m. Sotelo's men only flew two afternoon reconnaissance sorties over Crame, including the very public tour with General Tadiar during the EDSA-Ortigas showdown. Other rebel sympathizers in the air force obeyed orders to ferry Loyalist troops in C-130 transport planes. Those routine flights were taken, as the rebels planned, to be concrete evidence of the pilots' dependability.

Judging from his fire-breathing ''warhorse'' speech, the ruse did

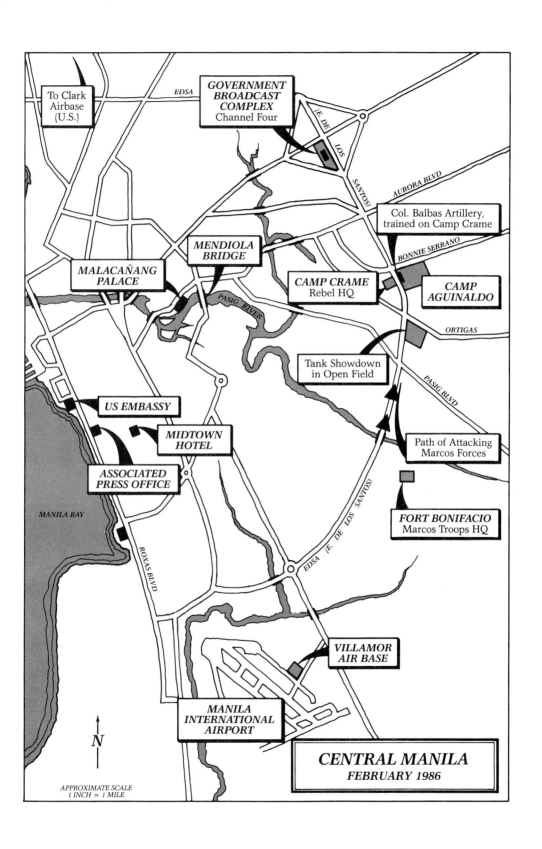

To Clark Airbase (U.S.)

EDSA

GOVERNMENT BROADCAST COMPLEX Channel Four

(E. DE LOS SANTOS)

AURORA BLVD

Col. Balbas Artillery, trained on Camp Crame

BONNIE SERRANO

MENDIOLA BRIDGE

MALACAÑANG PALACE

PASIG RIVER

CAMP CRAME Rebel HQ

CAMP AGUINALDO

ORTIGAS

Tank Showdown in Open Field

PASIG BLVD

US EMBASSY

MIDTOWN HOTEL

ASSOCIATED PRESS OFFICE

MANILA BAY

Path of Attacking Marcos Forces

FORT BONIFACIO Marcos Troops HQ

ROXAS BLVD

EDSA (E. DE LOS SANTOS)

VILLAMOR AIR BASE

MANILA INTERNATIONAL AIRPORT

N

APPROXIMATE SCALE 1 INCH = 1 MILE

CENTRAL MANILA **FEBRUARY 1986**

First Lady Imelda Marcos plants a kiss on her husband's forehead, shortly after the Marcos-controlled National Assembly declared him winner of the February 7 presidential election.

Below, Jaime Cardinal Sin is mobbed by cheering crowds at a post-election mass where he encouraged Filipinos to keep guarding ballot boxes.

General Fidel Ramos (top left)
watches Defense Minister
Juan Ponce Enrile intently as
the two rebel leaders
announce their defection
from the Marcos government.
Within hours, thousands of
Filipinos arrived at the
Ministry gates (below), with
sacks of rice, bags of donuts
and home-baked cookies for
the rebel soldiers.

Minister Enrile and his supporters (top left) surge out of their camp on Sunday afternoon to join General Ramos at Camp Crame. Security chief Gringo Honasan, in a flak jacket, leads the procession.

Less than a mile away, a column of Marine tanks (bottom left) sit like beached whales at the corner of EDSA and Ortigas Avenues, blocked by thousands of defiant civilians.

(Top right) Ferdinand Marcos, flanked by his loyal military henchman General Fabian Ver, assures a TV audience that his troops have the rebel camp surrounded.

(Bottom right) General Ramos makes a premature leap for joy on Monday morning, after reports that the Marcos family has fled the country.

Within hours of the rebel "victory", Marcos was back on television. The newsboy above peddles his papers with that news at the barricade protecting Malacañang Palace.

Amid the confusion, rebel forces seized the government's Maharlika TV station after a short, fierce fire-fight. The pro-Marcos soldier in the middle of this mêlée is held by Reformists.

The "nearly bloodless" revolution turned violent at the Maharlika shoot-out. The rebel soldier above stands guard over three dead pro-Marcos defenders.

The pro-Aquino crowd at the Mendiola Bridge fashions barbed wire into crowns of thorns and taunts the Marcos Loyalist soldiers guarding the main entrance to the Palace.

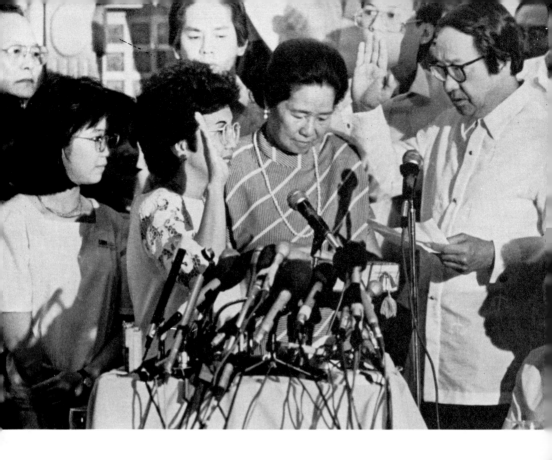

By Tuesday morning, the Philippines had two presidents. Cory Aquino (above) is sworn in at 10 a.m., with her mother-in-law Doña Aurora Aquino in the background, and two thousand supporters as witnesses.

Two hours later, President Marcos took his own oath of office before delivering this fierce speech from the balcony at Malacañang, which turned out to be his farewell address. By 9 p.m., he and Imelda were on their way to Hawaii.

wonders for the President's morale. Indeed, from Malacañang's perspective, the situation on Sunday night must have seemed well in hand. The loyal air force gave them complete control of the skies, the mobility to move troops at will, and an awesome sledgehammer to "annihilate" Camp Crame whenever they wished.

Shortly after dawn on Monday, however, the rebels would enjoy most of those advantages. By noon, Malacañang was the fortress under siege.

Colonel Sotelo woke from a short nap at 2 a.m. on Sunday, and fiddled with his bedside radio. Veritas had mysteriously disappeared off the air, but June Keithley was just down the dial on a station calling itself Radio Bandido. Sotelo remembers that she sounded frightened, reciting a long litany of rumored Loyalist attacks. Ironically, her main worry seemed to be his own helicopter strike wing. Every few minutes a listener would phone in with an ominous report about the gunships. The very word Sikorsky sent shivers through the civilian barricades.

The colonel woke his wife at 3 a.m. and asked her to cook him a nice breakfast. It was not necessary to add that it might be their last together. The food was great, he recalls, "but it tasted like wood to me. I felt like a death-row prisoner having his final meal."

He called the Sangley Point supply officer, asking that a box of M-16s and ammunition be sent to the guards at Villamor. The command was just camouflage, a make-work project to keep the men busy and their attention focused elsewhere. The guns and bullets he would need were already secured. Sotelo next ordered a subordinate to prepare the aircraft and awake the pilots. None knew where or when they would be flying.

At 4:15 a.m., the colonel said goodbye to his wife. "He said, 'We may meet again in the afterlife,' " remembers Lilian Sotelo, "but I didn't try to convince him to change his plans. I just gave him the rosary which I bought in Jerusalem and reminded him to keep on praying. There were no tears shed." The Sotelos' youngest son, Nick, was only nineteen, but he had an Armalite slung over his shoulder, and he was going with his dad. "He really insisted on being there," shrugs the colonel, "and he's a very good shot. So I made him my security. We just said goodbye very simply, with instructions not to use the phone. I kissed my wife, Nick kissed his mother, and off we went. The worst part, really, was after we got into my staff car and turned on the radio. The situation sounded pretty bad and it was deteriorating rapidly. We heard 'Eddie' Ramos appealing to Marcos and Ver to call off the attack. Then we listened while people on the radio told the civilians how to deal with tear gas. Being part of it, actually doing things, was not so bad. But it was very frightening to listen to them on the radio."

The colonel had barely arrived at his Villamor hangar, and begun checking the rocket tubes on his gunships, when he received the best news of the day. Two Sikorskys had been ordered to go to the Loyalist command post in Fort Bonifacio by 6 a.m. It was a phenomenal stroke of luck. Sotelo had been trying desperately to think of some reason, a cover story, for starting and warming the helicopter engines before the defection. Without orders to take off, such an action would be highly suspicious, and armed guards might seize his planes before they could get off the tarmac. Now he would seem to be obeying instructions.

There was one last briefing, one final chance for the pilots to reconsider: "Anybody who wants to back out, you're free to leave this room and go home in peace." No one budged. The nervous fliers even resisted the temptation to ask where they were going. At Sotelo's signal, the whole group simply pulled on their helmets and headed for the planes, trying to appear casual.

"Basically, we were just sneaking away," says Sotelo. "We had dragged all the helicopters out in front of the hangars to make it easier. Clearance security was very heavy at this point, and, of course, we had no clearance at all. We were just hoping the cover would work when we started up the engines. We hoped they would just say, 'Okay, those are the helicopters going to Bonifacio.' But I had a lot more than two. We had five gunships, two of the rescue Sikorskys, the white ones, and one small utility helicopter, the BO-105. There was supposed to be another utility helicopter going with us, but it wasn't able to take off. Somebody finally caught on and put a gun to the pilot's head and stopped them. The guards finally got wise to it."

For a few tense moments, Sotelo himself believed that he might have to shoot his way into the air. He was running towards his own helicopter at 5:55 a.m. when Colonel Ojelio de la Cruz came forward to ask where he was going. "He's a guy I know very well, a golf-mate of mine," says Sotelo. "But I was already running and I'd given my last instructions to my people, so I just kept going. I didn't even answer him. He tried to talk to me again when I was starting the engines, but I still didn't say a word. When I got to the plane, of course, I cocked my M-16, because, if he had shown any signs of stopping us, I would need to kill him. But, very luckily, he did not. He just stood there in surprise, and we took off."

(Sotelo was astounded, at 9:30 a.m. on the same morning, to meet his old golfing buddy again in Camp Crame. Colonel de la Cruz had defected by land, bringing a small number of air force troops with him. "I was just trying to find out if you were going to attack Crame," he explained to Sotelo. "If I'd known you were going to defect, I would have gone with you right then." The colonel had been so depressed by that wordless rebuff on the tarmac that he immediately left Villamor and returned home. By that time, he'd heard of the defection on the radio, and told his wife he felt humiliated by Sotelo's lack of trust in him. So he gathered some men, commandeered a vehicle, and joined his golf partner in the rebel encampment.)

Sotelo lifted off the tarmac, and heard the No. 5 gunship call over the radio: "Airborne." Instantly, he says, "I had a complete feeling of serenity. I think every one of us did."

Ramos, Enrile, and a few top advisors were aware of Sotelo's imminent defection. But the rise of the fully armed choppers into the red dawn of Manila threw everyone else into a terrified frenzy. Observers with walkie-talkies immediately flashed the word to Radio Bandido, where it was greeted as the fulfilment of a horrendous prophecy. Opposition newspapers had been full of stories describing the Sikorskys' firepower: seven rocket pods on each side, 20-mm cannon, 2,000-round-per minute machine guns. June Keithley could barely choke out the words as she told the human barricades what was coming their way. This time there was not much point in offering advice. No amount of calamansi juice would be of any use against the fire-spitting Sikorskys.

"We weren't aware of all the fear at the time," says Sotelo. "We were just so glad and relieved to be in the air, and we knew nothing could stop us now. In hindsight, the timing was terrible, because the people were told there'd be an attack at dawn, and that was exactly when we came. It was just a coincidence, but it caused so much terror. Actually, we had not radioed ahead to the camp, either. We lost contact with them late Sunday. Even Ramos must have wondered if it was really us in the air."

Apparently so. The General's men were crashing down three flights of stairs from the "war room" at the time, with shouts of "Look out! This is it!" Ramos could not have been greatly concerned, or he would have had his boys cowering under that orange shrapnel sheet. But the command group certainly appeared apprehensive as they ran out to face the choppers.

Their reaction was nothing, however, compared to the stark terror that gripped the rest of the camp. Soldiers were diving behind anything they could find: walls, trees, ditches, buildings. "Death was very real to me," recalls Lieutenant Graciano Victor. "I sat there and smiled at Colonel Ciron, who was beside me. He smiled back. It was as if we were saying goodbye. When the helicopters came, I stood up. We all stood up. We were not going to fire until we were fired at. But at that moment . . . I was thinking: 'This is it. Thank you, God, for the life I have had.' I was ready for death."

Civilians were even more panic-stricken. Thousands simply grabbed whatever they valued – including, in many cases, their children – and ran for their lives. There was very little warning, since it took the Sikorskys less than five minutes to zoom in from Villamor. Whole campsites were ripped apart in that time as vigilante groups scooped up folding chairs, food sacks, and radios, and headed for safety. The problem, of course, was that no safety existed. Those who tried to flee ran smack into each other, in Keystone Kops confusion. Almost nobody had left the scene when Sotelo's combat gunships came thundering overhead, the rising sun now glinting on their windows.

"It's surprising nobody was seriously hurt," says Eric Tadeo, a university student who crouched between a tree and Crame's outside wall. "I saw lots of people jumping off walls and falling down everywhere. It took a couple of minutes after the announcement on the radio for the real panic to hit. The word just kind of buzzed around outside the camp, and you could almost hear the news coming. I didn't have a radio, but I was startled right away by the sudden noise. Right away, thousands of people started yelling at each other in Tagalog. That alone was almost deafening."

As if to aggravate the tension, the Sikorskys circled once overhead, a manoeuvre most civilians took as a warning run. Actually, the 15th Strike Wing was worried about possible gunfire from below, and was checking out the landing area.

"We couldn't dip our wings or do anything to show we were peaceful," says Colonel Sotelo. "For one thing, helicopters don't have wings. We were coming in for a landing, and that's a serious matter. There is no room for extra movements with a helicopter. We were landing right by the grandstand in front of Ramos's headquarters. It's a small area, and we packed it tight with Sikorskys."

When did the crowd first realize it was witnessing the turning point of the Revolution? Probably it came on the second pass over Crame, when the helicopters dropped their wheels and someone inside Sotelo's chopper waved a white flag. Another airman leaned all the way out of another gunship to flash the L-sign with both hands. "Atin pala!" someone shouted. "It's ours!" There was a three-second sigh of collective relief as tens of thousands caught their breath simultaneously, then utter pandemonium. Civilians leapt into one another's arms and fell laughing onto the ground. Thousands started jumping up and down and trying to climb the walls. Inside the camp, soldiers near Ramos's headquarters were so delirious that half a dozen were nearly crushed under the choppers, all of them trying to rip the doors open and hoist the defectors on their shoulders.

The reaction was markedly less festive at Malacañang Park, where General Fabian Ver took the news over the telephone, and sat wordlessly at his desk. An aide asked if he was going to tell the President. "Piccio will tell the President," muttered Ver. "It's his air force."

Rotor blades were still whirring when Colonel Sotelo leapt from his cockpit to be pummelled on the back and lifted into the air. Microphones were shoved in his face from all directions as the world press surged in to record the moment. But the talkative colonel had remarkably little to say. "This is the best thing I've done in my life," he smiled, but he shook his head and fought back tears when pressed to explain the mass defection. "Not yet," he said. "First, I have to see General Ramos."

Soldiers quickly pushed a path through the crowd and led the defectors upstairs to the command centre. Sotelo stepped through the door, and saluted Ramos crisply, but did not try to hold back a most unmilitary yard-wide grin. "Sir," he announced. "Your air force is here!"

Juan Ponce Enrile's eyes were brimming with tears as he embraced the colonel and each of the pilots in turn. Ramos stepped forward to do the same. "The tide has turned," he announced, and clapped his hands like a school kid who had just scored the game-winning goal. He took Sotelo by the shoulders, and the two veteran soldiers just stood there, beaming at each other.

The whole group went to the windows to admire their proud new selection of killing machines. Even the nuns and the little children were doing the same down by the grandstand, affectionately stroking the metal flanks of the whirlybirds. Then, off in the distance, another lone BO-105 utility chopper limped into view. It circled briefly overhead, then settled unsteadily down on Crame's lawn beside the others. A single young pilot stepped out, threw a clenched fist into the air, and ran past the bemused crowd into the command headquarters. In all the excitement, nobody bothered to find out his identity, and he went unmentioned in press reports. But the strange straggler is one of the smaller, and more delicious, untold stories of the Revolution.

"Ah, yes," said Sotelo, when asked months later about him. "That was the biggest surprise of all. That guy wasn't even part of our group. He was just sitting in Villamor, eating his breakfast, when he heard about our defection on the radio. He looked outside and saw that nobody was guarding that helicopter, so he dropped his breakfast, ran to the airplane, and started it up. He didn't even have a co-pilot. He just hopped up into the air and came over to Crame. We were astonished when we looked out of Ramos's office and saw him get out of the plane.

"But that was part of the euphoria of the moment. Our morale had just gone up a thousand per cent, and the enemy's morale went down a thousand per cent. Suddenly the momentum was with us. The air was ours."

13 *VERITAS AND BANDIDO*

JUNE KEITHLEY WAS AFRAID of guns, death, Loyalist storm troopers, tear gas, Sikorskys, bombs, Marcos . . . and heights. Prime among those fears was that her two teenage sidekicks might be killed, and she would be responsible for their deaths. But the Mercado boys were up on the tile roof of the old building with their UHF radios and June could not bear to climb out, even to tell them about their escape route. She just huddled at the top of the staircase and listened to their radios squawk into the night.

"God, I was scared," says "General" June, who began the revolution as the giggly host of a children's TV show and ended it with a Legion of Honor medal. "I had these two boys with me, and no security at all. If we went on the air, I would be responsible for their lives. There was no way we could do it. I talked to the rebels at Camp Crame and they promised to send me some soldiers. But nobody came. I was just sitting there, shaking, and determined not to risk anyone's life."

It was just before midnight Sunday, and Radio Veritas had been off the air for five hours. Some say its backup transmitter failed; Keithley and others believe the Catholic station had a "failure of will". But it was no time for recriminations. Without Veritas, the human barricade was coming apart. There was no one to dispatch the civilian "troops" to bare spots in the defensive wall, no one to sound the alarm about tank movements, or broadcast the stream of inspirational messages. In the eerie silence, People Power was like a fleet of taxicabs without any central dispatcher. Thousands of the vigilantes wandered around aimlessly, hoping for the best. Thousands of others simply packed up and went home.

Up on the red-tile roof above Keithley, the radios crackled with Messages from Crame. "There is a priest here," someone shouted over the channel, sounding terrified, "who is asking when, in the name of God, will someone go back on the air. There's nobody left here. They're just drifting away and there's going to be an attack, a tank attack from the south. Please, God, someone tell the people to come back!"

And there was Keithley, trembling on top of a radio station. It was a wreck of a station, this DZRJ, with absolutely no credibility and hardly any audience. Worse, its ramshackle studio atop a building in Santa Mesa was virtually in President Marcos's backyard, right beside Malacañang. Still, she supposed it could be cranked up and put on the air . . . for a few minutes anyway, until the Loyalist soldiers found it and blasted it away.

Keithley went into the studio, plunked down in front of a dead microphone, and tried to find help. She called her friend Harry Gasser at Veritas, and suggested they join forces, using the facilities of DZRJ. No dice. "The bigwigs have just had a pow-wow," Gasser told her, "and they decided not to go on with it. You're on your own, girl." Perhaps not. A mildly independent station called DZRH had summoned the courage that afternoon to cover the tanks-vs.-nuns showdown. Maybe *it* would rally the people to Crame. Keithley found 'RH on the dial, and immediately screwed up her face in disgust. "They were playing Johnny Mathis," she recalls. "Johnny *Mathis*. I remember thinking: 'My God, how can anyone play Johnny Mathis at a time like this?' "

It was just after midnight, Sunday. Keithley pulled out the only record she had brought with her, a 1953 campaign song of the late Philippine president Ramon Magsaysay, and put "Mambo Magsaysay" on the turntable. It had become her signature tune, a theme instantly recognizable to the thousands of dial-twisters. Among the eager listeners, of course, would be those manning the military monitors at Malacañang, a few hundred yards away.

"Okay, switch it on," Keithley told the young technician in the booth. He had already done his part, fiddling with the station's crystals to adjust its frequency. DZRJ usually occupied 810 on the AM dial; now it had inched closer to Veritas's familiar 840 spot. In the excitement, few would bother to check exactly where the mambo was coming from. The record played twice, as thirteen-year-old Paulo Mercado and his sixteen-year-old brother Gabe scrambled down from their rooftop perch. Their mother was crazy with worry, phoning everywhere to find them. June wanted them out of there, too. But the kids were great with those walkie-talkies, staying in touch with a wide network of Father James Reuter's observers around the city, and communications was the whole point just now. Besides, it was too late to find replacements.

"Good morning, here we are again," announced Keithley, in that shrill soprano that listeners either loved or hated, but could not mistake. "This is DZRB, Radio Bandido. I can't tell you where we are, but we're around 810 on your dial. Here's a message for all of you out there: we need a lot of people at Camp Crame. I'm going to give you our phone number, so you can call in all the troop movements. But please, no crank calls, no opinions. Just give us the information, tell us where the tanks are. And please, please, go to Crame and protect the soldiers. Everyone's life is at stake now."

Things had been different at Veritas, where there was a semblance of objectivity and an attempt to provide both sides of the story. Bandido was Rebel Radio, pure and simple. Inside Crame, General Fidel Ramos whooped for joy and made a grab for the phone the instant Keithley went on the air. Patch me in, he demanded. Get our message out. Get people down here. Both Ramos and Enrile were on Bandido within the first twenty minutes, issuing impassioned pleas for support. But it was the General who virtually commandeered the new station and made it his main battle weapon.

The cigar-chomping Ramos often projected a Douglas MacArthur image during the revolt: a lead-by-example type who manned the front lines; a hands-on tactical wizard; the consummate cool commander, with fire in his belly and ice water in his veins. In truth, Ramos had delegated tactics, intelligence, logistics, and finance to trusted subordinates at the very outset of the revolt. Instead of trying to oversee the entire campaign, he concentrated on his own particular area of expertise: "psychological operations", or "psy-ops". Ramos is the Philippine military's acknowledged master of deception and illusion. He had taught the subject to various fighting units, including the noted "airborne special forces group" he formed in 1962. And he surrounded himself on Crame's third floor with similar-minded specialists such as General Eduardo Ermita, Colonel Noe Andaya, and Colonel Honesto Isleta. If the war against Marcos was to become a "psy-war", then Ramos was damned sure he would win it.

"I'd seen these things before," he told me months later, "and I knew the information side would be vital – perhaps even more crucial than hardware or weaponry. We were trying to avoid a shooting war. So what did that leave? Obviously a media war. And that was an area where we had a chance. At the beginning, we had the credibility, but Marcos had far more outlets. I'd been in Vietnam. I'd seen the Tet offensive, and saw the war of words there. You simply must have media outlets in this kind of a situation. . . . If possible, they should be under your total control."

With the arrival of Radio Bandido, that ideal became a reality. Ramos immediately opened a hotline to the pirate station and spent much of the time between midnight and dawn on the line to Keithley. He was not always on the air, but concedes that "almost everything she was saying was dictated by us. We didn't give her the exact words to say. We'd just say, 'Well, here's the situation; please make this kind of appeal.' We used the textbook formula for getting our message across. We followed 'Scame', point by point.''

Scame? The General is referring to S-C-A-M-E, a memory aid he drilled into the heads of his psy-ops students. The letters stand for the five basic principles of propaganda warfare: Source, Content, Audience, Medium, and Effect. For anyone who will listen, Ramos is only too glad to offer an on-the-spot lecture on the intricacies of winning hearts and minds.

"First," he smiles, "the Source must be very credible. And who was credible last February? Ramos was. Me. That's why I went on the air so often with the appeals." The General does not draw the obvious corollary: that his rebel partner Juan Ponce Enrile had far *less* credibility with Filipinos, and therefore concerned himself with behind-the-scenes political manoeuvring. "Content? It must be as truthful as possible, even if you are trying to distort things. It must be essentially true. Audience. That's your target group. Are you addressing the people or the Marines? Very often I pretended to be talking to the people, but was really speaking directly to the Loyalist troops. As for Medium, the electronic means was the most effective and persuasive. But we tried everything: face to face, wife to wife, classmate to classmate, buddy to buddy. We even dropped leaflets.

"Finally, there's the Effect. That's the most important, because you must always work backwards. You establish that objective first, decide what you want them to think. Then you work back and devise a way to convince them of it."

The General's psy-ops formula explains much about his own behavior during the revolt – particularly through the tense hours before the Monday dawn attack. His apocalyptic radio appeals throughout that night simply *terrified* the human barrier outside his headquarters. Many observers wondered at the time if he did not risk scaring thousands of them away. But the talk of an ''overwhelming force arrayed against us'' was not aimed at them. Ramos was speaking directly to Colonel Balbas and his Marines, an appeal he supplemented with personal notes delivered to the colonel by intermediaries.

"Sure, it was a ploy," he smiled later. "But remember what I said about the Content. It must be basically sincere. Those were honest-to-goodness messages. Some of them were slightly slanted, you might say, for the purpose of generating a certain reaction."

To Filipinos, the combination of June Keithley and Radio Veritas is like green mangoes and *bagoong* shrimp sauce. Inseparable, synonymous, two halves of a whole. Perfectly rational people still insist they listened to Keithley on Veritas all through the revolution's first night on Saturday, and tell rapturous stories of the Catholic station's courage. When Keithley received the Legion of Honor and Veritas the cherished Magsaysay Award, the nation nodded in wholehearted agreement. The twin media heroes had reaped their just reward.

Actually, this scenario is a complete fiction, a form of national amnesia. Keithley and Veritas are oil and water, fire and ice, the Karpov and Kasparov of Philippine radio. Even months after the revolution, any mention of the station sets Keithley's teeth on edge and she brandishes the "welcome" note handed her by a Veritas manager during the first hours of the revolt: "Sorry, June, but we have decided that only priests and Veritas staffers can go on."

"The truth is that Veritas just wouldn't allow me on the air," she says angrily. "I went out there as soon as I heard about the revolt, and got on for a few minutes. I told listeners there were only thirty people guarding the White Plains gate, and we needed more. Then there was a knock on the studio glass and they handed me this note. They asked me to leave. I had about three minutes of air time, and those were the last words I ever spoke on Veritas. . . . There is no doubt in my mind that [Veritas] simply chickened out. The upper echelon, I mean. The announcers and reporters wanted to go all the way, but the higher-ups wanted to protect the station. It was obvious to me . . . they thought Enrile and Ramos were going to lose."

Such bitterness is more than just personal animosity. Indeed, the Veritas-Keithley wrangle touches all the key elements of the Philippine media: anguish, courage, cowardice, corruption, the Catholic Church, and an almost supernatural fear of Ferdinand Marcos.

Radio Veritas cannot fairly be cast as the villain of the piece. By local standards, the station mounted a heroic defiance of Marcos after the August 21, 1983, assassination of Benigno Aquino. Malacañang had its boot on the media's neck back then. The few newspapers that dared to oppose the dictatorship were padlocked, and offending journalists were invited to "meet" the military. Crony newspapers were staffed with obsequious apologists, some of whom drew twenty times the normal salary to kiss, in daily print, the feet of Ferdinand and Imelda. Aquino's brutal murder horrified the world, yet caused barely a ripple in the Manila press. Instead of outrage, local papers were filled with the official version of events: that a communist gunman had somehow slain Aquino all by himself.

It was the Big Lie, employed by a regime with the power to enforce it.

But Veritas refused to play along. Almost overnight, the tiny religious channel with a negligible audience was reborn as the "Station of Truth and Love". It cancelled its August 21 programs and simply stayed with the Aquino story long past sign-off time. Program manager Orly Punzalan got a call from the government's Office of Media Affairs (OMA) ordering him to stop the coverage. When he refused, he was told to at least "tone it down".

"Tone it down?" he replied. "Somebody's dead. We don't know who killed him. How can we possibly tone it down?"

The station clung tenaciously to the story, twelve to fourteen hours a day, while its chairman lobbied the authorities to permit the coverage. Ordinarily the man would have found himself in jail and his facility sold to a more congenial owner. But the chairman of Veritas is a certain Jaime Cardinal Sin, and its banker is the Roman Catholic Church. The Media Affairs office fumed in frustration as the Church station provided saturation coverage of the extraordinary Aquino funeral. Two million marched in tears and song, while the Philippine media averted their gaze. All except Radio Veritas, whose announcer cried along with his countrymen.

Much had changed by November 1985 when President Marcos told David Brinkley he was calling a snap election. Manila's press had grown bolder since the Aquino killing, with several opposition papers now on the streets, and new ones in the works. A rumored government crackdown was kept at bay by American demands for reform. Anyway, a show of force would be unseemly on the eve of "free and fair" elections.

But there was little shift among the electronic media. The government's Maharlika TV network was a Marcos house organ, its camera crews trailing the First Couple like photographers at a wedding. Day and night, Maharlika's powerful Channel 4 spent the campaign showing the President's weary face repeating the same tired harangue about Communists and foreign meddlers – while its announcers swooned over the "brilliance" of his oratory. The standard Marcos election speech included a twenty-minute ramble about Indonesia's bloody 1965 uprising, with dire predictions of a local repeat under Mrs. Aquino. Channel 4 played the tirade so often that Filipinos knew it by heart, and started mocking their leader by repeating it in unison with him.

Symbolic of the station were a pair of cheerleading hosts named Rita Gaddi-Baltazar and Ronnie Nathanielsz, whose unctuous on-air manner and deference to all things Marcosian made them (after the Marcoses and General Ver) the fourth- and fifth-most-hated people in the country. Filipinos called them "the *tutas*", the Tagalog word for lap-dogs; foreigners gaped in amazement at the most slavish, one-sided political commentary any of us had witnessed. "I've only been here two days," said the Irish member of one international election observer team, "and even *I* want to kill them. How do they stay alive here?" (It wasn't easy: Nathanielsz travelled with two red Fiera vans full of security men, and during the heated post-election period, there were even motorcycle cops to clear the way for his "convoy".)

The situation was not notably different at the other four TV stations, all owned by cronies such as Marcos's fraternity brother Roberto Benedicto. An occasional announcer would be so bold as to air tape of the massive Aquino rallies; but such people quickly found themselves "on vacation" until after the election. "It is the most helpless feeling in the world," says Lucy Orara, who worked for the crony Channel 2. "I was interviewing Butz Aquino, and they just cut us off the air. The Philippines was the world's best news story, and Filipinos were the only ones who couldn't cover it. After a while, we realized there was no sense interviewing anyone from the opposition, because it would never be broadcast." Orara found a simple solution. She quit, and went to Radio Veritas.

But if Veritas seemed a courageous beacon of truth, that was largely because of the shadow cast by its timid Manila competitors. Government control was more lax in the provinces, where a chain of seventeen Catholic radio stations and one TV outlet often lambasted Marcos in no uncertain terms. They were linked together by the Philippine Federation of Catholic Broadcasters – a group, says its executive secretary, James Reuter, to which Radio Veritas was actually afraid to belong.

"They were scared," says Father Reuter, an American Jesuit who has lived in the Philippines for forty-eight years. Reuter was arrested in 1976 on seventy-three charges of sedition, and has long been deeply involved in the country's broadcasting, arts, and politics. He was a ferocious anti-Marcos campaigner, and minces no words in assessing the Catholic flagship station. "Veritas thought the Federation was too radical," he snorts, "and that we were going to get into trouble with Marcos. They had that new transmitter at Malolos [about 20 miles outside Manila] to protect, so they couldn't risk making the government too angry at them."

Enter June Keithley. A *mestiza* of mixed American and Philippine heritage, she is a sometime actress, singer, comedienne, and children's TV host who spent the month before the elections in a numbing fit of upper-class angst. She was wracked by anxiety and guilt, and found herself constantly in tears about the Aquino-Marcos showdown. "No matter what I tried to do, I ended up crying," she says. "I went to a psychiatrist and she gave it to me straight: 'Look, there are thousands of Filipinos all over the country going through the same thing. They have to make a choice. They have to put themselves on the line. That's what you're afraid of.' My husband and I had already decided to leave the country if Marcos won. For ourselves, for our son, we couldn't go on like this. How can you teach your child values when all he sees is cheating and corruption?"

Keithley happened to be a protégé of Father Reuter, who had directed her in college theatre, so she was aware of his planned presidential vote count. She volunteered to spend election day manning a computer terminal. But the Jesuit had other things in mind. His broadcasting Federation had enormous resources, and had lined up an impressive network of men and machinery to cover the polls. "Every one of our stations had a base transceiver and four mobile units," he explains. "And here in Manila I had eleven mobile units and three hand-held units, because we knew this was a deadly area. The elections were so important, and everyone knew they'd be crooked as could be. The fraud would be colossal. So we wanted to get a count as quick as possible and foil his [Marcos's] plans. We were linked up everywhere. We had thirty of my boys here in Manila alone, manning the units, watching out for foul play."

What Reuter did *not* have in Manila was a radio station. For that he needed Radio Veritas, but he was afraid it would censor his most sensational revelations of cheating. Eventually he cut a deal with the station's executive vice-president, Bishop Ted Buhain: the Federation would feed its news to Veritas – but only if it was allowed to put its own reader on the air. And guess who was nominated?

"I had June, and it seemed a shame to use her for office work," smiles Father Reuter. "Anyway, I knew she would tell the stuff straight and not back away from it. I gave her the two boys [Gabe and Paulo Mercado] to link up with us, and turned them all loose on Veritas."

It seemed simple enough, before election day. Both the government's Comelec and the independent NAMFREL had promised a quick count. It would take only a few hours, overnight at most, until the nation knew its president. Few realized that the February 7 vote would dissolve into a tragic fiasco, a day of killings and beatings followed by a night of delay, deception, and intrigue. In retrospect, it is apparent that both NAMFREL and Comelec quickly realized Cory Aquino was winning. But they had diametrically opposite reactions. While the citizens' group raced to get the word out, the government ballot-counters did a superb job of fouling the machinery in red tape. The two groups had agreed on an intricate validation procedure, but Comelec supervisors simply melted into the dusk and left the count in limbo. When NAMFREL publicized its results without the seal of approval, the government dismissed them as "spurious" and threatened to shut down the citizens' arm.

Operation Quick Count became operation slowdown, as Comelec stalled for time and cast about for a new plan. Its strategy was not hard to divine. Posted returns came out in dribbles, completely at odds with NAMFREL's count. Top Comelec officials, meanwhile, seemed to spend fourteen hours a day on Channel 4 – damning and threatening their NAMFREL counterparts. But the plot was blown sky high by the thirty-one computer tabulators who yanked the floppy disks from their machines and stormed out of the government's vote-count centre, charging that "there is something terribly wrong here . . . they're doctoring the results, and we won't be a part of it."

In the midst of this chaos, apple-cheeked June Keithley somehow became a star. No one, least of all Keithley herself, quite knows why. She had been in the media for years, and was among the last people anyone would turn to for hard news: she was a glib lightweight, a socialite who chattered about fortune-tellers and hairdressers on the inane "June and Johnny Show". Worse, her voice had a fingernails-on-the-blackboard quality, a reedy squeal that veered on occasion into dog-whistle range. Her voice seemed forever on the verge of hysteria, and was hardly the ideal tone for a crisis. Yet, at 6 p.m. Friday, when the polls closed and Veritas began its coverage, she simply took command of the airwaves. By morning, June was incarnated as *the* voice of Veritas, the Voice of Truth and Love. Within two days, opposition papers were calling her the Angel of the Airwaves.

"I can't explain it," she shrugs. "I was aware that some people didn't like my voice, so I tried hard to keep calm this time and tone things down. Strangely, people said they found me very calming all through the election and the revolution. Maybe I stood out from the reporters because I'm female. Or maybe it was because I had most of the hard news to read.

"Right at 6 o'clock we had solid information. The first thing I read was a report on beatings and violence. It was hard-hitting stuff. It galvanized people. The listeners didn't expect it, and I don't think Veritas did, either. I think the events simply overtook Veritas. It all just happened. The first few hours, whenever news of terrorism would come on, they just passed it over to me. That became my role. It started with Father Reuter's information, all the things his boys could find, and then it just grew from there. Suddenly, everyone was listening to Veritas. And I was up front.''

Whether by design or accident, Radio Veritas found itself thrust into a media war. Channel 4, other crony stations, and the main daily newspapers all trumpeted Comelec's "Marcos-in-the-lead" results and began a vicious hatchet job on NAMFREL. The citizens' watchdog had just one powerful defender: Cardinal Sin, chairman of Radio Veritas.

It was radio-vs.-television, hammer and tongs. And television spoke with one voice. There were no low-budget opposition stations to oppose it, no Catholic TV channels to mediate, just the sneers of Baltazar and Nathanielsz – reinforced by a roster of high-profile *tutas*. Things reached a climax just before Sunday night's computer walkout when NAMFREL executives appeared on Channel 4 to defend themselves. The result was a savage inquisition, as painful to witness as a physical beating. The Philippine ambassador to Britain, a Marcos loyalist named J. V. Cruz, arrived abusively drunk and proceeded to pour invective all over the citizens' group. When they dared to reply, Nathanielsz cut them off contemptuously.

(Enraged Filipinos picketed the station with "Kill Nathanielsz!" posters the next day, and at least one group took the advice literally. The SMK urban guerrillas staked out a nearby TV station with plans to "blow his fucking head off", but were dissuaded by the massive security escort in those red Fieras.)

Television's wild attacks on NAMFREL, however, only heightened the credibility of radio. Even in the wee hours of election night, it was impossible to walk through downtown Manila without hearing Radio Veritas. Fruit vendors, jeepney drivers, students, and shopgirls all huddled around beat-up yellow Toyota taxis with their windows rolled down and their radios blaring. Money-changers and prostitutes sat transfixed along the Mabini bar strip as Veritas reporters checked in from NAMFREL headquarters with the "real" election count, and Keithley told tales of ballot-box snatching and thuggery all over the country. A neutral listener might have rated Veritas nearly as biased towards Cory as Channel 4 was pro-Marcos. But neutral Filipinos did not exist. And now, given a choice between J. V. Cruz on TV and Cardinal Sin on radio, there was little doubt whom the majority believed.

The election tug-of-war dragged on for days as President Marcos shifted the vote count to his rubber-stamp National Assembly and Cory Aquino held massive "victory" rallies. It became a media struggle, with each side wielding different kinds of power. Aquino, solidly backed by the international press, appeared the clear winner in American living rooms. But Marcos had a stranglehold on the domestic media, and squeezed with all his might. He realized that tensions would lessen once the election became a *fait accompli*, so the plan was to ram his proclamation through parliament and present a business-as-usual face. Channel 4's job was to lend the Assembly canvass a veneer of legitimacy, and to ridicule the opposition's "childish" protests.

Mrs. Aquino desperately needed to increase the pressure at home, to focus the nation's outrage. She would draw two million people to a raucous Februry 16 rally at Rizal Park, and unveil a civil-disobedience package – including boycotts of crony banks, businesses, and media – designed to bring the government to its knees. But she needed a booming voice to send that message across the country. She needed the Voice of Truth and Love.

To this day, most Filipinos believe that she was given that voice, that Radio Veritas broadcast her rallies and became the medium for a series of nightly "fireside chats". The true story, much less flattering to the Catholic station, is one of passionate in-fighting, shouting matches, and outright lies.

Veritas did broadcast Mrs. Aquino's early rallies and two of the promised "Talk-to-Cory" shows. But enormous pressure was applied by the Office of Media Affairs, and the station's staffers could feel the management begin to bend. Cory Aquino began her chats on a Monday night. By Wednesday, June Keithley was on the air telling listeners that "you'll no longer have the voice of Cory to listen to." That touched off a behind-the-scenes screaming match, the first of many. Veritas had planned to drop Cory quietly; now the station was shamed into restoring the broadcasts, but with the stipulation that Veritas could edit her message. Tapes were supposed to be at the station by 5 p.m., for later airing. But Cory's campaign managers and confederates inside Veritas intentionally held them back until broadcast time. Veritas executives fumed, and the Aquino campaign went looking for another radio station.

The hidden battle came to a head at Aquino's largest rally in Rizal Park, where she announced the long-awaited boycott. The mobile units of Radio Veritas were quietly withdrawn from the park, amid complaints of "technical problems". An enraged June Keithley went on the air and blew the whistle again.

"All hell broke loose that time," she recalls. "They wanted us to *lie* about it, tell people there was a technical problem. Imagine, a Catholic station and the priests are telling us to *lie*. I got into a huge shouting match with Bishop Buhain. He said: 'I don't care about politics. My only concern is to keep Radio Veritas on the air. We have to protect this station.' And I said: 'Look, Father, we just can't desert them now. We can't give up.' I was in tears and white in the face. That was it for me. Everybody remembers me being on Veritas after that, but I wasn't. Just those few minutes on the night of the revolution, before they kicked me out." Veritas still maintains its decision was not political, but its own staff debunks that notion. "Of course we were capable of covering it," says one insider. "We didn't, because Bishop Buhain said, 'No!' "

The public knew nothing about the wrangling. To them, Radio Veritas was still the Voice of Truth and, more important now, the Voice of Cory. Before the dissension bubbled into the open, two men named Enrile and Ramos made it irrelevant.

There are still those, including Enrile, who claim that the revolt was a spur-of-the-moment move, a purely defensive reaction to President Marcos's roundup orders. But no one who listened closely to Radio Veritas can be among them. As early as Thursday afternoon, forty-eight hours before the February 22 breakaway, Veritas began broadcasting veiled hints that something was afoot: "Any time now we will have an important announcement from the military establishment." Nothing happened that day, and an embarrassed announcer later explained that it had been postponed. The following day there was another enigmatic bulletin: "You remember the very important report we promised you yesterday? Well, it will not push through today. Perhaps tomorrow." A similar message was aired on Saturday morning, just a few hours before the "surprised" minister took refuge at Camp Aguinaldo.

"Our correspondents were tipped off days in advance," explains Veritas anchorman Franky Batacan, Jr. "Actually, they were almost held hostage over at Aguinaldo by Colonel [Eduardo] Ermita, the PR man there. He was sort of holding them at bay, keeping them on standby, because he knew something would happen and he'd need media coverage right away. He was keeping them informed, but not really spilling the beans. He just gave us enough to keep us there.

"The [military] officials are now fudging that Thursday and Friday business. But they had the information, all right. Even we had an inkling. We suspected it was going to be a coup d'état. By Saturday, we were paranoid already. There we were, out on a limb, sort of flim-flamming it on the air. And now it looked like it might not push through. Finally, they set the press conference for 6 p.m.

"Enrile won't spell it out now, because he doesn't want it to seem premeditated. But if *we* knew it, he certainly must have."

Only a few of the Filipino opposition media – Veritas and the newspapers *Malaya*, *Philippine Daily Inquirer*, and *We Forum* – were waiting at Colonel Ermita's knee. After the dramatic Saturday press conference, all of the local newsmen knew two things. First, this was a great story. Second, they might be rounded up and jailed that night for reporting it.

The tension was greatest at Radio Veritas, whose suburban Fairview studio was at the revolution's very core. The Catholic station was no longer a medium; it had become a key player in the political drama, and would be a major piece on the military chessboard. Staffers could only wince when they looked towards the front gate and found a pair of poorly armed private security guards. There was nothing at all to stop the inevitable Loyalist attack. As it turned out, General Ver was thinking the same thing. Shortly after 8 p.m., he barked a crisp telephone command to General Fidel Singson: "Take a platoon to Radio Veritas, and destroy it!"

Singson was in charge of an armed forces intelligence unit housed behind the Defense Ministry in Aguinaldo. By coincidence, he had just contacted the Enrile camp, testing the waters before deciding which side to support. Keeping his options open, he dispatched a team to check out the Veritas compound. "No problem," a captain radioed back. "We can take it any time you order." General Singson merely nodded and ordered the troops home. He had decided to join the rebellion.

Veritas was a madhouse. The antiquated station is a sprawling old barracks on the very outskirts of Manila, with long, dank corridors, cubbyhole studios tucked in unlikely spots, and just four telephone lines. Two had been assigned as direct lines to Camp Aguinaldo and Cardinal Sin. Everyone assumed that the Cardinal would comment on the Enrile-Ramos breakaway, but initially he refused even to answer their calls; Jaime Sin was busy elsewhere, "imitating Moses" and communing with the contemplative nuns. Meanwhile, thousands of Filipinos flooded the other two lines, with a chorus of remarkably similar messages: "Don't trust Enrile. This must be some kind of Marcos ploy. Pray to God that these guys are really on the level."

At 10 p.m., production assistant Lucy Orara glanced into the Veritas lobby and nearly fainted. The place was full of soldiers in military fatigues. Armalites clanking as they hoisted them about. She backed into an office, but ran into two fully armed men. "Who are you?" she demanded. They replied that "the colonel" had sent them. Okay, thought Orara, this is it. They're from Marcos. "I was so scared I could hardly talk. But I asked them what colonel they meant. 'Santiago,' they said. That's when I began to breathe again. Santiago was on our side.''

Mariano Santiago was not actually a colonel, having quit the military in disgust some months earlier to become a transportation commissioner. But this was the Philippines, where no colonel ever hands in his guns, his rank – or, apparently, his camouflage fatigues. Santiago rounded up about twenty military buddies within an hour of the press conference and headed for Fairview bristling with rifles, pistols, and grenades. Santiago's little army needed no one's approval to join the revolution, and met no resistance from the frightened guards at the Veritas gate.

The rebels back in Aguinaldo also realized Veritas might be their best hope of survival. Butz Aquino had already been on the air with his plea for ''People Power'', and the Cardinal was preparing to second that motion. But the tiny breakaway group was still helpless to defend their camp, much less secure the media outlets. They sent a small team to reconnoiter the Veritas compound, discovered Santiago's men, and breathed easier. If Ver wanted to occupy the station now, he'd have to fight his way in.

But Fabian Ver had an ace up his sleeve. For once in the four-day revolt – and *only* once – he would outsmart the opposition with a deft tactical manoeuvre. The Veritas studios were in Fairview, but its gleaming new $5-million transmitter was twenty miles away in Malolos. This time, Ver did not give the job to his bungling and reluctant military units. He turned instead to the private army of Eduardo Cojuangco, billionaire warlord and beer baron who had become the No. 1 Marcos crony. Ostensibly a businessman, Cojuangco had secured his holdings with the help of an Israeli-equipped fighting force estimated at three thousand men. What is more, he had just added an extra contingent of strong-arm specialists during the recent election, and his storehouse of gleaming black Galils was augmented by five hundred high-powered M-16s from Ver's stockpile.

No crisis of conscience here. No hesitation or self-doubt. Cojuangco's hitmen were well-trained mercenaries, not poorly paid soldiers from the boondocks, and they trashed the Malolos outpost with ruthless efficiency. Sixteen of them tied yellow bandannas around their heads and pulled on yellow T-shirts, pretending to be Cory supporters come to guard the transmitter. It was the old Trojan-horse trick, and the Veritas security guards fell for it completely. Delighted at the arrival of reinforcements, they threw open the gates and were immediately chopped down by clubs and gun butts. The invaders knew exactly what they had come to destroy, and they did a neat job. For an agonizing ten minutes they bashed in all the crucial control panels, smashed all the machinery they could, and roughed up the operators . . . as Veritas staffers back in Manila listened in helplessly.

"It was terrible," says Lucy Orara. "A technician called on the radio to tell us what was going on, and we could hear the gunshots in the background. The technicians and the guards were hit with fists and clubs, and you could hear all the glass smashing. They were calling for help, but what could we do? The thugs even stole their watches, jewelry, and money after they finished destroying the place."

The 5 a.m. attack silenced Veritas's national and international voice. But a decrepit 10-kw backup transmitter at Fairview could still provide a weak signal in Manila itself. Cardinal Sin's eloquent pleas became increasingly wavy and unclear as they were replayed over and over during the early morning. By noon Sunday, it was difficult to understand the warnings of tanks and Marines on their way to the EDSA-Ortigas showdown. Then, as the nuns stared down the Marines, Veritas executives came face to face with their own test of courage. "We got a note, a warning, that if we didn't stop broadcasting by 8 p.m., they would start shooting at this building," says program manager Punzalan. "I think it was the same people who blew up the Malolos transmitter. There was no doubt they meant business."

By its own account, the station never had to meet that challenge. Veritas executives say their wonky backup transmitter grew progressively weaker during the day, and finally conked out an hour before the terrorists' deadline. But Father Reuter and June Keithley raise skeptical eyebrows at that claim. "There's a report that Veritas's standby transmitter didn't fail. They just went off the air because they were afraid," says the Jesuit. "All we know for sure is that they went off when they were told to."

"I don't know about the transmitter," shrugs Keithley, "but I do know that Veritas could have continued, and chose not to. When I reached DZRJ, they were already patched into it. They used its facilities for a while, and guess what they were playing when I got there: Peter, Paul and Mary. I think the song was 'Blowing in the Wind'. What does that tell you about their commitment?"

Father James Reuter was astonished, and very angry, when he got Keithley's call on Sunday morning. "What do you mean, you left Veritas? This is no time for petty squabbles. There's a revolution going on. Get back in there!"

"Look, Father, I've got news for you," replied Keithley. "They don't want us. We're not welcome there."

There was a long pause on the other end as the blunt-spoken priest did his imitation of a human typhoon. Finally, his temper under control, he growled at Keithley: "Okay, just stay where you are. I'll get you another station."

Reuter first checked with Bishop Buhain at Veritas, and found the situation just as he'd been told. "Buhain was afraid to have her there," he says now, struggling still to maintain his Christian charity. "They were timid. It's hard to condemn people for that. Their transmitters were smashed and I guess they were afraid they were all going to get killed. They'd had enough."

Though an American by birth, seventy-year-old James Reuter is something of a Philippine institution, a linchpin of the so-called "Jesuit mafia", with strong ties to both anti-government radicals and the upper layers of the country's establishment. He had administered the marriage vows of many powerful people, including Johnny and Cristina Ponce Enrile three decades before. Now he called his old friend at Aguinaldo and outlined the situation. The minister, surprised and upset to discover that Veritas might go under, almost shouted his reply: "Find us another station, Father. We've *got* to have a radio station."

The priest spent Sunday calling in every I.O.U. he had collected over a half-century career. By early evening there were two strong possibilities. The first was DZRH, the mildly independent station that had dared to broadcast some of Cory Aquino's speeches and had provided sympathetic coverage of the revolution. Reuter believed he had obtained a commitment to put Keithley on the air. When she arrived with the two Mercado boys just before 9 p.m., however, the tropical night air had developed a distinct chill.

"It was obvious that something was wrong from the moment we walked in," recalls Keithley. "This guy [news director Rey Langit] had his feet up on a desk, and you could see from his face that we weren't welcome. I said: 'I thought you were called. I thought we had an agreement.' But he told me he had his own reporters, his own mobile units. He asked me to leave my phone number, the old don't-call-us-we'll-call-you routine."

Langit's feet were right beside his phone. Keithley snatched it up and called Father Reuter. "There's been a mistake," she told him, freezing the news director with a glare. "This guy doesn't want us here." The

Jesuit sighed and offered a backup option: the small Protestant station DZFE in Bulacan, Malolos. "Wait a minute," said Keithley. "Malolos? Isn't that where they blew up the transmitter? No way."

That left only DZRJ. Reuter considered this scruffy little station a last resort, since it had virtually no audience and was only a few hundred yards from Marcos headquarters. Once popular, it had been taken over by the military and become a virtual government mouthpiece. Ironically, the military man in charge of the yappy propaganda outlet was a certain minister named Juan Ponce Enrile.

Keithley agreed to put 'RJ on the air, then had a revealing exchange of views with Langit. She and the boys were preparing to leave when the DZRH executive shook her hand and apologized. "Sorry," he said. "These are difficult times. It's very scary right now."

"I was so shocked," says Keithley, "because that was when I first realized he thought Marcos was going to win. It seemed incredible to me. I got angry and said: 'Look, don't you realize this guy is going to go? He's right on the edge. We can push him out. What are you scared of?' He just looked at me and asked: 'Do you really think so?' Marcos still had people buffaloed. They couldn't imagine him losing."

By 10 p.m., Veritas had been in hibernation for three hours. It was now hooked up to DZRJ, but was playing folk music while executives huddled in Bishop Buhain's office. Keithley arrived at the Jacinto Building, took one look around, and fought off a shudder. The place was twelve storeys high, but the elevator stopped at the eighth floor. From there, a winding cement stairway led to the top-floor radio studio and the roof. The only possible escape route involved leaping from the tiled rooftop across a yawning four-foot gap to the next building. The Mercado kids might make it; Keithley couldn't even bear to go up and look.

There was a teenage secretary, a young disk jockey, and a couple of technicians at DZRJ. They were drinking coffee, listening to the piped-in strains of Peter, Paul, and Mary, and waiting for developments. Keithley checked with Reuter again, and he suggested she alternate air time with Veritas. That idea was quickly quashed when her friend Harry Gasser called in from Fairview. "They've just decided," he told her. "They're not going to continue with 'RJ. You're on your own, girl. By the way, do you realize where you are? You've got your back to the fortress."

"Huh?"

"Malacañang. It's right behind you."

"Oh, Jesus," was all Keithley could say. Father Reuter had carefully avoided telling her that.

For a priest, in fact, Reuter was remarkably single-minded and cold-blooded that night – a posture he takes no pains to hide. Within a few minutes late Sunday, he had two nearly hysterical women on the phone. June Keithley, in tears, called from her rickety radio perch and refused to go on the air without security. And Monina Mercado, mother of the Mercado boys, screamed at him on the other line: "My boys are in danger of death. Please give them back to me!" Reuter sat in his ramshackle headquarters overlooking the Pasig River and calmly gave each woman the same message: This is war, lady. Straighten up and get on with it.

"I said, 'Oh, for God's sake, Monina, your boys don't get a chance to be heroes every day. Give them their chance.' I mean, my God, you have to die *some time*. What they were doing was very important and I just felt she shouldn't make those kinds of decisions for them. They're good boys. They knew they were in danger, but they loved it. Anyway, we had to have them. If June was on the air, who would handle the radios?"

As for Keithley, the Jesuit dismisses her refusal as "just a case of fear. I didn't have much sympathy, I'm afraid. She was scared, but the soldiers *needed* her. I told her I'd get her some protection, that I'd get her some nuns. We called the convents and they were wonderful. The nuns went over and just filled that spiral stairway all night. We couldn't plead for help over the radio because the Loyalists were looking for June, so we turned to the nuns."

They made an extraordinary sight, packed into the clammy stair-case in their white habits, fingering rosaries, reciting Mysteries, Psalms, and other prayers, sending timid emissaries above to find out what was going on, and eating the baskets of food they had lugged in from the convent. Monina Mercado finally persuaded Father Reuter to reveal her boys' whereabouts, and rushed to the Jacinto Building in a taxi. When she burst out of the elevator on the eighth floor, choked with anxiety and dripping sweat, she could hardly believe her eyes. "There were wall-to-wall nuns," she reported later. "It was like being dropped in the middle of a convent."

When Radio Bandido finally went on the air at 12:05 a.m., it was as if someone had suddenly thrown the light switch attached to People Power. Observers and activists were scattered all over the city with good, solid information to relay. But they had been seething in frustration for hours, watching the human barricades crumble and Marcos troops begin to move freely. Keithley's "Mambo Magsaysay" theme song was just fading from the airwaves when the first woman called in on her walkie-talkie. She was atop the Meralco Building at the EDSA-Ortigas intersection, and had seen an armored column make a right-hand turn. Keithley flashed the word on the air. "Let's go. Let's get some people out there to stop them. And please, all of you, pray to God for deliverance. Pray to God we all get out of this alive."

Loyalist troops never did find Bandido. Many Filipinos believe this was yet another instance of divine intervention: God just would not let them find *His* radio station. A more secular explanation lies in something called "triangulation": the three-cornered method of tracking down radio waves. Military men say DZRJ was too close to Malacañang for General Ver's henchmen to find it. Still, it required only a little logic (Ver knew, after all, that Enrile controlled the station) and some diligence to locate the outlaw station. So the Loyalist hunt was probably bungled by the over-centralized Marcos command post. General Ramos would have set a good man to the task, and moved on to another problem. General Ver and his officers dithered and dickered, trying to handle every detail themselves, and wound up running a Keystone Kops offensive. While Bandido was signing on the air, Colonel Braulio Balbas and his thousand Marines had already been twiddling their thumbs on a roadside for three hours. They sat there listening to the opposition station for nearly three more hours, until Ver's gang could organize transport for his most loyal and powerful strike force.

Aside from her Mambo record and two kids gathering information on a radio, Keithley was singularly ill-equipped for her task as "General" of the civilian forces. She had a handbook on civil disobedience, and spent the slower moments preaching to the masses on the efficacy of calamansi and wet towels against tear gas. And she kept rerunning the taped psy-war messages from General Ramos. But, by the dawn attack, she was numb with fear and began reciting a stream-of-consciousness prayer that boomed at the Marines from thousands of radios:

"Lord, you know that there are many people out there. You know what we are going through right now. There are many of us and we are trying to do our duty. We ask you please to guide us, Lord. You teach us to always turn the other cheek. We ask you now to show us in many concrete ways that truly nothing good can come from evil. Show us, Lord, that only good will work in this world. Please take care of all who are out there. . . . There are children out there, young girls and boys, parents, brothers and sisters, husbands and wives. Lord, I am not good at this, but I just ask you please, in Jesus' name, please save our people."

She cannot recall what made her tell everyone to turn on their lights and go out into the streets with their radios. "It was just instinct, a gut reaction," she says. "We put the military hymn on the turntable, then the national anthem. We could hear the tear-gas attack on the UHF radio . . . all the people begging and crying, and the Marines cocking their rifles. That was just deafening, the sound of all those rifles."

The sun came up at 6:08 that morning. Keithley remembers it exactly, because she and the Mercado boys and all the nuns in the stairwell were praying for it to rise. The terror inside Bandido's studio reached a peak, then suddenly doubled and quadrupled. The walkie-talkies crackled with a terrible message from Villamor Air Base: "Oh, Christ, there they are! The Sikorskys are coming!" Keithley could barely find breath to relay the news to the hordes around Crame. "We *knew* they were going to attack," she recalled months later, her eyes damp with tears even then. Those crammed in the DZRJ studio lived the ultimate radio nightmare, a drama they could hear but not see; only a brick wall was visible outside their window as the gunships and the helpless thousands below flooded their imagination. Observers with hand-held radios filed frantic reports, their voices jagged and jumbled as they all called at once on the same frequency. "Rockets! They've got rockets. . . ." "There's two more white ones. . . ." And the lady atop the Meralco Building, her voice almost drowned by the thunder of their engines: "They're here! They're right here!"

But wait a minute. What's that? Isn't that the Laban sign? "They're landing! They're landing! They're on *our* side!"

The celebration inside Radio Bandido was a mini-version of the pandemonium at Crame. A few moments passed before someone thought to tell the nuns, touching off a most un-Sisterly chorus of whoops, cheers, and howls down the staircase. Nobody used the phrase "turning point", but an unconscious dam had burst. Months later, Keithley and other key players in the revolt would remember that moment as "the first time I really knew we would win. The relief was . . . just beyond description."

In all that euphoria, however, the bandit station made a terrible blunder. Keithley had blurted out the DZRJ phone number and invited calls. The listeners who now responded were either badly informed or part of a brilliant Marcos psy-war gambit. Either way, they came perilously close to derailing the revolution.

"I've just had a call from my sister in San Francisco," one breathless lady from Makati informed the station. "Marcos is gone! They just saw him step off the plane in Guam." Within seconds, another call, then another. Seven in all, with an identical story: The dictator and his immediate family had flown the coop, leaving General Ver behind. Marcos was in Guam, probably on his way to California or Hawaii. All the informants were society matrons, who claimed they had been called by relatives in the States. The U.S. Cable News Network (CNN) was reporting that Marcos had left, they said. There was even a phone call from a man claiming to be a lieutenant in the Presidential Security Command. "It's true," he said. "I saw Marcos and [son] Bongbong get on a helicopter . . . they're gone."

The most important call came from Crame. "Yes, June," said General Ramos, and she could actually hear him smile over the phone, "we've seen the same reports. It's confirmed."

Giddy with joy and exhaustion, Keithley hugged nuns and technicians, kissed everyone she could find, and searched the DZRJ library for an appropriate goodbye to Marcos. She spotted the old 1960s rock song "He's Not There", and slapped it on the turntable. Everyone thought it was a hell of a joke.

Including Marcos himself. The song rang loud and clear in the nearby Malacañang office where the amused President and First Lady listened to the announcement of their departure. Marcos was on the phone a minute later, chuckling at the news with army commander General Josephus Ramas, making sure that all was well.

"No problem, sir," said Ramas. "The guns are in place. We are just awaiting your order to destroy Crame."

14 *"FIRE ON TARGET!"*

"I can't put out of my mind the fact that – and nor should any of us – his leaving the islands was preceded by his denial of permission to the military . . . to take action. The one thing [Marcos] did not want was bloodshed or civil strife. And so he left rather than permit that." – United States president Ronald Reagan, July 8, 1986

"Balbas! Fire at objective and report compliance! You'd better fire your cannons, because the President is on the other line, waiting for confirmation." – Philippine army commander General Josephus Ramas, Feb. 24, 1986

COLONEL BRAULIO BALBAS and his men were startled by the sudden commotion at Crame. They had driven their LVTs and their V-150s and tons of lethal hardware right through the captured gate and up onto the golf course at Camp Aguinaldo just after dawn. Then they had promptly and efficiently begun setting up the artillery. It was a routine operation, a walk in the park. Nobody opposed them, nobody even seemed to know that they were there. If Balbas had bothered to bring his clubs, he could have strolled over to the fifth tee and knocked a few balls past the long, muddy ruts his armor had carved into the fairway.

But now, all hell had suddenly broken loose on the other side of the wall. What was going on? What was all the cheering about? The colonel sent a Marine over to take a peek, and switched to the AM band of his radio. There was the unmistakable voice of June Keithley, and her euphoric message: "It's the dawn of a new day. . . . All you Marcos soldiers, you are not fighting for anything or any one any more." Marcos was gone!
phoric message: "It's the dawn of a new day. . . . All you Marcos soldiers, you are not fighting for anything or any one any more." Marcos was gone!

Hmmmph, thought Balbas. They don't call General Fidel Ramos a psy-ops wizard for nothing. It was a pretty good ploy; it sounded almost genuine. He got on the two-way radio, checked with the commanders back at Malacañang, and was told not to worry. The "Apo" was still there, and the plan remained the same: Set up the mortars, get your artillery in place, and wait for further instructions.

The colonel put down his walkie-talkie and bent over one of the filthy grey LVTs. The 105-mm howitzers mounted there are "bore-sighted", which means the gunner can look right down the barrel at his target. Balbas did exactly that, and found himself staring at the third floor of the Constabulary headquarters in Crame – into the window, in fact, of the rebel "war room". It was outrageously easy. Two hundred yards, no obstructions. They could have *thrown* the damn shells that far.

One glance at Balbas and his howitzers would have wiped the grins off half a million faces across the street. But the human barricade had not the faintest idea he was there – or, indeed, a care in the world. My wife, Vangie, and I were with them outside Camp Crame's walls when Radio Bandido hailed the "new dawn", and we wondered if the Loyalists had shifted from tear-gas to laughing gas. People were literally intoxicated with ecstasy, limp with joy. Victory! Out of nowhere! It was too good to be true. Two men wove towards us, propping up a girl between them like drunken sailors, and shouting the news: "Happy independence day! He's gone!" Soldiers from inside had somehow clambered atop the twelve-foot walls and were beaming their confirmation. "Yeah, it's true! It's confirmed!" They had Cory headbands, yellow bows tied to the snouts of their M-16s, and more ribbon wound around the barrels of their guns. Kids in rubber flip-flop shoes were trying to scale the rough walls and clasp hands with the rebels, but could not quite reach. The hordes surged past us, chanting "Marcos, Marcos, Marcos defeated!" on the way to their cars.

It was a beautiful morning, the cool 7 a.m. sun blazing over palm trees and glinting off the camp's whitewashed walls. A great celebration, a great day in the history of the Philippines, seemed to beckon. But Vangie and I exchanged dubious looks and shook our heads in unison. "No goddam way," I said. "Not Marcos." It was not great prescience on our part; we had simply learned to believe *nothing* about the Indomitable Ilocano. The guy was a sleight-of-hand master, a political Houdini. With him, there was one only one rational approach: listen to what you were told, and believe the exact opposite. He had said it himself a thousand times: "Neither bullets nor ballots will defeat me." *That* you could believe. His departure was too good to be true, all right. Much too damn good.

Vangie tried to dissuade a few celebrants, and persuade them to hang around until we knew for sure. Nothing doing. They were streaming in two directions now, some heading home for their first shower in days, others pushing to Crame's front gate to join the celebration. We ducked in a side entrance to find out what was going on.

The camp was more orderly than the street, but just barely. A truckload of bright yellow ribbon seemed to have exploded overhead, draping soldiers, priests, children, even the tripods of sinister M-60 machine guns, in sunburst streamers. Nuns in neat blue habits sat beside the Sikorskys that had defected barely an hour earlier, looking like contented kids with their security blanket. These were now *God*'s gunships.

Strangely, the buzz of conversation was all about a tear-gas attack that had been repulsed around dawn. Heroic nuns had refused to give in, and the gas had blown back in the Loyalists' faces. . . . A wonderful story, one that utterly contradicted the actual events of 6 a.m. Amid the rejoicing, truth had become irrelevant and the rebels were passing around this happy apocryphal fairytale. Not a word, not a hint, about Balbas and his guns.

The crush around General Ramos's headquarters threatened to push in the plate-glass front doors. Five burly Constabulary officers were leaning forward at a sixty-degree angle, holding back a noisy throng of well-wishers, journalists, and officers. I dug out my press pass, plunged into the melee, exchanged elbows to the head, neck, and solar plexus, before hurtling into the lobby like a bar of soap squeezed out of someone's hand. The press was gathered in a small upstairs conference room, where Ramos and Enrile were to appear any moment. "Sorry," said an aide, "but they are receiving congratulations from all over the world. They're talking to the U.S. right now."

Actually, General Ramos was on Radio Bandido, fielding the questions of callers like a baseball manager on a sports phone-in show. He sounded bubbly, elated, completely in charge. What would happen to General Ver now? a lady wanted to know. "They are taken care of by the police," declared Ramos. "General [Narciso] Cabrera and his men are now on their way to Malacañang. It is their duty to arrest common criminals." Listeners could hear Keithley and the Bandido staff laughing and applauding in their crowded studio. Ramos grew serious for a moment and addressed all the "wayward" commanders who had yet to surrender. "You can call me on the radio," he said. "The new frequency is one-two-zero. I repeat, one-two-zero."

The small press room had a makeshift wooden stage with TV monitors on either side, but not nearly enough room for the dozens of television crews trying to set up equipment. American and French cameramen started pushing each other's VTR packs aside, jockeying for the best angle, flexing sweaty muscles. Like everyone else, the newsmen had not washed in days. The place smelled like a high-school locker after gym class.

Suddenly, a change in priorities. Enrile and Ramos had decided to thank their men first, and were headed downstairs. The media crush behind them was so thick you could descend a staircase without touching it. Back-pedalling as their flashguns popped, photographers smashed and elbowed each other, astonishing the guards at each floor. In three days these hardened revolutionaries had not seen such violence.

The enduring image of the next few moments is the famous news photo of General Ramos leaping for joy, his arms thrown into the air. It was a hard shot to miss, as the exuberant General obligingly made the leap half a dozen times – aides clinging to his waist, so that he would not tumble off the grass terrace. "Actually, I'd been leaping like that even inside my office, even when things were going badly," he told me later. "It's a warm-up exercise for jogging, and I really enjoy it. I did it constantly during the revolt, to relieve tension and just charge people up, make them enthusiastic."

While Ramos bounced up and down in his Tiger training shoes, Enrile was making grave Tagalog pronouncements over the microphone: "Starting today, no president will ever rule in our country who will cause the same suffering. Starting today, the people of the nation will never be afraid of their government again. And anyone who commits the crimes Marcos did against [the murdered] Aquino and Javier will be met with justice."

"John-ny! John-ny!" Camp Crame's gates had not been opened, but the chanting crowd inside the camp was heavily civilian. Enrile, still in his green flak-jacket and jeans, then declared February 24, 1986, as Philippine Independence Day, and pledged that it would be celebrated throughout the country's history – a bold promise that would be forgotten within a few minutes.

Ramos was less bombastic. "We have won," he declared, "only because we were protected by the vast multitude of People Power. The people are stronger than tanks, cannons, and mortar fire." The General then switched to address the "discredited army of Marcos and Ver", and issued an ominous warning: "Lay down your arms. From here on, if you do not lay down your arms, we will assault you. We will not spare you."

Cheers and chants washed over the leaders as they left the headquarters building and marched purposefully down a brick roadway to the front gate. People Power must also be thanked personally. Excited soldiers fell in behind the parade, still clanking in their armor. To my eyes, the weapons seemed irrelevant now, almost like Christmas toys swathed in all that ribbon.

It was an absurd perspective, quickly shattered by an equally absurd event. Dozens of us were striding along beside a stocky Constabulary sergeant when he somehow managed to whack loose a grenade from his own belt. It was a smooth, modern one, not the old-style pineapple, and its first bounce on the red-brick walkway sent it four feet in the air. Jesus Christ! Smack in the middle of a victory celebration, and we were all going to get our legs blown off. The grenade hopped right down the sloping roadway like a stray rubber ball in a school playground. *"Grenade! Grenade!"* the soldiers yelled, and we all dived for cover. I took refuge behind a foot-high cement planting box, grinding my face into the pavement. Time froze, and somewhere a soldier began counting down the seconds: "Five . . . six . . . seven".

The assembled military minds eventually decided that the thing was not going to blow, and the sergeant ambled over to retrieve his errant bomb. He had the grace to look apologetic as he re-hooked it onto his belt. We civilians all dusted ourselves off, shrugged, and struggled to assume an air of indifference. The soldiers, more honest, rolled their eyes and made the sign of the cross.

Enrile and Ramos, meanwhile, had begun slowly sinking into the roof of a white Fiera van. They had climbed atop it outside the front gate as the entire human barricade chanted their names. But Colonel Gringo Honasan had to be up there too, to protect his minister, and someone else needed to hold a five-foot Blessed Virgin statue over their heads. Then there was the Ramos aide, the guy with the ATOM banner, and a dozen other essential celebrants. Within minutes the van's roof began collapsing beneath their weight. The rebel leaders hardly noticed. They did a reprise of the speech they had given inside, this time more extravagant in its praise of People Power. The crowd was like a massive heart, pulsing with love for its heroes. Tens of thousands poured in when the speeches began, and by now people were even pressed against the far wall, the wall of Camp Aguinaldo . . .

The wall where, just out of sight, Balbas and his men lounged on their hardware. Listening to the speeches, they were fascinated by the unfolding drama, and mightily apprehensive about the role they would soon play.

• • •

It was now approaching 9 a.m., and the first hints of imminent danger were beginning to penetrate Camp Crame. Many in the crowd had radios tuned to June Keithley's Bandido station, where the puzzling sound of gunshots could be heard in the background. The firing came from a Quezon City media centre that housed Channel 4, and it baffled Keithley, too. She had picked up the noise on a walkie-talkie, and simply held her UHF radio to the microphone. "There's some shooting there, we can hear shooting at Channel 4," she said. "We are told there are sixteen armed gunmen there . . . I don't really know why."

Colonel J. C. De La Cruz was pressed against the front gate, accepting my congratulations, when Bandido came back with a startling bulletin: Ferdinand Marcos was on television. He and his family had appeared on Channel 4, claiming they were still in Malacañang. "No," said the colonel. "That's a typical Marcos trick. It's a tape. The intention is to buy time . . . so he could reach Guam. It's not real." Marcos, finally aware of his credibility problem, had foreseen that reaction; he was gazing glassy-eyed into the camera from behind a copy of *that morning's Daily Express.*

Suddenly people around us began to cast uneasy glances skyward. The two F-5 fighter jets had been up there all morning, drawing lazy smoke patterns as they criss-crossed Manila in tandem while Crame's joyful vigilantes had occasionally waved and cheered them on. It was just assumed that they were "ours". Now, however, they hovered above us as deadly question marks. Whose side were they on? It had been the helicopters of the 15th Strike Wing that defected. The two F-5s, volunteered a military man, were from an entirely different unit called the 5th Fighter Wing. Did anyone know whether they had come over to the rebels?

No one, including General Fabian Ver, really did know. But the Loyalist chief of staff was in Malacañang's reception hall that very minute, informing the nation that he was about to unleash those fighters on the sitting ducks below.

It was true that a televised Marcos press conference was under way, though only a handful of press were in attendance. A few reporters had gone to the Palace to witness the end of the Marcos era. Instead, they were greeted by a grateful information minister Gregorio Cendaña, who ushered them into a room with a camera, a few chairs, and the familiar Presidential Seal. Sure enough, Marcos and Imelda arrived minutes later, with son Bongbong in his camouflage fatigues, daughter Irene and her husband Greggy Araneta, daughter Imee and Tommy Manotoc, the Marcos ward Aimee, the entire Ver clan, and just three other generals. The ruling circle had shrunk down to a tight little two-family compact. Gone were the row upon row of military officers who usually flanked the President on such occasions. In their place were today's newspapers, a clock, and squealing grandson Borgy Manotoc – who squirmed out of Imee's grasp and romped joyfully across the podium, oblivious to his family's perilous circumstances.

The televised conference began as a simple question-and-answer session, with the President umming and ahhing through the standard questions. Yes, he would take his oath tomorrow. Of *course* he would take his oath. "I am the duly elected President." General Ver paced off-camera to the left like a nervous guard dog, hitching up his green fatigues and tugging at his camouflage cap. He kept edging closer and closer to the microphone, visibly eager to get in his own two centavos' worth. Finally, when a reporter asked Marcos whether he would accept civilian casualties to end the impasse, Ver could wait no longer.

"All I would ask," answered the President, "is that the civilians stay in their houses, because . . . uh . . ."

Before he could finish, Ver had wrested a microphone from an attendant and begun gesturing frantically for attention. The studio camera swung over to put him on screen. "We have come here . . . we are sorry, Mr. President, to butt into your program," he blurted out. "We just wanted to show you that we are still here and that we are strong and organized and ready to neutralize any force. The air force is ready to mount an air attack. We request the civilians to leave the vicinity of Camp Crame immediately, Mr. President. That's why I come here on your orders, so we can immediately strike them."

It was impossible, unprecedented. *Nobody* interrupts Ferdinand Marcos during a nationally televised press conference; certainly not his dog-loyal bodyguard. The ensuing scene was even more bizarre: Ver, towering over the slightly-built President and shouting into the microphone, proceeded to argue with his boss for a full three minutes, in plain view of the world press and the Philippine nation. Videotapes of this unique set-to are now cherished possessions in many Filipino homes, and it is worth repeating with every "ah" and "uh" intact. The roster of great comic duos – Laurel and Hardy, Mutt and Jeff, Bert and Ernie – was suddenly one pair richer: Marcos and Ver.

The President turned to his henchman with remarkably little surprise, blinked repeatedly (the tip-off that he was lying), and began to respond: "Ah . . ."

But Ver would not be stopped. "We have to immobilize the helicopters that they got," he interrupted. "We have two fighter planes flying now to strike at any time. Because your orders, sir . . ."

Marcos: "My order is not to attack. . . ."

Ver (not listening, talking right through his boss): "We insist that all civilians leave the area!"

Marcos: "No, no, no, no! You hold on! Uh . . . You are not to attack . . . uh . . ."

Ver: "Sir, we are left with no options but to . . . uh . . . do so."

Marcos: "Uh, yes. But . . . uh . . . you will . . ."

Ver was manic now, completely out of control. He was shouting at the top of his voice, his free hand clutching the air as if grasping for words: "Our negotiations and our . . . our prior dialogues have . . . eh . . . have *not* succeeded, Mr. President!"

Marcos: "I understand General Ramos is issuing orders like a chief of staff. All I can say is . . . uh . . . we will . . . we may have to reach the point where we will employ heavy weapons. But . . . uh . . . uh . . . you utilize small weapons and . . . uh . . . hand or shoulder weapons in the meantime."

Ver: "Can we give the commanders, sir, the option to decide what is best under the situation?"

Marcos: "If they are overrun. If there is . . . uh . . . any attempt to take . . ."

Ver (interrupting): "Our attack forces are being delayed. I understand you gave them orders to wait."

Marcos: "I told them to . . . uh . . . wait, because . . ."

Ver: "They are massing civilians near our troops and we cannot keep on withdrawing. You asked us to withdraw yesterday."

Marcos: "My order is to disperse the crowd . . ."

Ver (leaning forward, pushing his microphone almost into the President's face, the two men talking simultaneously): "We cannot withdraw all the time, Mr. President!"

Marcos: ". . . without shooting them. No, no, no, no. Hold on! You disperse the crowd without shooting them. You may use any other weapon."

Ver stepped back smartly and, as if touched by a magic wand, regained his composure. He saluted and quietly acquiesced: "We will obey your order, sir."

This extraordinary on-air confrontation touched off its own debate as to whether the whole thing was staged. Marcos loyalists insist that it was absolutely genuine, and paint the President as a dignified statesmen who held back his bloodthirsty four-star general. The outrageous Ronald Reagan quote at the beginning of this chapter indicates how thoroughly this interpretation has been swallowed by the White House. Even now,

President Reagan uses the "restraint" shown by Marcos to justify continued leniency towards his old pal, the man he once called Asia's "bulwark of democracy".

This notion is a total fiction. What's more, it is a fiction known only too well by residents of the beautiful estate on Manila Bay that houses the U.S. Embassy. American diplomats knew *immediately* that Marcos was putting on an act for their benefit. Indeed, they viewed it as a colossal joke, one of the few light moments in a tense four days.

"It was a show, a put-on," admits Embassy spokesman Allan Croghan. "That was certainly the interpretation here. It was a 'moro-moro'." This was an ironic reference to Marcos's own use of the Tagalog term for play-acting. The President instructed prosecutors in the 1985 Aquino murder trial to: "magmoro-moro na lang kayo" ("just play-act your way through"). He could have given the same advice, word for word, to General Ver on that Monday morning. The pair were fully agreed upon the real course of action, and transmitted their order to Colonel Balbas at 9 a.m., thirty minutes *before* the televised charade.

So why stage an elaborate spectacle? "Well, it's only speculation on whose benefit it was for," smiles Croghan. "But it's a matter of public record that we had warned Marcos not to use heavy arms against the rebels or the civilians. . . . In retrospect, some of the things he did and said at the time seemed to be in preparation for the future. His inauguration, for instance, made it possible for him to claim he is still the duly elected president."

And the public fight with Ver was enacted so that he could blame the General when Colonel Balbas reduced Camp Crame to shards of rubble, bone, and blood. If Marcos won, there would be no need to apologize. If he lost, there was now a ready scapegoat.

It was about one minute after 9 a.m. when Colonel Balbas's radio burped to life with three seconds of static. Then the clear voice of army commander General Josephus Ramas crackled out. "Balbas," said the Loyalist ground commander, "fire at objective with cannons, and report compliance." The Marine colonel's response was automatic: "Yes, sir!" But he did not pass on the order to his gunner. In fact, he did nothing but stare from his v-150 armored vehicle at the big howitzer just behind Camp Aguinaldo's wall. "The cannons were in perfect position," he shrugged, in an interview four months later. "But I did not take any action. I waited."

Response was not long in coming. At 9:12 a.m., General Ramas was back on the radio: "Balbas, I say again, fire on Crame and report compliance. I want you to fire three rounds initially with your cannons, and then report for compliance."

Balbas barked another "Yessir!" and set down his radio. He had run a textbook operation to this point, with three howitzer-mounted LVTs just behind the walls, ideally situated to destroy the rebel headquarters with minimum danger to civilians. He had lined up his trio of V-150s behind the howitzers in a neat, symmetrical row. Further back, on the golf-course fairway, there was a line of six bazooka-like 90-mm recoilless rifles. Behind them stood nine more 81-mm mortars, carefully spaced near the officers' quarters and pointed at the Constabulary Headquarters across the street. Nearly eight hundred battle-hardened Marines and thirty-five officers were strategically deployed to guard the emplacements. Everything was neatly laid out like a miniature battlefield with tin soldiers on a dining-room table. There was no last-minute jockeying or fiddling to do. So Balbas just stood there, knowing that further developments would not take long.

At 9:30 a.m., the colonel got his third call from Josephus Ramas. This was precisely the moment that President Marcos and General Ver entered Malacañang's reception hall to muted applause from the assembled press. Balbas, of course, had no way of knowing that. His only contact with the Palace was through the man on the walkie-talkie, and General Ramas's messages were angrily one-sided.

"The third time, he sounded upset," Balbas recalls. "He told me that the President was on the other line waiting for compliance. He said: 'You'd better fire your cannons, because the President is on the other line waiting for confirmation.' All I could say was 'Yes, sir' again. But General Ramas was army, so, after that third call, I started calling up the commander of the Marines" – the familiar General Artemio Tadiar, of EDSA showdown fame – "for confirmation. Many, many people would have been killed if I fired the heavy weapons. Before doing anything else, I wanted to make sure it was a real order, that it came from President Marcos himself."

The delay reveals much about the fractious Philippine military. Colonel Balbas was far outranked by the army's pre-eminent commander, but as a Marine he felt virtually beyond the law. Balbas was not likely to massacre people in any case, but he sure as hell wouldn't do it on the say-so of an army officer. Aside from inter-service rivalry, moreover, there was another reason for the double check: the dubious reputation of Josephus Ramas as a *"tuta"* of the First Lady. Everyone knew the army leader was Imelda's boy, her post-Marcos insurance policy. If kidney failure had finished off the President, his successor would need a finger on the military trigger. General Josephus Ramas was Imelda's trigger-finger, her bargaining chip. Whenever Fabian Ver made a grab for the brass ring, he would need to cut the First Lady into the action; General Ramas would see to that. So it was not unnatural for Colonel Balbas to be suspicious of Ramas's orders. They might indeed come direct from the President. Then again they might be Imelda's own contribution to the revolt.

Balbas had trouble finding General Tadiar. He used a telephone, so that army intelligence would not pick him up on the military radio, but his boss was not at Fort Bonifacio. Someone thought he had gone to Malacañang. Balbas asked for General Brawner, but no one had seen him, either. Finally, after wrestling with the dilapidated Manila phone system for twenty minutes, the colonel tracked down Tadiar at the community hall in Malacañang Park. He had been ordered to appear on the TV press conference, but had not actually shown up in front of the cameras.

"Sir," Balbas told his superior. "I have a problem. I have received repeated orders from General Ramas to fire the LVTs at Camp Crame. Do you know if this has been cleared by the President?"

Tadiar replied crisply: "Hold your position. Just wait there for a while and I will verify." The Marine general checked with Ver just before 10 a.m., mere seconds after the televised Laurel and Hardy routine. Ver did not bother to disguise the charade. He immediately confirmed that the President had given the firing order that morning. Within five minutes, General Tadiar was back on the phone to Balbas. "The order is confirmed by Malacañang," he said. "You can fire now."

Balbas stood in silent shock for a moment, then began pleading with his commander. He knew that his military career was finished if he disobeyed such a crucial order. That was at the very least; at worst, he could be jailed or shot. Yet it was less than twenty-four hours since he had seen Tadiar himself bend the rules at EDSA. Balbas grasped at that straw, drawing parallels and appealing to the General's compassion. "I told him about the situation at Crame," says the colonel. "I told him there were thousands out there and they would be killed. They were outside celebrating and they didn't know the tanks were right around the corner. We had been together at EDSA, so I told him the crowd was even thicker now. He started out very firm, but then he became calm on the telephone. I told him: 'Sir, I just cannot fire. Thousands will die.' "

There was a brief pause on the line before Tadiar replied: "I understand," he said finally. "Use your own discretion, Balbas."

The General's understanding was some comfort, but Colonel Balbas remained on the hot spot. Now he was certain that the orders were genuine, and still he could not bring himself to fire. All that talk about civilian casualties was partly sincere, but also a smokescreen. The bore-sighted howitzers are absolutely accurate at such short range, and the Marine gunners could have virtually planted a missile in General Fidel Ramos's hand-carved cigar box. There was no need to lob shells into the compound to gauge distance; no need even for maps or coordinates. It was a case of pointing a gun at the rebel war room and pulling the trigger. The only civilian casualties would be newsmen inside and those hit by flying debris.

Balbas admits as much, albeit indirectly. "I knew most of the officers inside [Crame], and liked them," he says. "I could almost see their faces, and I didn't see them as my enemy. This situation, with all these pressures . . . I had to use my head. All the way I'd been obeying orders and telling myself to obey as long as they were legal. Now . . . the foremost thing in my mind was not to commit atrocities against the Filipino people or my fellow soldiers.

"I had several things to consider. I knew that if I disobeyed and Marcos wins, then I would be arrested, court-martialled, and maybe face a firing squad. I could not defect to Camp Crame, because my family was back in Fort Bonifacio and maybe they would be hurt. I was between the devil and the deep blue sea."

In the midst of his anguish, the Marine colonel was confronted with a more routine problem. The rebels had finally realized the danger he posed, and had taken steps to neutralize his force. On his right flank, Aguinaldo's security battalion of two hundred men had moved into position and now stood in plain view – apparently hoping to intimidate the attack force. On the other side was a platoon from the El Diablo group, an organization of Reformist soldiers who supported the RAM officers. They had been banned under Marcos, but regrouped into a fighting unit at the start of the rebellion. At the far rear, hidden from the Marines' sight, was a small, elite unit called Task Force Delta, one of the "surgical strike teams" formed by RAM many weeks before their breakaway.

The rebels had the Marines surrounded, but they were vastly outgunned by all those howitzers and recoilless rifles. In retrospect, it is clear that the two sides made quite different strategic assessments. The Reformists believed that they had the situation in hand – while Balbas dismissed them as a minor irritant.

"We had sixteen Marine instructors with us in Crame," says RAM's intelligence chief, Colonel Red Kapunan. "And we sent a couple of them over in civilian clothes, trying to convince Balbas's people to move to our side. They came back saying that, as far as the key NCOs were concerned, they weren't going to fight us. Balbas himself . . . well, we didn't know for sure." In purely military terms, the rebels also considered Lt.-Col. Jerry Albano's security battalion on the flank a strong deterrent to any attack. In their version, he "warned" Balbas that he would strike him from behind if a shot was fired. The rebels felt fully capable of "hitting" the Marines.

Balbas recalls the episode with the contempt of a man playing with boys. His soldiers, after all, were *Marines* – and armed to the teeth, at that. His recollection of Colonel Albano's "warning" is very different from the rebel account: "He came to me and said, 'I'm on the other side.' I said, 'So? What do you want?' He was asking me not to attack them. I said it was really not our intention to attack. His force was quite small, ours was big. They had no armored vehicles, we had a lot. We could have eliminated them immediately."

Rebel negotiators inside Aguinaldo did not know what to make of Balbas. He was reputedly a principled officer, sympathetic to General Fidel Ramos and, by extension, to their cause. Yet he replied to every peaceful overture with cold arrogance and a stunning disrespect for superior officers. It was General Pedro Balbanero who dispatched Colonel Albano to negotiate. Balbanero was in charge of Aguinaldo's peace-keeping force, and now realized that the camp was about to blow up in his face. One stray shot on either side and his golf course would become a war zone.

"Look," pleaded Albano, after being escorted to Balbas by grim-faced Marines. "Can we just talk this over? You know very well that many civilians will die if you fire your cannons."

"I have my orders," Balbas replied icily, betraying no hint of his inner turmoil.

"Yes, you have your orders," continued Albano. "But I also have mine: to assault you and fight it out with you the moment you open fire. I pray it will not come to that."

Balbas just glared in silence. Inside, his guts were twisted in an angry knot. These Reformists acted as if they had cornered the market on morality. What did they think of him? Did he want to kill people any more than they did? And the threats . . . *threats!* Imagine this pipsqueak army colonel threatening a Marine. Did he think the LVTs and V-150s were rooted to the goddam ground? Didn't he realize they could turn and blast his security force to bits any time they wanted?

Albano, unnerved by the sphinx-like Balbas, tried a different tack. "Sir," he said, "General Balbanero wants to speak with you about this matter."

"That's fine," replied Balbas evenly. "Tell the General to come here."

Albano could barely contain his surprise. His eyes widened, his mouth dropped open, and he took an involuntary step backward. A colonel ordering a general to come to *him*? It was outrageous, an absolute violation of military procedure. Still, Balbas had the guns, and the rebels were desperate to buy time. "All right," he agreed. "I'll get the General to come. But please don't take any action until you confer with him."

That would not be difficult, for there was little action the beleaguered Balbas could reasonably take. He had already decided not to fire the guns, and could not risk defecting to Crame. Back at Fort Bonifacio, meanwhile, there was a jail cell or a firing squad awaiting him. They wanted him to hang around the golf course and wait, did they? Well, that was fine with Balbas.

15 OFF THE AIR

ENRILE AND RAMOS WERE in full oratorical flight at 9:30 a.m. when an aide scrambled onto the sinking roof of the Ford Fiera and tugged at the General's sleeve. "Sir," he told Ramos. "Please finish what you are saying and come with me. We've got a problem. Marcos is on television. We think it might be genuine." They collected Enrile and tried to climb off the van as unobtrusively as possible – not an easy trick with half a million people cheering your every move. Then they sprinted up the brick pathway back to headquarters (stealing occasional glances at the cruising F-5s), and flopped in front of Ramos's office TV. Incongruously, the first thing they saw was the President's grandchildren romping carelessly before the cameras.

Ramos cursed and glared angrily. "Is this for real?" he demanded.

"We're not sure, sir," replied a colonel. "We thought it was just a tape, but it looks very real. He's got today's newspapers and he's been talking about things that happened this morning. They mentioned the [helicopter] defection."

Enrile had an idea. When in doubt, why not call the guys who always know what's going on? "Rene, get in touch with the U.S. Embassy," he ordered his friend Rene Cayetano. "Get Bosworth on the phone."

Ambassador Stephen Bosworth seemed in remarkably high spirits that morning. Instead of giving a straight answer, he gently mocked the inquiries from rebel headquarters. "Do you have a TV set?" he asked Cayetano. "Is it tuned to Channel 4? Well, there's your answer. What you see is what you get. Marcos is still in Malacañang." Was the ambassador sure about that? "You bet I'm sure. I just talked to him fifteen minutes ago."

Thanks a lot, Steve. Cayetano put down the phone and nodded to Enrile and Ramos. "It's for real. Marcos is still there." Some aides say it was the only time during the four-day revolt that they saw the General agitated; they claim that Ramos looked worried and upset, and began stalking about the room. Others in the crowded office say he merely stood up and said: "Well, gentlemen, we still have work to do." There is unanimity, however, about Juan Ponce Enrile's reaction to the setback. The Defence Minister wiped a handkerchief across his brow and fixed General Ramos with a mischievous smile. "General," he said, "I think it's time we had our *own* TV station."

The assault on Maharlika's broadcast centre had actually begun an hour before when Colonel Mariano Santiago took his fellow-rebels from Radio Veritas and boldly rode up to the door of Channel 4. At the time, Santiago believed that Marcos had left the country and so was simply taking control of the "people's" TV station. What he encountered was yet another of General Ver's incredible blunders: an absurdly small force, only five duty soldiers and a dozen Scout Rangers, guarding his most vital media outlet. Civilians and priests were already arguing with the Loyalists through the compound's steel gates when Santiago, grandly decked out in a yellow Cory headband and flak jacket, arrived to demand their surrender. The Philippine revolt had established a pattern for such situations: an uneasy standoff, plenty of talk, hordes of intervening civilians, and a non-violent compromise. But that mold was broken at Channel 4. Almost immediately, cool negotiations gave way to gunfire.

Each side claims that the other fired first, but the only certainty is the eruption of a vicious five-minute fire fight – the one heard flaring in the backround over Radio Bandido. One Loyalist soldier was killed outright, another was injured, and a Channel 4 technician died of a heart attack. Civilians, accustomed to a talk-talk-talk revolution, were taken completely by surprise. As usual, People Power ran towards the danger instead of away from it, the sound of gunfire bringing carloads to the scene within minutes. But they weren't prepared for the hail of ricocheting bullets. People dived behind cars, trees, walls, and barriers as the M-16 automatics chattered back and forth. Windshields exploded all along Bohol Avenue and several onlookers were cut by flying glass.

After the first exchange of shots, the station's employees could be seen scurrying out a side gate, lugging their possessions. During the brief respite, the rebels also noticed Loyalist soldiers sneaking away in civilian clothes, but they did not try to stop them – the fewer defenders the better.

The odds shifted decisively just after 9:30 a.m. when Lt.-Col. Teodorico Viduya roared in from Camp Crame with a combat-ready strike force of 128 men. Viduya's troops had drilled weeks in advance for an assault on Maharlika as part of the original RAM coup plot. But with Marcos and Ver already on the airwaves, there was no time to fight it out with the defenders. "We'll knock them off the air first," Viduya told his squad. "And then worry about taking over the station."

Thunk-thunk-thunk-thunk-thunk! Thunk-thunk-thunk! The rebels opened up on the broadcast tower from two directions. They were equipped with rifle grenades, but did not want to start a fire, or blast civilians by mistake. So they tried to knock the tower out of commission by hammering away with their assault rifles. Thwack! At exactly 9:56 a.m., somebody got lucky. There was a small explosion near the top of the tower, and a puff of grey-black smoke rose into the cloudless blue morning.

In Malacañang's reception hall, the three TV monitors suddenly went blank, fizzing with white noise. The First Lady let out a small cry of surprise and put her hand to her throat, but Marcos appeared to be more annoyed than concerned. He waved Gregorio Cendaña over to fix the set and fidgeted while the Information Minister played with the controls. After a few seconds, someone noticed that the other channels were all coming in loud and clear. Cendaña threw a pleading look towards a man working on another set, but the technician just shook his head. The President's close personal aide, Colonel Arturo Aruiza, hurried in from the doorway and conferred briefly with his boss, obviously explaining what had happened.

Marcos did not pass on the news to the assembled press. He simply set his jaw and – his face the color and texture of putty – fielded another half-dozen questions. Someone asked again how he planned to deal with the civilian barricades, and the President flicked his wrist in dismissal: "If you are going to be frightened by . . . uh . . . two thousand civilians," he scowled, "then let's not even talk about running a government."

There were closer to two million in the streets, and the fall of Channel 4 struck them like a lightning bolt. It was miraculous, phenomenal, beyond comprehension. Thousands came running out of their houses, onto balconies, into the streets, shouting the news: "They killed Maharlika! They blasted Channel 4 right off the air!" People stood by the dozens in the front parlors of total strangers, and stared at the buzzing blankness. Turn the channel! Sure enough, the other stations were still on. Filipinos were ready, most of them, for the fall of Ferdinand Marcos. They had dreamed about it, read about it, prayed and campaigned for it. Omnipotent and sly as he often seemed, the President was at least mortal. Marcos could *die*. But Channel 4 was something else. Channel 4 was *eternal*, an incessant litany of lies from Ronnie and Rita that could never be staunched. Perhaps the Germans had felt the same way forty years before about Paul Joseph Goebbels and his minions.

A little tailor shop across from Camp Aguinaldo's side gate provided a perfect illustration. I rushed there on Monday morning in desperate search of a telephone, only to find the tailor's entire family and friends sitting on a moldy brown sofa, staring fixedly at the blank screen. They were ravenous for news of the revolt; four other TV channels were still churning out up-to-the-moment bulletins. Yet the tailor, his kids, and his neighbors were glued to the void left by Channel 4. "We're afraid it will come back on," he said, and smiled weakly; the comment was not meant as a joke.

Too late, General Ver grasped the importance of the takeover, and dispatched three truckloads of Marines to the station. But a tide of pure elation stopped them cold. This time there was no need for frantic radio appeals: People Power had already made a spontaneous beeline for the media centre, thousands marching arm in arm from all directions. The last few Loyalist guards had appeared at the station's door after the tower was blasted, waving in a "Don't shoot!" gesture. Colonel Santiago's men rushed in to find forty terrified technicians running through the building, pleading for their lives, diving out windows, or trying to flush shredded tapes down the toilet. Soldiers swear that they discovered Rita Gaddi-Baltazar cowering under a table in an upstairs room, and took pity on her. "Just lock the door and stay there," they told her. "If you try to go outside, the crowd will tear you apart."

And what a crowd. Vigilantes blocked the streets by simply picking up cars, plunking them down in intersections and tearing off their wheels. Policemen with fire trucks arrived just north of the media complex, but were soon immobilized by the mob. The cops and firemen sat there for the next three hours, calmly smoking hand-out cigarettes while Ver's Marines tried to deal with the masses.

The thirty Loyalist soldiers came barrelling down Bohol Avenue towards the station, then stopped in confusion when they ran into People Power. Serene little girls, in Cory-yellow print dresses, white "Madonna" socks, and shiny patent-leather party shoes, tried to jam flowers down their gun barrels; men stood in front of the jeep-trucks with arms extended, like Jesus on the cross. But this was serious business. The objective was less than two hundred yards away, and the officers had been told to retake the station at all costs. Gunfire erupted, with Colonel Viduya's rebels firing from atop the station's walls. A civilian went down in a pool of blood when a bullet creased his skull, and was carried off by the crowd, like a grain of sugar borne by ants. When the Marines stopped firing and went into a huddle, the human barricade huddled right around them. Men offered cigarettes, women held up fruit and flowers. Oblivious to the shooting, middle-aged Filipinos could be seen handing their nine-year-old nieces garlands of sampaguitas and urging forward another wave of tiny peacemakers.

One Marine had had enough. He accepted the flowers and draped them over the oily barrel of his M-16, then cupped his head in his hands. Those near by said he was crying as people cheered him and chanted ''Co-ry! Co-ry!'' Finally, the Loyalists gave up. They climbed back in their trucks and sat there awhile, surrounded by wary civilians who feared a trick. But no, the drab-green trucks eventually turned tail and rode off, tarpaulins flapping in the breeze.

In the press room at Camp Crame, meanwhile, the morning's bizarre events had taken a toll on the rebels. Sergeants and lieutenants frequently dropped in to watch the TV, and their reactions were highly revealing. If General Ramos had been caught off guard by the Marcos reappearance, his men were utterly flabbergasted. ''It can't be real. It must be some kind of psy-war,'' one disgruntled sergeant told another. ''You know Ramos. He probably planned the whole thing.''

''He wouldn't do that,'' said the second NCO. ''They can't deceive us like that. It's got to be one of Marcos's tricks. It could be *his* psy-war.''

Days, weeks, a year later, journalists and commentators still ask that same question about the False Victory. Some American newspapers and TV networks reported it as a Ramos masterstroke, and quoted an unnamed Philippine colonel who called it a ''beautiful operation of psy-ops''. Even Colonel Gringo Honasan went on record saying the ''euphoria which followed'' the bogus victory was a powerful psychological weapon, touching off a stream of defections from Marcos.

But that was almost certainly an accident. Anyone of even passing importance on the rebel side was interviewed for this book, and they remain as puzzled as the rest of us. In retrospect, even Ramos and Enrile cannot fathom why Marcos would attempt such a ploy. All they know for certain is that *they* did not – and they can hardly imagine that the whole thing happened by chance.

''I'm flattered that people believe I engineered it,'' smiles General Ramos. ''But that just isn't true. I believed the reports were absolutely genuine. If it was one of our tactics, there'd be no reason to hide it now. . . . As you know, there were many wild rumors flying around at the time, so we had a tight system at our headquarters. Everything had to be verified by at least two credible sources, and we had two excellent sources for this report. To tell you frankly, I got it from our operations and intelligence centre. They said: 'We got a call from our assets in Malacañang that they [the Marcoses] have left.' And so I replied: 'This is too good to be true. Have it verified.' They went back and got it confirmed by another source. That's when I phoned June Keithley to put it on the air.

"Was Marcos behind it? I don't know. Keithley was getting the same reports from entirely different sources. I'll tell you something for sure: I consider those kinds of things too vital to play with. It did not come from me."

The denial may seem questionable, since the False Victory ultimately favored the rebels. But Juan Ponce Enrile still shudders when he thinks about what might have happened at Camp Crame after the aborted celebration. "What if Marcos had stayed quiet for another hour or so?" asks the minister. "We didn't know he was there. We were out celebrating, the crowds were dispersing, our soldiers were completely off-balance. What if he'd let us whoop it up for another hour and then hit us? It's something I've thought about since then. . . . Why didn't he wait, and spring the trap?"

No one is sure there *was* a trap, but the weight of evidence points strongly in that direction. In the rumor-mongering capital of Asia, it is remotely possible that "assets" inside Malacañang and blue-haired telephone ladies all happened to be purveying the same gossip at the same time. It is not, however, a very plausible scenario.

That leaves Marcos, and the intriguing question: Why didn't he spring the trap? The most probable answer is that it *did* snap shut – on his own foot. The military reported a wave of Loyalist defections in the wake of the False Victory announcement. Obviously Marcos's own forces believed the Radio Bandido reports and heeded the calls of June Keithley and General Ramos; when their new "commander" issued radio frequencies for surrender, dozens of units checked in immediately rather than risk being considered renegades. With his woeful credibility, it was all the President could do to convince his own soldiers that he was still in the country. If he had waited another hour, there would have been no Loyalist troops left to command.

The morning had been a series of turning points. Now, minutes after Channel 4 went up in smoke, General Fidel Ramos switched the rebel forces from defense to offense. He had a whole fleet of Sikorskys sitting on Crame's parade grounds, loaded down with rockets like May Day floats in Red Square. What the hell? Why not give Marcos something to think about?

In the official account, a lone gunship was sent to knock out the radio transmitter atop Malacañang Palace. "But, that's bullshit," according to one Reformist officer who requested anonymity. "You like to believe that everything you do has a tactical reason. But, really, we just wanted to scare the hell out of Marcos. It was what we call a 'persuasion' mission. Pure intimidation. We wanted him to know that we ruled the air and we could hit him any time we wanted."

"The whole idea," confirms Colonel Antonio Sotelo, "was to let Marcos know our capabilities. We just sent one helicopter, one pass, and he fired six rockets. Actually, he was only supposed to fire four, but the trigger is very delicate and the pilot held it a bit too long. It wasn't a grenade-launcher, as everyone reported. They were small rockets, 2.75 inches, twice the size of a grenade, but they sound like grenades when you fire them. We weren't shooting at the Palace, just the premises. I think he shot up the First Lady's garden, and we heard that General Ver dived under the table. I would have given a lot to see that."

The attack was absolutely brazen, almost a daredevil stunt. The rebels intentionally sent Captain Wilfredo Evangelista over the Palace all alone – without the usual cover from a backup chopper – to demonstrate their complete invulnerability. Evangelista swung the Sikorsky out over Manila Bay, ducked down among the buildings surrounding Rizal Park, and used the Manila Post Office as a screen to sneak up on Malacañang, which allowed him to come out of nowhere as he screamed in low over the Palace. Soldiers scurried across the grounds, firing wildly with their assault rifles. Two or three tanks swung around to take shots at him, but they were far too slow. Evangelista squeezed the trigger and watched his rockets skate through the air before kicking up fire around the Marcos sanctuary. One put a hole in the metallic blue Mercedes-Benz convertible of Marcos's son-in-law Greggy Araneta. Another exploded near the First Lady's bedroom. A third did slight damage to the white-and-blue presidential escape Sikorskys sitting on the lawn.

Evangelista also heard a hollow "clank!" somewhere in the back of his chopper. An M-16 bullet had lodged in the tail assembly, but did little more than scratch the paint.

Lieutenant Ferdinand Golez was on the wrong end of the assault, diving for cover as an aide-de-camp of General Ver. "A Sikorsky S-76 gunship hovered from a distance," he wrote in his report, "and fired a salvo of rockets. Three explosions were distinctly heard, but it could be more, since the rockets were fired simultaneously. The troops at Malacañang scampered for any available cover. They did not know what actually hit them. At first, some thought the explosion came from mortar fires or any other light artillery pieces. The recovery of some fragments confirmed that they indeed came from anti-personnel rockets [2.75 inch]. Fortunately, no one got physically hurt, but the psychological damage was certainly great."

Nobody can confirm Colonel Sotelo's rumor about General Ver diving under a table, but insiders say that officers were still scrambling to buckle on flak jackets long after Evangelista's gunship had disappeared into the east. The First Family were all in one room, well away from windows. But Marcos himself would later go on television to tell the nation that his family was "cowering in fear".

Seconds after the attack, the President phoned military headquarters across the Pasig River and ripped into his chief of staff. What the hell are your people doing? he asked Ver. Why wasn't there any warning of the attack? My own *grandchildren* are here! They are crying in terror! General Ver passed the outraged questions down the line to his son Irwin, a 38-year-old colonel who had never seen battlefield action. Nepotism had placed the unfortunate Colonel Ver in charge of the Presidential Security Command, but his father's influence had proved to be a poor defense against live rockets.

It was not long before the cauldron of Loyalist anger and recrimination came boiling down on the head of Colonel Braulio Balbas. By now, he had been fending off firing orders for a full ninety minutes, his refusals becoming more and more inventive – if less and less plausible:

– "Uh . . . sir, we are still setting up our guns. I will call you when we are ready."

– "Yessir, the guns are in position now. We are simply trying to find our maps and . . . uh . . . check our co-ordinates."

– "Yes, we have the maps, sir. But they are old and there appears to be some problem with the co-ordinates. We are still checking, sir."

This comic routine had not drawn many laughs in the office of General Josephus Ramas, the desperate army chief. He was in Fort Bonifacio when the rockets struck the Palace, but he found out about them in a hurry. General Ver was on the phone within seconds of the attack, screaming his favorite four-letter word. Just what the fuck was going on with the artillery in Aguinaldo? Ver demanded. To hell with Balbas! If you can't get him to shoot the fucking guns, Ramas, then send somebody over there who will. Find someone who knows what a trigger looks like, and tell him to *pull* the fucker!

Ramas tried to radio Balbas for the umpteenth time, but found him busy. While the senior Ver had been chewing out his army commander, his son had gone to work on Balbas.

"It was about 10:30 a.m. when I started receiving calls from

Malacañang, from Irwin Ver," recalls the Marine colonel. "I had been making excuses about the maps, but of course they knew I didn't need maps at that range. Now, this was different; Colonel Ver was not ordering, he was screaming. He told me to fire my cannons, mortars, and attack Crame with my men. He wanted me to throw everything I had at them. He told me the Palace had been attacked by helicopters and they had sustained many casualties. He made it sound like a real war over there."

Josephus Ramas finally broke into the radio transmission and added his own account of terrible devastation at Malacañang. He repeated all of Colonel Ver's orders, and this time he would not accept a perfunctory "yessir" in response.

"General Ramas sensed I was not going to obey," says Colonel Balbas, "so he told me just to wait right there. He said he would send General [Cirilo] Oropesa to supervise, to take over my command. He wanted my exact location, so Oropesa could find us. Then his radio just clicked off."

This was the moment of truth for Colonel Braulio Balbas. Was there any moral difference between firing howitzers himself and handing them over to someone else to fire them, with the same devastating results? He had promised himself that he would obey legal orders, and the transfer was strictly by the book. But could he stand aside and watch General Oropesa open up on the crowd? Might it not be wiser to fire the guns himself, to ensure that they hit no civilian targets?

The colonel did not linger long, however, in the ethereal realm of pure ethics. His was an applied science, where moral dilemmas must yield to other imperatives. And the crux of the matter for this hardrock battle commander was very simple: Cirilo Oropesa was an *army* general, and no goddam army officer was going to take over a brigade of Marines.

"I thought about many things," says Balbas, "but the decision was taken very quickly. When he came, I would not give up the command of my troops. There would be some sort of fight between me and Oropesa. It is true that he far outranked me, but . . . well, there was no doubt about the loyalty of my men. He is army; I am a Marine.

"If there is any conflict, the men will always follow the Marine. I had the weapons. I had the men. What could Oropesa do against me?"

16 *THE NOOSE TIGHTENS*

THE COLLISION BETWEEN General Oropesa and Colonel Balbas was averted by a small band of soldiers with headphones clamped over their ears. They made up the Reformist radio team, which had been together for months, secretly assembling monitors from spare parts, concocting and hiding elaborate aerials, hoarding radio crystals for every imaginable frequency – and eavesdropping on President Ferdinand Marcos. Two weeks before, they had spent election day glued to their sets. It had been dispiriting work, sitting listening to Malacañang Palace dispatch false ballot boxes, club-wielding thugs, and armed hit-teams across the country. Now the rebel "signals corps" was actively involved, playing a vital role in the fight against Marcos. It was an unnoticed, unglamorous role; holed up near the garbage dump in a far corner of Camp Crame, its equipment stacked behind a beat-up army truck, the group did not rate a second glance from the hordes of reporters who wandered past their sanctuary. But the radio men spent the entire four days stealing transmissions from the Loyalist high command.

They heard General Josephus Ramas order Colonel Balbas to stay beside his guns. Five minutes later, a fascinating follow-up crackled over the air from Fort Bonifacio to Villamor Air Base:

"Colonel, prepare the Hueys for a mission. There will be a drop on Crame . . . and expect General Oropesa. You will supply him with transportation to Aguinaldo."

Marcos obviously planned to use his last five helicopters – the outmoded but still powerful US-18 Hueys – to launch a desperate air-drop of Loyalist soldiers on rebel headquarters. Two dozen Ranger commandos, armed with rockets and recoilless rifles to knock out the Sikorskys, would be ferried over Camp Crame's walls and landed near the gunships. One chopper would make a stop along the way, delivering army general Cirilo Oropesa and a small escort force to the guns on the golf course at Aguinaldo. There, Oropesa would take charge of Colonel Balbas's Marines, and put his itchy finger on the triggers of those three howitzers. Rebel headquarters would be blasted from within and without.

But not if the RAM radio team could help it. They immediately relayed the attack plan to rebel intelligence, which passed it at once to Colonel Antonio Sotelo. The 15th Strike Wing commander took about three seconds to formulate a defense. They were going to blow up his Sikorskys, were they? Not if he found those Hueys first.

"When I heard about this, the first thing was to get my choppers off the ground," recalls Sotelo. "And what better way than to send them out looking for the Hueys? Maybe we'd be the ones to catch them napping. Unfortunately, we had no idea where the Hueys were. If the Loyalists were smart, they'd have them in the air somewhere out of our sight, or move them over to Bonifacio, where they'd be safer."

Squadron leader Captain Charles Hotchkiss was given the job – and a set of marvellously vague instructions. "Take three gunships up and look around for other helicopters," Sotelo told his hard-nosed subordinate. "I don't care what they are, Hueys, utility choppers, whatever. When you find them, shoot them. Air or ground. I want them out of commission right *now*." Hotchkiss and his trio of gunships left Crame in the usual hot-wings fly-boy fashion: as if they had been ejected from catapults. The Sikorskys resembled the cartoon characters whose legs churn in the air for a moment before they go zinging off the screen. It took the whirlybirds a few seconds to become airborne. Then . . . poof! They evaporated into the south with a single high-pitched screech.

There were no helicopters on the ground at Bonifacio, just Loyalist soldiers scurrying in all directions. They believed their own officers' exaggerated reports of the attack on Malacañang, and reacted to the approaching gunships as if to the Apocalypse. Hotchkiss dipped to take a look at the fleeing ants below him and angled right. "Let's check out Villamor," he told his pilots. Within three minutes the Sikorskys were churning in place, while the pilots grinned in triumph at what they saw on the ground. The five Hueys were trapped helplessly on Villamor's tarmac, fuel lines sticking from their bellies like umbilical cords. Absurdly, the targets were lined up in a neat single file, making it easy for any attacker to cruise over and destroy them all in one pass. Hotchkiss radioed the good news back to Crame.

Instead of congratulations, however, he was greeted by an anxious voice in the rebel operations room. "Charles," pleaded an air force captain. "Make sure everybody gets out of the way before you shoot. Give them time to clear out. Those are my boys down there!" Captain Ramon Cruz had defected to the rebels with only part of his crew. The rest were down on the flight line, making last-minute checks on the Hueys.

So, in this ultra-civilized, eminently Filipino battle, the attack force made lazy circles around the target while the commander negotiated with his intended victims. "Look . . . you guys better get out of the way," Hotchkiss radioed down to Villamor. "I'm asking you to vacate the area entirely. I have orders to destroy the helicopters. Just go away, get lost, disappear. I have . . . Repeat! . . . I have orders to destroy the helicopters."

The return message was remarkably free of panic: "Yeah, Charles . . . Is that Charles? Yeah, Charles, can you make another circle? We're not ready here. We'll have to send someone out to tell them." Captain Hotchkiss had his own office below in Villamor, and remembered that he had left someone behind to run it. He flicked on the radio and got his own man on the line: "Get out of there and run over to the flight line," he ordered. "Clear everyone the hell out of our way."

Comic as it may sound in retrospect, the scene was not very amusing for those trapped on the ground. "I was at the [Villamor] command operations centre," recalls Colonel Pablo Gonzalez, "and my first impulse when they started shooting was to shoot back. Their main mission was to disable the 'copters, to stop possible retaliation. But the choppers on the ground weren't armed. When they destroyed four helicopters . . . I was very upset. We didn't like it at all. We almost fired back.

"Still, you know, it was a beautiful war. If you have to fight, that's the way to fight. We knew each other's frequencies and we talked for quite a while. They circled three or four times to give us a chance to get out of the way. . . . The whole thing was so Filipino. We are all family men, you see. We are human beings. The Filipino armed forces are not the German Wehrmacht or the Japanese. We are not military fanatics."

It was nearly noon, ten minutes after Hotchkiss and his men had arrived on the scene, before someone on the ground said, "Okay, we're clear. Come and get them," and the 15th Strike Wing finally struck. It was a minimal operation: just a few lightning bolts from the 50-caliber machine guns mounted on each side of the Sikorsky's snout. One Huey exploded into flames and burned to a twisted shell. The others just toppled over at absurd angles and sat there smoking on the tarmac. None of the Fokkers, Falcons, or Hercules transport planes near by was even grazed by a bullet.

The commandos who were supposed to drop on Crame and destroy it had not even arrived yet. They pulled up shortly after the tarmac shoot-up, and found themselves spectators at an impromptu bonfire. Eventually they loaded their rockets on a truck and bumped back across town towards Fort Bonifacio. General Cirilo Oropesa also had not arrived at Villamor – another reason the choppers were such fat targets on the ground. Now there was no reason for him to go there. The Loyalists could no longer transport him to Camp Aguinaldo, to fire Colonel Balbas's unused guns.

Balbas never did figure out what happened to Oropesa. When asked about it months later, the Marine just shrugged and shook his head. "I made up my mind to resist the general," he said. "But, fortunately, he never arrived. Nobody told me why not, and I didn't ask. The next time I heard from anybody at headquarters, it was General Tadiar."

"In case no one has informed you," the Marine general told Balbas, "they've strafed Malacañang with helicopters. Have you fired your cannons yet?"

"No, sir," replied the colonel. "In this situation, it is impossible. I am entirely surrounded by hostile forces, sir. We will suffer very heavy casualties the instant we attack." (This, of course, was in direct contradiction to Balbas's actual feelings: that he could swat the rebels aside like a cat toying with mice. The story was strictly for head-office consumption, as Tadiar undoubtedly knew.) "He sensed I would not budge," explains Balbas. "So we began talking of ways to bring the troops back to Bonifacio."

"How bad is the situation?" asked Tadiar. "Can you get out of there?"

"It won't be easy, sir."

"Okay, talk to the rebels. Let them know your plans. Tell them you just want to come back here, then move your unit out of there."

"Yessir."

Balbas had his doubts about going home: "We had no idea what was waiting for us."

As it turned out, leaving Aguinaldo was no trouble. The camp's security chief, General Balbanero, did everything but leap for joy when he heard of the retreat. It was only when the Marine brigade got outside and began to rumble down Shaw Boulevard that all hell broke loose. A great yellow army of roaming civilians and media were waiting. The Marines who had been so completely ignored when they were poised to strike and destroy the rebel base were now surrounded by tens of thousands – when all they wanted was to slink back home in peace. "Marines! Marines!" shouted the hordes of walkie-talkies and UHF radios that linked People Power. Immediately, anyone who could walk or crawl made straight for this "new" Loyalist threat.

It made no difference that Balbas was headed *away* from Crame, announcing to anyone who would listen that he was in retreat. No, the human barricade had perfected the art of stopping Loyalist troops, and they were not about to miss another opportunity. The Marines were the most awesomely equipped soldiers of the entire revolt, literally stooped beneath the weight of their machine guns, mortars, and bandoliers of M-60 bullets. They were Evil incarnate, the very *image* of Marcosian power. And they must be stopped at any cost. Dozens of young men in Cory T-shirts and cut-off jeans threw themselves onto the street before Balbas's lead jeep. When he eased to a halt, thousands swarmed around him and his men, pleading with them, even trying to bribe them, not to attack.

"Here, take my watch. Take it!" a Filipino commanded a soldier in the back of one truck. "Take anything we have. Just, please, don't attack." The embarrassed Marine alternated between grins and grimaces as dozens picked up the chant: "Take it! Take it! Take it!" No soldier accepted the offer. Newspaper photographers were everywhere, their motor-drives going "kachunka-kachunka" as they snapped countless dramatic shots of unarmed citizens "halting" the ferocious Loyalists in their tracks. Even the foreign press eventually got wind of the event and descended on the beleaguered Balbas. They peppered him with questions, and got only his battle-commander's glare for an answer. At the time, none of us had the faintest idea what a pivotal role the colonel and his men – and their unused guns – had just played. But we wrote about him anyway:

"Their vehicles were pointed in the wrong direction and they were well and truly stuck in the crowd," noted British journalist James Fenton, in his book *The Snap Revolution*. "I went up to the officer in the first jeep and asked him what was happening. He was rather tight-lipped. All they wanted to do, he said, was get back to their base at Fort Bonifacio. But the people wouldn't let them. As he said this, the soldiers in the back seat were making Laban signs at me. The crowd had given them bags of bread rolls.

"The officer seemed to think the people were being thoroughly unreasonable. . . ."

Balbas sat in that jeep for more than three hours as it crawled back to Bonifacio through the jeering throng. He spent the entire time giving the same answer to the same question: "We are going back. We are retreating. Please let us pass." The man who was in fact the revolution's anonymous hero appeared in Tuesday's newspapers as one of its laughing-stocks: the impotent Loyalist commander who had pleaded with the crowd to let him go home.

When he finally reached base on Monday night, Colonel Balbas was immediately stripped of his command and assigned to a support unit, amid rumors of his imminent arrest. His superiors, however, had more important things to deal with for the moment.

It was about this time – early Monday afternoon – that a middle-aged Filipino couple were seen edging their way through the crowd at EDSA with two large wicker baskets. The man seemed like a mechanic or repairman of some sort, with large, gnarled hands and a grease-streaked pair of jeans. He kept pushing the square basket ahead of him through a mass of vigilantes, then waiting impatiently for his wife to catch up. They finally reached a small clearing, a traffic island not far from the famous EDSA-Ortigas intersection, and set down the boxes. What happened next was a small, touching ceremony, performed without fanfare. The couple just yanked open the doors of the baskets, and a flock of fifteen to twenty doves struggled into the air above them.

It is tempting to describe them as "snow-white doves" and to tell how the sun glistened off their backs. Actually, the birds were a dirty seagull white, and they emerged under a cloud patch. Their flight went unnoticed at first, but people soon began poking each other and pointing skyward. Everyone got the symbolism immediately, nodding their heads, clapping their hands. A few even embraced the pair with the now-empty wicker baskets. Inevitably, a nun in a blue habit delicately sank to her knees, and a prayer circle formed from nowhere.

The strange new emptiness in the sky above the doves was equally symbolic. The two F-5s had vanished; even their smoke trails towards the northwest had now evaporated. The masses on the ground never *did* find out which side they were on. In truth, even the fighter pilots themselves did not know the whole story until they landed at Clark Air Base in nearby Pampanga. They were outraged, absolutely livid, when they found out.

"The true story has never come out because . . . well, we're a bit embarrassed about it," explains Colonel Tito Legaspi, the RAM insider who helped neutralize the 5th Fighter Wing. "We had a classmate in one of the planes [Major Francisco Baula], and he had made a commitment that they wouldn't shoot. They didn't agree actually to join us, but they pledged to stay neutral, not to fire their guns for either side. When [General] Ver ordered them into the air over Crame, they went. That's why Ver figured he had their loyalty. We knew all the time that they wouldn't shoot, and when Colonel Sotelo defected with the helicopters, he checked again with them on the radio and got the same commitment."

By mid-afternoon on Monday, there was no longer any pose of

neutrality. With the rebels in command of the air, the two F-5s made brief "persuasion" runs over Loyalist headquarters before landing at the U.S. air base. The complication arose when RAM "bought a little insurance", just to make sure that the lethal fighters could not be persuaded to erase Camp Crame from the map of Manila.

"We had a backup plan," smiles Legaspi. "We got the technicians at their base to foul up the electrical circuits on the F-5s, to screw up the firing mechanisms so they would essentially be helpless. They didn't know it, but they couldn't shoot at anyone that day. Afterwards, we had some trouble. The pilots were saying, 'What's the matter, couldn't you trust us?'· Major Baula was really peeved because we sent him over Malacañang and Fort Bonifacio on a couple of 'persuasion passes'. The air space over both of them is absolutely restricted, so there could have been firing. And there were the F-5s, thinking they could easily defend themselves . . . when they actually had nothing at all.

"We had to patch it all up later. There were some hard feelings."

General Ver was among the last to know about the F-5 defection. He was on the phone to air force chief General Vicente Piccio by 1:30 p.m., ordering yet another air attack on Camp Crame and asking what the hell had happened to the Huey air-drop of the commandos. All he got in response was a litany of disastrous news. The Hueys, the last Loyalist gunships, had been disabled at Villamor; the T-28s from Colonel Sotelo's base at Sangley had jumped to Clark, and were sitting there without fuel; as for the F-5s, well, the goddam F-5s "have started menacing *us*, sir," reported Piccio. "Let's hope they don't attack, because I do not have any pilots or planes to send against them."

At this point, the truth dawned on Ver, as his next action demonstrated. He called in air force colonel Romeo Ochoco from the operations centre in Malacañang Park for an important mission: Ochoco was to evacuate Mrs. Edna Camcam and her children from the Philippines. Manila gossip had long held that Mrs. Camcam was Ver's mistress, but it was not until a few weeks later, when Cory Aquino's government began its "hidden wealth" probe, that Filipinos would learn the full extent of the General's devotion. He had provided his female friend with a $10-million Manhattan apartment, allegedly paid for with U.S. tax dollars diverted from the military's bottomless "intelligence fund".

Ver was playing safe with his "hidden assets", but he had not given up the fight. The 42nd Infantry battalion had just arrived from Quezon province, apparently loyal and willing to obey orders. In a tense planning session at Fort Bonifacio, Ver suggested that the 42nd and a detachment of Marines could still cut through suburban Greenhills and reach the rebel camp's Santolan gate. Army commander Josephus Ramas, sick of launching the same attack on the same objective, opposed the idea. Generals Tadiar and Brawner were on the verge of rebellion, perhaps outright defection. But Ver repeated the sacred mantra that had elevated him to chief of staff ("This is the President's order. I am doing the will of Mr. *Marcos!*") and the high command yielded. They would send a team of their most disciplined and well-trained soldiers on a test run. If that worked, a full-scale assault on Camp Crame would follow the same route.

Why should this plan succeed when others had fizzled? There was no reason, really, except the Loyalists were now more desperate . . . and sneakier. This time they would ride through People Power while flashing broad smiles, making the L-shaped Laban sign and waving M-16s with yellow ribbons tied to their barrels.

At first the 120 soldiers in a procession of armored vehicles found that the tactic did indeed sow confusion among civilians. Bewildered students in front of Polymedic Hospital just stared suspiciously at the waving soldiers as their jeeps rolled towards Crame. But the kids had not spent three days at the barricades without learning something. "Hey!" someone shouted, "they're not wearing armbands! They don't have the flag patch!" Right. Rebels sported the Philippine flag on their sleeve as more than a badge of patriotic honor. It was a carefully planned countersign, rotated 90 degrees clockwise every morning to separate the good guys from the bad. These Marcos soldiers had removed their own countersign, the white armband, but had not bothered to counterfeit the rebellion's signature. "Hindi kakampi yan!" people shouted. "They are not ours! Man the barricades!"

Young men raced into the EDSA intersection with their palms up, like traffic cops flagging down motorists. In this case, the wayward vehicles happened to be army trucks studded with machine guns, assault rifles, and fixed bayonets. That did not seem to bother the students, most of whom had driven in the day before from a university in Los Banos, two hours to the south. They had no weapons or shields, just banners and signs. So they waved their slogans, held out their hands, and hoped for the best.

No one will ever know whether flags and shouts alone would have stopped this particular Loyalist test run, carried out by crack troops. Rather than test their unwillingness to shed blood, someone had the much better idea of commandeering a truckload of natural gas and pushing it into the intersection, bouncing it over a traffic island to beat the soldiers to the crossroads. The students climbed atop the pile of cooking-gas canisters and met the oncoming troops eyeball to eyeball. One shot, even a spark, would have turned the whole block into a fire storm, and the soldiers knew it.

One of the armored carriers tried to go around the obstacle and got stuck near a fence, engine roaring, wheels spinning. The delay was enough to bring in civilian reinforcements: a dozen middle-aged ladies raising their arms to the sky and praying "Lord, help us. Virgin Mary, help us."

"The people stood their ground," wrote L. B. Flores, one of those on the gas truck, who that day earned the right to a little grandiloquence. "Men and women admonished the armored carriers to retreat. At first, the drivers refused to budge. Non-verbal communication at that instant revealed the following in slow motion: The people pressed their bodies against the armor. Their faces were pleading but they were clothed in nothing but raw courage. In that decisive and tense moment, the soldiers atop the armored carriers pointed their guns of every make at the crowd, but their faces betrayed agony. And I knew then, as the crowd too must have discerned: the soldiers did not have the heart to pull the trigger. . . . The pact had been sealed. There was a tacit agreement: 'We keep this street corner, you retreat.' And sure enough, the armored carriers rolled back and applause echoed.

"The face of that soldier struggling in agony over the decision to shoot or not, on the verge of tears, will forever remain in my memory."

The advance team retreated and reported back to headquarters. Passage to Camp Crame, they told the high command, would be impossible without massive civilian casualties. Generals Josephus Ramas and Cirilo Oropesa passed word to the Palace: the attack was not feasible.

General Ver's options had dwindled down to the point where he was willing to try anything. He rounded up half a dozen pilots and put them in an air-conditioned office near his headquarters, then began hunting for airplanes. None materialized. Even some C-130 Hercules transports that were supposed to be ferrying Loyalist troops from the south had disappeared. Reports on their whereabouts were highly pessimistic. At the very least, their pilots had abandoned the President; at worst, they had gone over to the rebels.

Marcos and Ver still had their personal fleet of four Sikorskys at the Palace, but those could not be risked in an attack; they were the President's escape route, his lifeline to the outside world. About 4 p.m. Monday afternoon, General Ver got word that the Sikorsky pilots, the President's *personal* pilots, were missing. It was assumed that they had fled the Palace compound. When Ver went looking for the spare pilots he had assembled earlier, they too had evaporated. It was not until later that Monday night, after dinner, that the chief of staff had the heart to break this news to President Marcos.

Meanwhile, General Artemio Tadiar – "Tadjak" Tadiar, the Marine hardhead – secretly gathered his unit commanders and staff officers for a conference. The Marines had now done Marcos's bidding for forty-eight hours, with nothing to show for it but a humiliating series of misfires. "I, for one, am growing weary of pointing guns at civilians and nuns," Tadiar announced. He was tired of making empty threats and then retreating in frustration. It must be one way or the other. Either they were willing to shoot, or they were not. If not, let's be soldiers about it. Let's say so openly.

Tadiar sat in silence, waiting for some response. His top staff had developed a consuming fascination with their fingernails and the table top. No one looked up. No one said a word. "Do I have a consensus here?" the General asked. He did indeed: The Marines would no longer take part in any operations against unarmed civilians. Henceforth, they would play a purely defensive role. They would defend the President, the Palace, the Republic itself. They would under no circumstances point any more Armalites at Sisters of Mercy, housewives, and small girls bearing peace offerings.

At the same time, the Philippine Military Academy – a combination of Sandhurst and West Point, the intellectual breeding ground for Colonels Honasan, Kapunan, Legaspi, et al. – announced its own preference for the rebels. "We finally decided to choose sides," recalls intelligence officer Colonel Greg Cagurangan. "We called all the PMA officers and cadet representatives, but even before that the cadets had already polled the whole corps: 91 per cent for Ramos and Enrile; 8 per cent for Ver. It was a choice between Ver and Ramos. Marcos and Aquino were only incidental. The bottom line was who would lead the armed forces."

In terms of military strategy, there was no doubt which side had made all the errors. Throughout the revolt, even with the odds lopsided in their favor, Marcos and Ver had been too conservative. General Ver had overestimated the rebels from the outset, hesitating over the slightest move, never daring to expose his flanks, when an all-out attack of combined forces would have wiped out the Enrile-Ramos forces. Ver had chosen to make a series of tentative forays against his enemy, husbanding the main body in defence of the Palace, as if terrified of an impending attack. Now, however, the Marcosian paranoia was no longer paranoia: the threat was real. The air force had flown en masse to the other side. Navy guns were poised in Manila Bay, pointed in the direction of Malacañang. The Marines would not fight. Trusted personal pilots were melting into the city, whose streets were loud with the sound of mass rebellion.

"And now," says RAM intelligence boss Colonel Red Kapunan, "Malacañang became an absolute fortress. They had been letting us off the hook for two days by being so defensive. But after that helicopter attack in the morning . . . it was just amazing. They brought *everybody* back to the Palace. That's why they were so concerned about getting Balbas to return. If he wouldn't attack, they wanted all that armor to defend themselves. They sent out a few probes on Monday afternoon, but that's all. After that, it was as if they were preparing for a siege. We could hardly believe the intelligence reports. Every time we checked on a unit, the news came back that they'd gone to Malacañang. The place is gigantic, but it could hardly hold everyone. Tactically, it was all wrong, totally absurd. They just gave away the offensive. They handed it to us on a platter. Ver and his people had no idea how to run a battle."

As the Loyalist forces withdrew into the Palace grounds, it was like a noose closing around the presidential neck. Inevitably its knot tightened at Mendiola Bridge.

Mendiola is a small, unimpressive link between the Palace and the neighboring university belt, nothing more than a glorified ramp over a branch of the Pasig River. But it is Manila's symbolic barrier between the rulers and the ruled. Students from four nearby colleges had mounted heroic, often bloody, charges over that bridge when martial law was imposed in 1972. They were repeatedly driven back by tear gas, truncheons, water cannons, rubber bullets . . . and lead ones, too. When you talk politics with a thirtyish Filipino university grad, the word "Mendiola" arrives with the second round of cold San Miguel. It is the Filipino Kent State: more a rallying cry than an actual place.

The Palace defenders had blocked the far side of Mendiola with five-foot-high "iron horse" barriers, long steel triangles wrapped in strands of shiny barbed wire. Soldiers pulled on their riot helmets and flak jackets, set transparent Plexiglas shields in neat rows beside them, and gazed over the wire from behind M-16s. For the first two days, a small crowd of civilians had merely stared back. Now the human wall was growing – both in size and in audacity. Street toughs and macho young college students started to challenge each other to get closer and closer. Teenagers would creep right up to the barriers on their hands and knees, almost daring the troops to shoot. When they held their fire, the kids would lie on their backs, flash broad grins to their more timid companions . . . and begin to *unravel* the barbed wire.

Crack! Thunk-thunk-thunk-thunk! One defender fired a pistol in the air, another opened up with his Armalite. The kids ran in apparent terror . . . but only across the street. There, safe for the moment among Jollibee hamburger joints and decrepit hardware stores, they punched each other in the shoulder and began goading up for a repeat performance. The heroes of the moment sat on the curb, carefully forming the stolen barbed wire into an L-sign or a crown of thorns. To *wear* that crown, with its religious and sacrilegious overtones, its anti-Marcos defiance, its advertisement of sheer guts, was the ultimate in revolutionary street chic. Every ten or fifteen minutes, someone would summon the courage to crab-crawl back across J. P. Laurel Street, and the cycle started all over again.

The drama at Mendiola went virtually unnoticed until the "People's Channel 4" snapped on the air like a ghostly apparition, a bizarre rebel parody of the Ronny and Rita station. It started when someone at the studio hastily drew a dove-of-peace logo on a piece of foolscap and shoved it in front of the camera. The image hung there at 1:30 p.m., completely unannounced, until a pair of radio announcers and a priest stared out from the screen. They were seated along a "public affairs panel" set, looking apprehensive and excited. Orly Punzalan, who had hurried over from Radio Veritas, hesitated a moment before speaking the first words on the "free" national network: "Channel 4 is back on the air," he said, "to serve the people. . . . This is now the place where you get the truth. This is where you'll get correct information."

The scene at the media centre studio was utter chaos. Virtually no one was behind the cameras and hundreds were battling to get in front of them. Maharlika's technicians had fled in terror when the rebels arrived, hiding among the rabbit warren of upstairs offices, or simply running for their lives. As a result, there had been radio appeals for anyone who could handle a control panel or a video camera to please come to the studio. Instead, the station was besieged by Manila's army of semi-celebrities, lugging their guitars and make-up kits. Third-rate nightclub singers, "variety show" hosts, the socialite wives of millionaires . . . everybody wanted to show off their Cory T-shirt and flash Laban signs on People's Television.

It was the wildest television station imaginable. One camera was simply anchored in place, its unwavering gaze pointed at the same spot for a day. The other video eye kept wandering aimlessly around the studio, regardless of who was talking. Colonel Santiago showed up in a yellow headband to beat his chest and take full credit for Channel 4's capture – while the real soldiers of Strike Force Delta seethed in silence. General Ermita came over from Ramos-Enrile headquarters with an update on the strategic situation, but was only half finished when the camera looped the loop and ended up pointing at a folk singer. An inane comedy trio (Tito, Vic, and Joey; every bit as bad as they sound) got on the air for a while, before somebody realized that they had been front-line campaigners for Marcos.

Almost in spite of itself, however, Channel 4 also provided a remarkable window on the revolt. The uprising had involved the middle class to such an extent that every well-heeled Filipino with a home video camera had rushed into the streets, their lenses trained on the action. Meanwhile, because the new TV station could not find so much as a Cory Aquino photograph in Maharlika's Marcosian library, Channel 4 was ravenous for raw footage, first-hand accounts, anything that might show what was going on outside. So it was not long before the unedited home movies began jiggling uncertainly across the TV screen.

McLuhanites might have predicted the stunning effect of such footage, but it took the rest of us completely by surprise. The juxtaposition of mundane and dramatic images was strangely hypnotic, almost addictive. Personally, I was bashing out a news story at the Midtown Hotel, desperately trying to be everywhere at once, when the first home-made videos flickered onto the screen. After a quick glance, I could not take my eyes off a dream-like sequence in which a ten-year-old girl floated up to an armored personnel carrier with flowers . . . causing painful miracles to unfold in the face of the Marine who accepted them. It was all shot in slow motion, as if happening underwater, and was unforgettable. The embarrassed amateur cameraman narrated the scene himself, apologizing profusely for the slo-mo "mistake". He had only bought the camera a few days ago and had accidentally pushed the wrong button.

The best was yet to come. Someone had crawled up beside the daredevils at Mendiola with a telephoto lens, and had lovingly captured the kids unravelling barbed wire. Then there were gunshots, people running everywhere. A teenager was clipped by a bullet and went down. Blood splattered the sidewalk. Heroes dived on top of the victim, dragged him across the jagged cobblestones to safety. Wow! Even the studio hosts were breathless at the sequence. They played it over and over and over.

I took one look and made straight for Mendiola Bridge. Thousands of others obviously had the same reaction; by late afternoon we were gathered across from the barriers behind a knot of Manila policemen, ducking away from the sporadic "thunk-thunk-thunk" of M-16s on the other side. The presence of the police seemed ominous, since the city's cops are a notoriously corrupt and thuggish bunch, more concerned with supplementing their meagre incomes than with enforcing the law. But they were on their best behavior that Monday afternoon: courteous, careful, totally neutral in the street battle, sucking in their paunches and staying out of trouble.

"We are just here to maintain law and order," a police colonel named Reyes told me, when asked which side he favored. "We are just hoping for a peaceful transition. The rebel supporters taunted the soldiers, and then there was about fifteen minutes of firing. The people were forced back across the bridge and some were trampled. They got caught between the barricades." The Palace defenders had apparently retreated to a second line of defense, but charged the bold demonstrators who tried to follow them across Mendiola.

To underline his own neutrality, the police colonel had abandoned his uniform for a pair of blue jeans and a long-sleeved red-and-white-checked shirt. He leaned against a taxicab about a hundred yards from the barriers and remained there for an hour, arms folded above a generous gut.

"You don't look much like a cop," I told him.

"I've got a gun, but not a gun belt," he smiled, and patted a lump behind his left hip.

"Where is your loyalty now?"

"I'm loyal to the commander. Police commander, I mean."

"What about Marcos?"

"I don't know where Marcos is. . . ." Then a shrug, and a self-contradiction: "I think everyone knows where he is."

Over at Camp Crame the people had formed a crowd, a mass action, a sit-in, a human barricade. But the Mendiola gang was a mob. Nobody who watched them tearing at the barricades or spitting insults at the soldiers would talk of a middle-class revolt. The students were vastly outnumbered by the *"halang ang bituka"* ("guys with criss-crossed guts") from the streets. "You don't want to fight with such people," a Metrocom sergeant named Perez lectured me. "They don't care if they live or die. They'll fight with knives against guns. Tough guys. We've got a lot of them in the Philippines. Get them alone and maybe you can kill them.

You dump their bodies in the river and nobody will care. But all in a group like this . . . ? Better to stay away. They don't care about the revolution. This is just an excuse for them to make trouble. That is their fun."

Perhaps. But among the mob were members of the University of the Philippines Vanguard Society, an ancient and elite military fraternity in which Ferdinand Marcos himself claimed membership. "We're here to wash the dirt off the face of the Vanguard Society," said a young man who identified himself as the brotherhood's corps commander. "Marcos and Ver are goons and criminals. We never, ever, want to see them here again." Around him, a dozen dirt-smeared faces nodded in solemn agreement.

I7 "TIME TO CUT – AND CUT CLEAN"

AT DUSK, COLONEL SOTELO took his rebel Sikorskys into the purple sky above Camp Crame and flew directly into the sunset. He figured that it would not be safe to stay overnight on the ground, since Loyalists could sneak in with the appropriate flag patches on their arms and blow up the whole fleet. It was better to get them over to Clark Air Base, where U.S. soldiers man the gates. That would be a headache for the Yanks, but *they* could worry about that.

Indeed, the flight opened a huge can of diplomatic worms in Washington. Clark is the biggest and most sophisticated U.S. air base outside North America, a sprawling mid-sized city of bowling alleys, ballfields, the Merv Griffin show, and Kellogg's Special K. Its ultra-Americanism, in fact, had rubbed local pride the wrong way for decades, before a series of cosmetic changes were finally instituted. Drunken airmen who insisted on busting up girlie bars could no longer escape justice by hiding on the base. The Philippine flag now fluttered *above* the Stars and Stripes at the gate. And a Filipino "commander" had even been placed in nominal charge.

That seemed strictly pro forma at the time, but it had suddenly become an American nightmare. For the Filipino base commander, Colonel Romeo David, had that Monday afternoon announced his formal defection to the Reformists, thereby making Clark a rebel base. The Pentagon's carefully crafted pose of neutrality was being torn apart at the middle seam.

"It is a tricky situation, very technical," explains U.S. Embassy spokesman Allan Croghan. "And I don't know that anybody has an absolute handle on it. Our bases are not Philippine bases in the sense that their units aren't based there. It is a Philippine base on which U.S. military units are housed. If the Filipino commander gives an order to refuel the rebel planes, for instance . . . Well, it's American gasoline, from American tanks, with American locks on it, and Americans doing the pumping. It's *very* technical. Who do you obey? If we *do* pump the gas, does that make us partisan? Or are we just obeying legal orders? Obviously, the situation was never foreseen."

Colonel Sotelo was plagued by no such uncertainty. He spat out a colorful set of Tagalog profanities when he landed at Clark and found his T-28 fighters still on the runway with empty tanks. They had been refused fuel for nearly twelve hours, since shortly after the dawn helicopter defection. "I want them gassed up *now*," said the colonel. "And I want fuel for my choppers, too. We're going right back out of here in the morning." The rebels had just seized control of the air, and now the Americans were about to ground the entire attack wing. What was *that*, if not interference? What was *that* but taking sides?

Clark's U.S. officers responded to this dilemma in the time-honored manner: they dumped the whole thing in Washington's lap, then shrugged amiably every time Colonel Sotelo demanded an answer. "That happened often during the night," says Sotelo, now a general and still fuming over the incident. "We kept demanding, and they kept referring us to Washington. The night was slipping away, and there we sat . . . like beggars in our own country." Juan Ponce Enrile was on the phone to both the base and Ambassador Bosworth, offering to pay for the fuel with his own personal check. But he, too, was referred to Washington.

Finally, just before 4 a.m., the Pentagon's bureaucrats handed down their decisive ruling: Yes . . . and no. The helicopters could have fuel, but the T-28 fighter-bombers must stay where they were.

"It was the ultimate in fence-sitting," says Sotelo. "I suspect that, if there had to be any fighting, they didn't want us to escalate it. The helicopters could strike at local targets only. Also . . . I don't know if I should say this, but the Americans told me they were giving fuel to the Sikorskys only under the guise that they be used as rescue aircraft. Not for combat. Well . . . uh, what can I say? They were gunships. We had machine guns, rockets, everything, fully loaded. The whole thing was obviously a fiction."

In the Philippine imagination, Ferdinand Marcos is a cat with nine lives – too cunning and too damn bloody-minded to die. So there was no surprise on Monday night at his wraith-like reappearance on television. Filipinos did not curse or shake defiant fists. They just gathered around TV sets in stolid resignation, straining to catch every word, sifting each gesture for a clue. Marcos was a dangerous animal at the best of times; a wounded and cornered Marcos was the most lethal creature his countrymen could possibly imagine.

By chance, my wife and I watched the show in a wretched noodle-and-rice joint on Santa Monica street. The place was about twelve yards square, with dirty grey Arborite tables, a pitted cement floor, and cockroaches the size of my ring finger. There was no front wall, and the TV set blared out onto the street. So when Marcos's voice suddenly boomed at us passers-by, we turned like automatons to its source.

The transmission was a complete mess. The Palace had hooked up with the crony TV channel 9 – apparently over the telephone – and the emergency hook-up produced a series of bizarre technical glitches that would have appealed to Monty Python fans. It began with a blank screen and the President's disembodied voice: "Is this being broadcast on TV, or radio only?" "Uh . . . Mr. President, you are on TV and radio," replied a deep, announcerish voice. The invisible Marcos was not convinced: "But I can't *hear* myself any more."

Video eventually cut in, revealing the gaunt Marcos sitting all alone in a casual blue windbreaker. "Forgive me the informal dress," he apologized. "We are all dressed . . . uh . . . prepared for any contingency, whether in daytime or at night." Gone were the generals and the government officials who normally surround him during national broadcasts. The camera panned awkwardly, showing only his family huddled on stiff, high-backed chairs against a wall to his right. Grandson Borgy was once again in perpetual motion, with son Bongbong chasing him in his fatigues. Imelda Marcos sat rigid and pale as a Tussaud's wax model, hands folded on her lap, lips pressed into a thin line.

Marcos displayed a copy of Monday's *Daily Express* and said: "I am holding it up to show you that I am here today. . . . So . . . uh . . . if there are Loyalists losing morale because they cannot see their President . . . well, here I am."

The broadcast used a press conference format again, but this time without any participation from the press. An announcer, a Loyalist general, and a police reporter from a crony newspaper served as the panel, though they were seldom visible. At one point, Marcos snapped off the air again, to return a few seconds later. Then he was drowned out by a telephone conversation in Tagalog which rose to a crescendo before slowly fading away. Crossed phone lines are the norm in Manila, but nobody in the noodle shop could imagine it happening to the President. They chuckled and hooted until people at the back shushed them into silence.

"We are not going to abandon the office of the presidency," Marcos pledged. "We are going to keep Malacañang. We are not going to give up Malacañang, nor the city, nor the country. . . . We are not going abroad. I have no intention of resigning. We will defend the republic to the last breath of our life, the last drop of our blood."

The panel's next question was lost in the buzzing transmission, but the President's response was crystal clear: "My family is here cowering in terror inside Malacañang Palace because of the threats of bombing by helicopter. . . . I am quite ready to go into combat if necessary. I am fit and strong." That caused a momentary hush in the noodle shop as patrons began to grasp the enormity of just *who* was quaking. A small man in a faded blue T-shirt muttered in Tagalog under his breath. He noticed me scratching in my notebook, straining to understand, and was glad to translate: "I said it was about time the son-of-a-whore started cowering." The man made sure I got it all down correctly, then turned with great dignity to watch the broadcast again.

The kidney ailments, two sleepless nights, and sheer desperation had taken a terrible toll on Marcos. He was raving now, blinking into the TV lights and pleading for support from the "little people" he seemed to imagine would flock to him. It was partly pathetic, but mostly terrifying. This man had held life-and-death power over fifty-five million Filipinos – roughly the population of the United Kingdom – for two decades, with no qualms about using it. He was capable of anything, and his talk now was all of raging fires and gunfights. "By all means," he shouted, "come over and we'll have a grand fire. . . . I am calling all my good friends to come to Malacañang. And we will demonstrate People's Power – especially if they bring their arms with them!"

Marcos was preparing to end the press conference when one of the panel obviously recalled his pre-scripted instructions. "Mr. President," he asked, "have you considered imposing a curfew?" There was a marvellous five-second pause while the wheels spun inside the presidential brain and every calculation was etched on his face. "Uh . . . now that you come to mention it," he replied, spreading his hands in magisterial admonition, "I hereby order a curfew from . . . uh . . . 6 p.m. to 6 a.m." What about night workers? "Well, uh, they will be fine . . . as long as they can explain themselves."

Never has an order been more blithely ignored. It was already past 7 p.m., but that was a moot point. The afterthought clampdown was the last of many hundred Marcosian decrees to descend on Filipinos over the years, and it was by far the least effective. An estimated one million people were in the streets surrounding Camp Crame, where the news was greeted with hoots of derision. Thousands more guarded Channel 4 or cruised through the streets with guns, daring anyone to enforce the curfew order. Nobody, least of all the city police, paid the slightest attention.

It is unlikely the President ever knew what became of his decrees. By this time he was confined to a few windowless rooms inside the Palace, entirely dependent on others for news of the outside world.

Supreme Court Justice Ramon Aquino (no relation to Cory) was scheduled to administer the oath of office at Tuesday's inauguration of President Marcos. Since the ceremony now seemed likely to be controversial, the good judge was fetched by Palace security on Monday night. Rumors of a rebel kidnap attempt were rife, so Judge Aquino and his son Manny were ordered to spend the night inside Malacañang. But even such honored guests could not enter through the barricaded gates. The Aquinos were taken to the military camp across the river, and then ferried in by boat. From inside, the Palace looked like a medieval castle under siege. Guns and soldiers were everywhere, with officers of the Presidential Security Command sleeping in every corridor. The President and the First Lady were supposed to join the Aquinos for dinner, but they did not appear. No explanation was offered. Instead, the Aquinos dined with Irene and Imee Marcos and their husbands, then sat at the table sipping wine until about 11 p.m. The girls tried to sound cheery, optimistic, and normal. Imee chattered about a series of pop concerts she was organizing, and Irene spoke of going out later to dance at a nightclub with friends. Only the two sons-in-law (Tommy Manotoc and Greggy Araneta) appeared worried about the situation.

Bongbong Marcos joined the dinner party for coffee, and seemed particularly pleased with himself. "Feel na feel ko ang get-up ko ngayon," he told the Aquinos, in a mixture of Tagalog and English that meant: "I really feel great now in this outfit." He would still be wearing it when the U.S. choppers came in to evacuate his family – a half-step ahead of the Mendiola mob.

The Washington "crisis management" team benefited throughout the revolt from the intercepted messages provided by their intelligence wizards. But by Monday night they needed no special intelligence to show them what was happening. With the Sikorsky attack helicopters on the rebel side, with navy guns trained on Manila, with the Marines now neutral and fearless crowds still ruling the streets, the eventual winner was obvious. Cory Aquino, still in hiding at her sister's place in Mandaluyong, had announced that she too would be inaugurated president the following day. The choice now was between a graceful Marcos exit and a savage civil war.

Washington used both push and pull to extract Marcos from the Palace. The stick was a grave formal message that "attempts to prolong the life of the present regime by violence are futile. A solution to this crisis can only be achieved through a peaceful transition to a new government." The carrot was a private message that Marcos, his family, and his entourage of cronies were all welcome to take asylum in the United States.

But that invitation must have seemed like a nightmare to Marcos. The Philippine president had taken inordinate interest in the 1979 downfall of Iran's Shah Reza Pahlavi, peppering his Tehran ambassador with daily questions and ordering him to extend the Shah "all possible assistance". And Marcos had obviously drawn deep lessons from the Iranian leader's fate. "I will never resign, never quit, never step down," the President told a close friend in 1984. "I don't want to end up like the Shah of Iran. They would hunt me and my family down like dogs."

Around midnight on Monday, Marcos summoned his family to his bedroom and they were present, arranged in armchairs at the foot of his bed, as he talked all night with them – and pushed at the buttons on his bank of half a dozen telephones. The calls were not encouraging. Just before 1 a.m., his labor minister, Blas Ople (the emissary sent to convince Washington that Marcos had won the election), called the Palace with the first batch of bad news. U.S. Secretary of State George Shultz believed that the Philippine president had lost both the election *and* the battle with Enrile and Ramos; only a Marcos resignation could avoid civil war.

His daughters Irene and Imee pleaded with their father in the small hours of Tuesday morning to consider the U.S. asylum offer. They were still at the foot of his bed, apparently in tears, when the President placed a 3 a.m. call to his old friend Senator Paul Laxalt.

Marcos was placed on hold for a few minutes as the Senator's office tracked him to a Capitol briefing session with Shultz and Habib. It was 2 p.m. in Washington, and Laxalt was astonished to learn that Marcos was on the line. "Have you been up all night?" he asked. The President, described by Laxalt as sounding "frightened and pugnacious", conceded that he had been. He told the Senator that his whole family, including his grandchildren, were "holed up" in the Palace. Marcos wanted assurance that he would not be punished if he accepted the asylum offer, and Laxalt told him "that would not be a problem." Strangely, Marcos seemed terrified by reports that U.S. Marines would join the rebels and steam up the Pasig River to capture Malacañang. Laxalt checked with both President

Reagan and Defense Secretary Weinberger and told him what Bosworth already had told him: that the reports were a fiction. (Both Marcos and General Ver repeated the accusation throughout their last day in the Philippines, and still insist, even in Hawaiian exile, that such threats were made.)

The Philippine president talked tough during the half-hour phone call. Despite the defections, he claimed to have the support of eighty-five per cent of the military, and said he was prepared to "fight it out". He also wanted to check whether the "peaceful transition" demand had come from President Reagan himself, and if it precluded a power-sharing arrangement. Laxalt knew that the message was valid, but he could not interpret the details. He begged Marcos to do nothing rash until he could check with Reagan and call back.

Laxalt and Shultz raced to the Oval Office for an immediate meeting with the President. The issues were clear-cut and the discussion was brief. It would be "impractical and undignified", Reagan decided, for Marcos to share power with Cory Aquino.

At 5 a.m. Manila time, the Senator called Marcos from a desk in the office of Admiral Poindexter, the National Security Advisor. He relayed the bad news about power-sharing, and Marcos paused to consider the implications.

"Does President Reagan want me to resign?" he asked.

That was a diplomatic hot potato for Laxalt, who explained that the United States could not officially ask the leader of a sovereign country to step down. In any case, the Senator could not speak for Reagan on such a delicate matter.

"What about you, Senator? What do you think I should do?"

Laxalt felt a "rush of sympathy" for his Filipino friend, but had an even greater fear of bloody civil war. He was no longer bound by the constraints of diplomacy.

"Cut and cut clean," he told Marcos. "The time has come."

The pause on the trans-Pacific telephone line seemed to last forever. Laxalt sat in Poindexter's office, listening to clicks and buzzes, waiting for some response, until he wondered if they had been cut off.

"Are you still there?" he finally asked, after two minutes had elapsed.

"Yes," replied Marcos. "I'm so very, very disappointed."

He hung up the phone, without indicating what he would do.

Chief Justice Aquino and his son had gone to bed around midnight in one of the Palace's dozen guest rooms. They had breakfast with Imee Marcos the next morning, served by uniformed waiters of the five-star Via Mare restaurant. (The regular Palace household staff had by now fled in terror.) Aquino, noting that Imee seemed exhausted and had deep circles around her eyes, asked how she had slept. She admitted that none of the Marcoses had slept at all during the night. Aquino was curious, but he dared not ask for details. Imee drank her coffee, read the morning newspapers, and volunteered no more information. Aquino thought ahead to the bizarre inauguration he would conduct later that morning.

Ferdinand Marcos was now down to his last three options: (1) Work out a face-saving, perhaps even a power-sharing, agreement with the rebels; (2) Proceed with the inauguration, then flee to his "solid North" home region to regroup for a full-scale civil war. The third option, of course, was to heed Laxalt's "cut clean" advice. But Marcos was not yet ready to admit defeat.

Shortly after 9 a.m., the phone rang at Juan Ponce Enrile's temporary office in Camp Crame. It was Marcos, an aide whispered, with an important proposal to break the "deadlock". Enrile had to smile at that one. Deadlock? He and General Ramos were just about to leave for Cory Aquino's inauguration at the posh Club Filipino. Already France had sent word that it would immediately extend diplomatic recognition; Germany and Australia would likely follow suit before the end of the day. Except for a last angry shot with his artillery, Marcos could do nothing to stop the inevitable. He was out of poker chips.

But he was still bluffing. The President made an effort to sound confident and controlled on the phone. He continued to address Enrile as a subordinate, while the Defense Minister called him Mr. President. "Johnny," asked Marcos, "how can we settle this problem? We must reach some kind of modus vivendi."

Enrile: "Well, I really don't know . . ."

Marcos: "Why don't we organize some sort of provisional government? All I want, really, is just a graceful exit. I will cancel the election and organize a provisional government. Then I'll just remain as an honorary president until 1987 . . . a figurehead only. You can run the government any way you want. I only want to leave politics in a clean and orderly manner."

Enrile: "Mr. President, I don't know about that. But we are not really interested in power. That was never the intention of my group. Our mission was never to establish a military junta or any kind of military government. . . . Besides, it is too late now. We have already committed ourselves to Mrs. Aquino. Our mission was to see that the people's will is respected, whoever won the election, whether you or Mrs. Aquino. But the men believe she was the one who claimed the mandate."

Marcos: "Well, can you talk to them about it anyway? Could you talk to Mrs. Aquino also, and get her reaction?"

Enrile: "Yes, surely. I can do that."

Marcos: "Do you think it would be safe for me to leave the Philippines?"

Enrile: "Why not, sir? This is your homeland and there's no reason for any one of us, least of all on our side, to harm you. If you want, we would be willing to protect you and your family."

Marcos: "But if I go abroad, do you think I can come back here and feel safe about it?"

Enrile: "Of course. You can come and go as you wish. This is your home."

Marcos: "How about General Ver? What about his safety?"

Enrile: "Mr. President, that is something that I cannot answer. I don't really know the attitude of the young officers towards him."

Marcos: "Well, can you try to explore these issues? You can call me back later today."

Enrile: "All right, sir. I'll try."

It must have been a humiliating few minutes for Marcos, begging for safe passage from his underling of so many years. But the remarkable aspect of the conversation was its near-total insignificance. Two days earlier, any hint of the President's intentions would have been scrutinized and debated by the entire rebel high command, plus Cory Aquino, Cardinal Sin, and a half-dozen other opposition heavyweights. On Tuesday morning, Juan Ponce Enrile would meet Mrs. Aquino just thirty minutes after the phone call from Marcos – *and not even mention it to her.*

The Defense Minister and General Ramos took a helicopter to Club Filipino, where 1,000 crowded inside and 3,000 more listened to Cory's oath-taking over loudspeakers on the front lawn. Enrile had wanted the swearing-in ceremony to be held at Camp Crame, citing the immense security risk. But Mrs. Aquino had already calculated the political consequences of being too dependent upon the military, and particularly upon Enrile. The venue might be uncomfortably patrician for a "People Power" President, but at least it was in civilian-held territory.

"I am taking power in the name and by the will of the Filipino people," Cory declared. "I pledge a government dedicated to upholding truth and justice, morality and decency, freedom and democracy." The seventh president of the Philippines wore a simple yellow dress with three-quarter-length sleeves and her trademark yellow-rim glasses. Her first act was to install Enrile and Ramos as defense minister and chief of staff. (It was politely forgotten by everyone concerned that Enrile had disavowed all political ambitions at the Saturday-night press conference where he had pledged never to accept another cabinet appointment.) The new government grasped hands and led the crowd through an emotional rendition of "Bayan Ko". Enrile and the just-proclaimed "President Cory" were on the same podium throughout the festivities. . . . Yet Enrile says he "did not have a chance to talk to her about the conversation with the President. Then, when I went back to Camp Crame, I was so tired, I went to sleep." That was the inglorious end to Marcos's proposal for a provisional government.

While the minister slept, however, General Ramos had his own telephone chat with Ferdinand Marcos. The General is the President's cousin and fellow Ilocano, and he had greatly admired Marcos at the outset of his administration. "I talked with Mr. Marcos as a younger brother speaking to an older brother," recalls Ramos, whose voice still softens respectfully as he recounts their final conversation. "I spoke with him in our dialect. I called him 'Manong Andy', because *manong* means 'older brother' and Andy is his nickname there in Ilocos. I asked Minister Enrile for permission to call, since we had agreed at the outset that he would do all the talking to the Palace. Even with General Ver, it was Enrile who talked to them. But Marcos was my cousin, so it was important to me to speak to him."

"Look," Ramos told Marcos, "this is the score now, in so far as the military is concerned. Manong Andy, I don't think you can expect any more support from these people . . ." and the General reeled off a list of confirmed defections to his side. "We have eighty-five per cent of the armed forces now. All you have left, really, are your troops there in Malacañang. Even some of them have filtered over to us."

"I was very respectful," says Ramos. "I always have been. After I told him all the facts and figures, he did not sound angry. He just said: 'Well, that's neither here nor there.' It was a very strange response. I mean, we were in a military situation and these were military facts, and he insisted they didn't matter. Maybe he looked upon me as a kid brother, or just a kid, you know. It was a strange exchange between us."

Even as he spoke to Ramos, the President must have known that the first trickle of Loyalists was gathering on the Palace lawn for his inauguration. They had been preceded by about two thousand hard-core civilian Loyalists who had answered Marcos's radio call the previous night. They brought handguns and knives and were issued with wicked 2"-×-2" clubs with nails driven through one end. Out at the Mendiola Bridge, knots of supporters coming for the ceremony were sheltered by soldiers as they waited for buses to take them in to the Palace. "We are waiting to see the President. We will congratulate him," declared Telesforo Santos, a 54-year-old movie stuntman already decked out in Marcos buttons and red-white-and-blue ribbons. "Whether you believe it or not, there are many people who believe in President Marcos and who voted for him." Santos said he and about a hundred friends had come in response to the President's televised call. "Cory Aquino knows she lost the election," he taunted. "Her people are like dogs barking in the street." His friends laughed and slapped high-fives in agreement.

Beyond the soldiers, hundreds of Cory supporters chanted "Sipsip! Sipsip!" at Santos and the Loyalists. Literally, the phrase means "suck", but the figurative translation is closer to "bootlicker", or worse. The Mendiola mob was in no mood to treat Marcosians politely. Their battle at the barricades had heated up overnight, with more than a dozen people shot and one – 25-year-old Emmanuel Lazo – struck full in the chest by a volley of bullets. An estimated three thousand civilian Loyalists did manage to enter the Palace for Marcos's inauguration, but many others were turned back near Mendiola. Several Mercedes-Benzes and Toyota vans filled with the President's supporters were stoned and rocked by the crowd before they prudently retreated.

It was a strange day in Philippine political history. The country began it without a sworn-in president, and now had one in a yellow dress. Soon there would be two presidents, two chiefs of staff – but still only one First Lady. "Thank God for that," went Tuesday morning's standing joke. "At least Cory doesn't have a First Lady." Not long after nightfall, the presidential head-count would again be down to one.

The butt of the cruel jokes was at her theatrical best during her husband's oath-taking ceremony. Imelda Marcos posed on the Palace balcony in her swept-back coiffure and elegant white terno – the formal gown with the sleeves puffed up at the shoulder – alternating between tearful resignation and brave defiance. She gazed into the distance in forlorn desolation, then grasped her husband's hand and raised a regal double chin to the crowd. Her famous entourage of Blue Ladies, eating free chicken dinners on the lawn below, waved and shouted and wiped away tears.

"Martial law! Martial law!" chanted the crowd when Ferdinand and Imelda first appeared on the balcony. "Kill the snakes! Kill the snakes!"

The reptiles in question were apparently Enrile and Ramos, although no one offered simultaneous translation. The Palace promotion staff had handed out small Philippine flags, to go with freshly sodded grass and a set of bleachers built for the occasion. But the lawn had turned brown and had begun curling up at the corners, so the invitees had ingeniously shoved the wooden flagstaffs into the ground as stakes. The brown dying sod, pinned down by a forest of little red and blue flags, made an incongruous scene. Within minutes, that tableau was littered with discarded chicken bones and pale-pink Styrofoam containers.

It was so obvious that no foreign ambassadors would, or could, attend the ceremony that none had been invited. The oath-taking was witnessed only by the crowd on hand and by Channel 9's doggedly loyal television cameras. Even that last link with the outside world was teetering.

Radio Veritas reporter Henry Omaga-Diaz received a call at about 10 a.m. reporting a shoot-out at the Channel 9 tower in Broadcast City. The crony station is only about 300 yards from Channel 4's own tower, so the assault might have portended a strong Loyalist counterattack on that station. The Veritas reporter rushed to the scene.

"Loyalist soldiers were already up in the [Channel 9] tower when we got there," he recalls, "and other Loyalists – Marines, I think – stopped us from entering. The guys in the tower had sniper rifles. They were shooting, but they didn't seem to be shooting at the people. They were targeting only uniformed soldiers, the rebels down below. The crowd was all over the place, hundreds of them. They were watching as if it was some kind of circus. The Reformists were also having a hard time, because wherever they tried to go, the people always followed them. They didn't want to miss anything. Here were all these bullets flying, and people were afraid they might *miss* some of the action.

"But it was funny: When the Sikorsky helicopter gunships finally arrived and started shooting, the people suddenly disappeared. You could not see a single person anywhere, because no one knew which side they were on. Everybody was afraid it was a Loyalist gunship. It took thirty seconds for everyone to disappear."

The choppers, of course, belonged to the rebels. This skirmish between the rebels and the Loyalists protecting the tower had been going on for hours, and one of the two snipers in the tower was killed by ground fire at about 11:25 a.m. But, by the time Marcos appeared on TV for his swearing-in ceremony, the Reformists had seen enough. They wanted him off the screen right away. Two of Colonel Sotelo's deadly Sikorskys were ordered to knock out the tower immediately.

"The first guy's body was already hanging there," Omaga-Diaz recalls, "and of course there was the usual cheering when he was shot. The Sikorsky just zoomed from behind a building and opened fire . . . several machine-gun bursts. . . . I think it took two or three bursts before they hit the other sniper. He got tangled up in the wires, too, when he fell."

Chief Justice Ramon Aquino had just stepped forward to administer the oath of office at that point, while the Channel 9 commentator spoke with the whispered solemnity usually reserved for golf announcers during a crucial putt: "And now," he said, "the moment you have all been waiting for . . ."

Bzzzt! Fttt! Right on cue, the screen went blank and high-pitched static squealed from the speakers. A voice came on to announce that "technical difficulties" had halted the broadcast, and asked us to stand by. But there was nothing to wait for, and nothing remotely technical about the President's difficulties.

Marcos began his speech at 11:55 a.m, just seconds after his last media outlet had been shot dead. "No man," he told the audience, "can be more proud than I am at this moment. . . ."

Juan Ponce Enrile accepted his final call from Marcos at about 5:30 p.m. He had just been told that the President's personal pilots had abandoned him, so he was in complete control when an aide handed him the receiver and said simply, "It's Marcos." There was no longer any pretense of a lord-and-master relationship. The President was frightened. He had called for help:

Marcos: "Will you kindly tell your security to come to the vicinity of the Palace to stop these people who are firing at the Palace towards our direction?"

Enrile: "But, Mr. President, we have no people there. Our men are not there."

Marcos: "Then who are these people? Who is shooting?"

Enrile: "No one is shooting. I don't think so. Maybe there are some provocateurs trying to agitate the situation."

Marcos: "Then will you please send a detachment to investigate and stop the shooting?"

Enrile: "Certainly. I will ask General Ramos to send a contingent to look at the situation and enlist the help of the police."

"I guess there were some people who were really sniping at the Palace," Enrile told me months later. "I was talking to him . . . well, deferentially, but not any more as a man who considered himself a subordinate. Because he was actually pleading with me, asking me to send people to stop the guys who were shooting at him. And I was thinking: 'Well, why should this man be asking me this? There must be a catch to it.' I was thinking he might be trying to draw us into this area and then capture some of our people.

"In the latter portion of our conversation, I sensed that he was really somewhat agitated about the whole thing. Then, when I mentioned that Ambassador Bosworth and I had just finished our conversation about a message from Washington, that's when he indicated he would leave."

Marcos: "Johnny, would you please call back Ambassador Bosworth and ask him to make available to me the group of [U.S.] General Teddy Allen as my security escort . . . to leave the Palace?"

Enrile: "Surely. I'll call right away."

"That was when I first knew that he was planning to leave," says Enrile. "But I said to myself: 'Why should he tell me this? Why does he not tell it to Ver? Instead of using me as his channel, why not order Ver to call the Ambassador?' This is something I cannot answer even now. Why? I just don't know. Maybe he had lost confidence in the men around him. Maybe he lost confidence in Ver."

At 9:05 that night, a U.S. Air Force Sikorsky lifted off from the Palace golf course with the Philippine First Family aboard. The next time President Marcos was seen in public was the next morning; he was helped off a U.S. plane in Guam wearing a blue golf hat with the presidential seal. His departure set off an avalanche of self-congratulation in Washington, where Defense Secretary Weinberger told Americans that the Pentagon had given "aid and comfort" to the military rebels. Despite U.S. knowledge of the instructions to fire the Marine howitzers, Secretary of State Shultz maintained the façade of Marcos's statesmanlike restraint, noting that the Philippine president's departure had "come peacefully, characterized by the dignity and strength that have marked his many years of leadership."

The U.S. reactions drew a stinging horse laugh from Colonel Gringo Honasan, who had become an instant media star, besieged by the press for his comments. "The United States," said Honasan, just hours after the flight of Marcos, "wouldn't touch us with anything. . . . They wanted to be sure of the outcome. Now they want to take the credit and create their own version of what happened."

Rene Cayetano answered his phone the morning after the wild victory celebration.

"Hi," said Phil Kaplan, number two man at the U.S. Embassy. "Look, Rene, I hope you understand that we could not do anything for your friend when you came to us. There was nothing we could do at that time."

"Phil, I will never understand it."

"I just want you to know that we could appreciate the human equation. We felt your anxiety for your friend. That much we understood."

"It's too late in the day," replied Cayetano. "It's too late to say all those things now."

18 *EXIT MARCOS*

THE EMBASSY OF THE UNITED STATES OF AMERICA is a fitting abode for a former governing master: its representatives are housed in an imposing colonial-style building on a huge tract of land beside Manila Bay. Fenced off from busy Roxas Boulevard, the U.S. headquarters is ideally suited for everyone's purposes. Diplomats need only stroll two hundred yards to the legendary Manila Hotel, a five-star landmark with elegant cuisine and solid marble washrooms. Protesters assembled at nearby Rizal Park to denounce the "U.S.-Marcos dictatorship" could hurl stones and epithets at their ease, while the Marine guards at the entrance stolidly stared them down from the other side of the fence.

For journalists, the site has another advantage: it is just up the street from the Associated Press office where many of us file our stories. And on the evening of Tuesday, February 25, the fourth day of the Revolution, that proximity paid large dividends. I had just stepped from the AP office, contemplating a quick beer at the Blue Hawaii, when there came that familiar overhead "thwet-thwet-thwet" of whirring propellers. Four or five Sikorskys, with American markings, were landing on the U.S. Embassy lawn.

Marcos. It had to be Marcos. The Americans must have scooped up the Philippine president from the Palace before that lynch mob at Mendiola could get at him. I stood stock still and watched the chopper blades whirling in the moonlight beyond the Embassy fence. Maybe they were giving him sanctuary there, or just stopping on the way to Clark Air Base. No matter, the Embassy guards would not let anyone in and the official statement would be bland. Far better to witness the denouement at Malacañang. After twenty years of Ferdie and Meldie, this was going to be some party.

I sprinted the two blocks to the Midtown Hotel, and nearly bowled over a massage-parlor girl drumming up business next door.

"Ano ba yan?" she asked. ("What's up?")

"Marcos. He's gone. The Americans have taken him."

"Ha, bolero!" she sneered, using the Tagalog word for bullshit artist, and waving her hand in dismissal.

Fortunately, my credibility is higher with my wife. Vangie had pulled on her shoes and was in the elevator before I could finish the details. She was at her mother's house with our children during the EDSA showdown, and had been regretting it for two days. This time she was not going to miss the action. But for my last-second lunge through an open back door, she would have left me behind at the taxi-stand.

"Malacañang," she ordered the driver. "Let's go."

He shook his head and shrugged. "Too many soldiers there. Too much problems. I'll take you to the street outside only."

It was 8:45 p.m., but Manila had entered some kind of timeless Twilight Zone. The city is *always* crowded, with the diesel-belching traffic slowing for just a few hours before dawn. Even during the Revolution we had been fighting through jam-ups day and night as the blockades played havoc with traffic. Yet here in this old, always congested, area, there was nobody in sight. The beat-up yellow cab cruised down J. P. Laurel Street at fifty miles an hour, all three of us staring in disbelief. Where the hell was everybody?

The driver slowed to drop us at a small side street leading to the Palace. I had been there yesterday, talking to the Loyalist soldiers at the barrier. . . . But wait a second. There were no soldiers. There was no barrier either. Instead, a row of grinning housewives and street kids had lined up along the sidewalk, and were now flashing the Laban sign, peering into the cab and waving us down the street. "Go on," they yelled. "Go ahead."

The cabbie did not wait for instructions. He gunned the engine and shot past the deserted army outpost with a flourish of squealing tires. He made a joke in Tagalog and laughed with Vangie. "He says he's never been to Malacañang in his whole life," she translated. "He's not going to miss it now." The two of them giggled as if they had been sniffing solvent with the Ermita street kids all afternoon. After being barred from the area for two decades, Filipinos found the prospect of seeing Malacañang a virtual intoxicant. "This is great," my wife enthused. "For us, it's like going to the Forbidden City."

In seconds we were outside the Palace fence. But the scene was completely unexpected. There were no celebrating crowds, no yellow banners. In fact, there were fewer than two dozen people in the street, standing away from the walls and gawking around in apparent confusion. I stuck my head out the window to ask questions, and froze instantly.

"Thwet-thwet-thwet. Thwet-thwet-thwet."

Sikorskys. The same four from the Embassy, now skidding in low over the Pasig River and landing in the Palace backyard beyond the fence. "Jesus Christ, how stupid can you get?" I cursed. "They weren't on their way out with Marcos. They're coming in to get him. The son-of-a-bitch is right there."

We leapt out, fumbled for money to pay the taxi, and stood helpless in the moonlight while one of the most dramatic scenes of the decade took place a hundred yards away – and out of sight. Malacañang's walls are ten feet high and topped with a spiked railing. There is no way to see over them and, though they can be scaled, it is much easier to climb one of the gates. That was going through my mind when, fortunately, someone else had the same bright idea first. A young man grabbed at the gate and began to climb. "Crack!" A sudden report and a flash of flame leapt from behind the gate. The shot did not hit anyone, but we all scurried for cover behind a monument and its low retaining wall a few feet away. The Sikorsky engines were still roaring inside, and we tried to tell the others that they were American copters, come to get Marcos. The only response was a smile and a shrug. Our companions were neighborhood residents who had wandered over out of curiosity when the Loyalist soldiers pulled out a half-hour earlier.

Their interests, it soon became clear, were non-political. While we stood waiting for the helicopters to re-emerge, they pried open a slick new Isuzu station wagon and proceeded to tear out its stereo. A ragged middle-aged woman, virulently pro-Marcos and utterly insane, appeared from nowhere, waving a Philippine flag and raining Tagalog obscenities upon the looters. They laughed, taunted her, pushed her away, and started tearing the seats out of the Isuzu.

The Sikorskys were only at the Palace for ten minutes, which did not allow us enough time to scale the wall and watch them load up the conjugal dictators, three dozen hangers-on, and the trunks of accumulated treasure. But for all the furtive haste and secrecy of the flight, an account can be pieced together from the servants, American pilots, and Filipino military escorts in attendance. It would appear that the final moments went something like this:

Neither Malacañang's huge service staff nor the Presidential Security Command were warned of the departure until nearly the last minute. They had been told nothing since the noon inauguration. The Marcos family had spent the afternoon huddled in a reception room above Heroes

Hall, with a pile of Armalites and machine guns on a stage beneath the Presidential Seal. The Marcos daughters spent the early afternoon in tears, pleading with their father to accept the obvious and go to the United States. The girls argued that everyone, including the grandchildren, would be killed if they stayed to fight. Most of the servants and cooks obviously feared the same scenario, for they had simply stopped coming to work two days before. But a few diehards stayed on to help with the packing and other preparations. At the nearby administration building, only three or four assistants were left to feed incriminating documents through shredding machines and to flush the paper down many toilets. "Our eyes were red from crying," says one Palace servant, who asked to remain anonymous. "The kitchen was shut down and we ate all our meals from those plastic boxes that were brought in. Even the President and First Lady were eating food from outside."

In fact, the Last Supper of the Marcos dynasty was interrupted by the Sikorskys. The first gate-crashers two hours later would find the half-eaten meal lying cold on the table, laid out on an elegant silver service.

General Fabian Ver, meanwhile, spent a frantic afternoon negotiating his own departure. Virtually unknown abroad, he had little of the Marcos bargaining power and was not included in the original U.S. asylum offer. By Tuesday, however, he made enough threatening gestures to earn a 1:30 p.m. phone call from Norbert Garrett, the CIA's well-known Manila station chief. Exact details of the call have never been revealed, but, immediately after talking to Garrett, the General changed into civilian clothes and began shaking hands with a few of his top aides. Ver was now part of the departure deal.

Just after 8 p.m. there was a great commotion when bearers were summoned to lug trunks, boxes, suitcases, statues, and paintings down the main Palace staircase. Even the military escorts were pressed into service; four trips were required to drag Imelda's omnipresent jewelry trunks from her bedroom. By 8:40 a convoy of the President's plainclothes security force left in limousines, making the trip to Clark Air Base by road.

That was when the First Lady, dressed in a traditional Philippine terno, made a tearful grand exit. She appeared at the top of the dark, polished staircase, bearing the standard Marcosian kiss-off: a stack of payroll envelopes stuffed with hundred-peso banknotes. The amounts, equal to $500 U.S., were stingy by First Family standards. A few of the security men and senior staff received 10,000 pesos, but by the time

Imelda's cousin Babes Romualdez took over the task the stipend was "down to only 5,000 pesos", says the servant, in Tagalog. "But anyway Ma'am took her closest people with her. The money was just for the rest of us."

The departure came with remarkable speed. One minute Imelda was handing out cash and striking tragic poses, dabbing at the tears on her cheeks. "And then the helicopters came and everybody was running and trying to get on at the same time. The ones carrying all the boxes . . . I don't think they knew if they were supposed to get on or not. We were all very afraid, and crying. All the ones with guns had suddenly disappeared. They climbed on the helicopters or went away in the cars. We didn't know what was outside. Maybe a mob would come in and kill us. Nobody told us what to do. Nobody was left to protect us. So we all went to the chapel and prayed for our safety. Some of us were still there [two hours later] with a priest when the looters came. But the priest waved them away, and they didn't bother us. He told them all the valuables were upstairs."

The grand finale looked different from the American side, where amusement mixed with open contempt. After aides put President Marcos on the first helicopter, right near the pilot, the most powerful dictator in Asia inquired politely about their destination. "I don't know, buddy," sneered the U.S. pilot. "I'm just the driver." The passengers were given ear plugs to soften the whine of the Sikorskys. Imelda sat across from her husband with the plugs stuck in upside down, apparently to avoid ruffling her famous coiffure. The Americans report, with malicious glee, that she spent most of the trip to Clark staring into a pocket mirror and fine-tuning her makeup.

Five months later, from his Hawaiian exile, Marcos would insist that he "had decided to die in Malacañang" and was "practically carried into the helicopter". Asked by whom he was carried, the deposed President said he thought "there were some white men . . . but we will not go into that." That is not at all how the Americans remember it. True, he was helped into the plane, and the Yanks joined his own men in lifting him through the helicopter door. But that was not because he was determined to go down fighting. "He was just weak," recalls a U.S. officer. "He wasn't protesting or resisting at all. He just needed the help getting on the plane. At that point, they were all good and glad to get out of there."

They certainly did not leave empty-handed. Crates of gold bars, boxes full of pesos, Imelda's jewelry trunks, suitcases stuffed with fur coats, two boxes containing two hundred video tapes, and "loads of other stuff" were shoved onto the Sikorskys by assistants. The packing job was so crude that some of the suitcases stuffed with peso notes still had the amounts taped on the outside. As the astounded Americans watched from the choppers, four men struggled towards them with a solid gold statue of the Santo Niño. It was "at least four feet high", according to one engineer, its golden necklace centred by an enormous diamond pendant. The Niño proved clumsy to load, but it was eventually nestled in the Marcos family helicopter. The Americans were too busy to count the boxes as they were shoved aboard, but the loot was later X-rayed at the U.S. Clark Air Base and dozens of high-powered weapons were confiscated. Among the more intriguing items on the Clark manifest was a cardboard box listed as containing "pornographic magazines". A day later, twenty-two crates would be impounded at the Honolulu customs depot. Official declarations said they contained money, jewelry, and a few hundred pounds of financial records.

The family of General Ver – complete with his officer sons Irwin, Wyrlo, and Rexor, their families, and a troop of more distant relatives – occupied one entire helicopter. The toad-like Armed Forces Chief climbed aboard last, holding his brocaded general's cap in one hand and an Uzi submachine gun in the other. An American crewman noticed that the gun was fully loaded, in violation of regulations, and asked Ver to remove the ammunition clip "for safety reasons". The General shot back a menacing glance, and a succinct reply: "Don't fuck with me."

Eduardo Cojuangco, the country's most powerful warlord and a first cousin of Cory Aquino, loaded his family and advisors into another chopper. Cojuangco controlled the Philippine brewing and bottling industry, owned half the island of Palawan and a fleet of personal jets, and commanded the Israeli-trained private army of at least three thousand men that had helped the Marcos cause by trashing the Malolos transmitter of Radio Veritas. But he scrambled onto the plane without luggage, in a pair of khaki pants and sockless sneakers. "The Apo [leader] had wanted to see me," he later explained. "The next thing I knew, I and my family were on our way to Guam." The billionaire Marcos crony left with "nothing but a handkerchief and 10,000 pesos. . . . When we reached Guam, the Boss lent me some clothes."

The first copter was already lifting off with Ferdinand, Imelda, and their loot when a young man in camouflage fatigues began pounding on a door of the second one. A U.S. officer poked out his head but could not hear the soldier on account of the noise. After much pointing and gesturing, the American hollered that he already had a full load – and found himself looking into the snout of a high-powered assault rifle. The door was opened and the shaggy-haired soldier shoved his way in. "I'm his goddammed son," he announced. Sure enough, it was Ferdinand (Bongbong) Marcos II, still in the military get-up that had made him feel so good the previous night.

The four blue-and-white Sikorskys and one French-made Puma helicopter that were supposed to be part of this final scene stood idle less than a hundred yards away. Both Marcos and Imelda had been imagining coup scenarios for years, and had spent millions of dollars to ensure their escape route. The centrepiece was this fleet of combat-ready jungle choppers, bought with siphoned U.S. military aid, specially outfitted for exactly this occasion, and grandly decked out with the Presidential Seal. But now the pilotless choppers sat like beached whales on the Palace lawn as the dictator absorbed the barbs of smart-mouthed Yankee pilots.

"The Marcos pilots had left their planes as early as Monday afternoon," explains air force general Antonio Sotelo, the man behind the earlier helicopter defection to Camp Crame. "And that, to me, is a pretty damning comment. These were the people you'd expect to be the most loyal to the President. They are the ones to whom he had entrusted his life, and the lives of his family. Yet even they left him at the most crucial moment. That must have terrified him. After the attack on Malacañang Monday, when he looked out and saw that his own pilots had abandoned him . . . he must have feared for his life."

The General has investigated the defections of the Marcos-Ver pilots, and paints an amusing picture of them tiptoeing out the door. "Basically, they just snuck across the fence," he says. "As I understand it, they went to the Palace gates, pretending to examine the outside area. You know, some business about looking for landing sites and so on. Then, when they got outside, they just made a run for it. They dashed out, took off their uniforms, and left. I'm not sure if they believed in the righteousness of the Ramos-Enrile cause, or were just afraid. Anyway, they definitely took off."

The Philippines' ruling couple had established another escape route: a trio of private jets at nearby Villamor Air Base. Indeed, the presidential Sikorskys were probably intended only to ferry the fleeing presidential entourage to Villamor. But with nobody to fly the helicopters, the Marcos-Ver gang would have been forced to make the three-mile trip by road – a dicey proposition in a city full of Cory supporters. "I know for sure he had a BAC-111 and a Falcon at Villamor," says Enrile. "And then also a Fokker jet. He could have used one to take all his family in one planeload. But I suppose he had no more pilots for those, either."

These multiple defections did more than just frighten the fleeing

President. They may also have averted a prolonged and bloody civil war. Until the very last, Marcos alternately pleaded for and insisted on two days' sanctuary in Paoay, the palatial Malacañang of the North in his native Ilocos province. There, surrounded by a populace that even today regards their "Apo" as the true president, he would have been impossible to dislodge without a massive military engagement.

His opponents vacillated on the demand all through Tuesday, their attitude changing as the strategic pendulum swung towards them. That morning, when a long siege of Malacañang seemed inevitable, they would have been only too glad to provide free passage to Paoay. "If he'd arranged it with us [then], we would have allowed him," concedes Enrile. "Why not? To get him out of Malacañang. Anyway, he would lose the capacity to govern at that point. It would be just a matter of time for him."

But the rebels' response hardened as the Palace defense crumbled. Finally, the request was channelled from Marcos to Ambassador Bosworth to Cory Aquino herself. The new president was at her sister's house in Mandaluyong when the call came at about 9:15 p.m., ten minutes after the lift-off from Malacañang. She had been in that "hideout" since returning from Cebu on Sunday morning, but only Loyalist incompetence (and perhaps Cory's beloved Blessed Virgin) had kept her safe for two days. The Aquino car had run smack into an armored column of Marcos troops just outside Manila's domestic airport. The driver pulled over to the side of the road, and Cory sat praying behind tinted-glass windows in the back seat as the APCs rolled past. A TV crew from the U.S. Cable News Network had followed her from the provinces, and trailed the car to the gate of her sister's suburban home. "They even *showed* the house on television," moans an Aquino supporter who watched the Revolution from a hotel room in Washington. "Even I recognized the place right away, and the Loyalists could have picked her up if someone from the [Philippine] Embassy had been watching CNN. Thank God, it didn't happen that way."

The phone call from Ambassador Bosworth presented Mrs. Aquino with the first hard decision of her presidency. And one insider says she came dangerously close to granting Marcos the detour. Cecilia Muñoz Palma, the former Supreme Court justice and opposition parliamentarian, was at the Mandaluyong house, along with Defense Minister Enrile, Rene Cayetano, and a dozen of Cory's aides and advisors. "Perhaps because Cory and I are women, we were inclined to agree to the request," she recalls. "But after discussing it with the others, we realized that, after two days, Marcos could then extend it to a week, a month, and much more blood would be shed."

With his own planes, of course, President Marcos would have needed no permission for the move to Ilocos. He could easily have made a run for it, forcing General Ramos into a tough decision: whether to shoot him down, killing wives, children, and grandchildren, or end up fighting a protracted battle on Marcos's home turf.

It is unlikely that any of this occurred to the pilots as they sidled out of the gates and ran for it. But that single act of betrayal may have saved thousands of Filipino lives.

From outside the Palace fence, the departure of the Marcoses made an idyllic tropical postcard. The moon was nearly full, and the American helicopters seemed to hang for a moment in the middle of it. Framed by palm trees and black against the moon, they rose one after the other, and then melted into the night.

It was 9:05 p.m.

My wife ran after them down the street, shaking her fist and hollering, "Good-bye, you bastard! Don't come back." I was jumping up and down on the spot, as if to get a better view two feet in the air. We hugged each other in jubilation as the last beating of the chopper engines died away. "I never thought I'd see this," Vangie laughed, near tears. "I'd have paid anything to be here now." It was a few moments before we noticed our companions, still standing on the far curb without much interest in the Sikorskys. "That was Marcos," we yelled. "He's gone. It's all over." They answered with shrugs and noncommittal nods. Two of the men slapped high-fives, but most were dubious. "That's what everybody said yesterday," grumbled one. "How do you know that was him?"

Good question. Even Cory Aquino was not to learn of the departure until a few minutes later, and she did not go on television to inform the nation until after 10 p.m. It was all speculation on our part, but it *had* to be Marcos. That was the only explanation for the pull-out of the Palace defense and the arrival of the U.S. helicopters. Anyway, it was no time for a debate with Doubting Thomas. We spotted a sizeable crowd of revellers down at Gate Four, and sprinted over two hundred yards of cobblestone to join them.

My behavior over the next five minutes was so monumentally stupid as to defy belief. The only explanation is that Vangie and I were both ten feet off the ground with excitement and certain that there would be an immediate celebration. So we rushed up to the gate, panting like a pair of six-year-olds who had arrived late for a birthday party.

There were perhaps 150 "celebrants", scattered on both sides of the locked gate. We figured that the lucky ones inside must have climbed over the fifteen-foot barrier and would open it for the rest of us. "Come on, open the gates," my wife pleaded. "Let everybody in." Someone inside looked shocked at this request, and demanded to know who we were. Foreign journalist, I told him, from Canada. That touched off a venomous outburst that should have sent warning bells clanging in my head. "This is all because of you!" his partner yelled through the grille. "You just tell lies about everything. You lie about the Philippines to the whole world."

As it happens, I am the sort of level-headed, peaceable guy who reacts badly to such remarks. "Look, Jack," I told him, "I don't give a damn about your opinion of the foreign press. This is a great news story and we need to get inside. Now, let's get the gate open."

Vangie was more diplomatic. "We just want to celebrate," she told them. "We want to be happy . . . like you guys."

This turned out to be one of the great ironic remarks of the Revolution, and momentarily stunned the "celebrants" on both sides of the gate into a belligerent silence. They stared at us, while our brains clicked away furiously. What the hell was wrong here? Why were these people so angry? That was when I first noticed that everyone in the crowd was wearing at least two "Marcos Pa Rin!" (it means "Marcos Again") buttons. Worse, they were carrying 2"-×-2" clubs with nails driven through the ends. Hmmmm. Maybe they had picked up the buttons as souvenirs from the Palace grounds. Or maybe . . .

"Jesus Christ," whispered my wife, pulling at my arm. "These are the Loyalists. Let's get out of here."

Unfortunately it was impossible just then to make an unobtrusive exit. A pack of burly toughs were pressing in around us, trapping us against the gate. One of them, covered from head to foot with Marcos ribbons and buttons, snarled that I was not allowed in the area, and demanded to know how I had got past the soldiers at the barriers. "They're gone," I told him. "They pulled out a few minutes ago." The murmurs of puzzlement and disbelief were still rising when I decided, what the heck, I might as well drop the other shoe. "Marcos has gone, too. He went out in those helicopters."

This conversational gambit was something less than a roaring success. A rough-looking character on the other side of the fence shoved his head through the bars and began spewing spittle and invective in my face. "That's a fucking lie!" he told me. "Our President is still here. We saw him only a few hours ago. He has been here all day. He would never desert us, and we will not desert him!"

"We are not *hakot*," insisted another, using the derisive Tagalog term for fake Marcos supporters who are paid to go off to rallies by the busload. "We will defend President Marcos to the death."

The mood, never friendly, had become distinctly menacing, and the talk of death was the last thing Vangie and I wanted to hear. But at least they were aware of danger, and that could be turned to our advantage. "Look," I said, adopting a conciliatory tone and appealing to a scholarly-looking kid of about twenty. "You are the ones left holding the bag. Everyone else has run away. For your own safety, you had better send someone to the Palace to find out if I'm telling the truth. Go and look for yourself at the barriers. The Marines have gone. It's only a matter of time until the Cory crowds come here to celebrate. There'll be thousands, hundreds of thousands. You'll never be able to defend yourselves."

That stirring speech separated the Loyalist sheep from the goats. They were all young, and wound up tight as the springs on a window shade, but they were obviously divided into two distinct classes. At least half of them were college students, including a dozen or so neatly dressed girls on the verge of emotional breakdowns. The others were plainly thugs, itching for a fight and led by a maniacal giant swishing a club over his head. The Monster was about 225 pounds, immense for a Filipino, and he now began dashing around the fringes of the group. One glance at his eyes – dilated and the size of baseballs – foretold that there would be trouble.

The clean-cut faction began discussing my point with evident concern but were cut short by the Monster. "No!" he shouted, pushing through to the gate. "It is all psy-war. The President is still here."

I was about to pursue the argument, but Vangie grabbed my belt and started tugging. "Let's go," she said. Sure enough, the debate had opened an escape route. We eased slowly towards the street, staying well clear of the Monster, then broke into a slow trot and finally sprinted for safety. Two dozen Cory supporters had gathered one hundred yards away, warily eyeing the crowd. Unlike us, they were smart enough to recognize a band of club-wielding Loyalists when they saw one.

The latest news was not encouraging. Someone had leapt the fence, trying to reach the Palace, and had been dragged back to a gate just a few minutes later, gushing blood from five stab wounds. Periodic shots could be heard from across the wall. My wife and I crept over to a low metal gate and peered inside, into the dark grounds of the Palace, which looked like a park in the moonlight. But the light also revealed shadows and shapes running silently from tree to tree. A small stone building near by seemed to be a servants' quarters and kitchen. It was abandoned, but a bonfire raged on the porch outside. Another shot rang out. We ducked and scurried behind the main wall.

Two youngsters were crouched near us, cowering in obvious fear. They turned out to be defectors from the "collegiate" Loyalist faction, and they remembered us from Gate Four. "Were you telling the truth?" asked the boy, while his girlfriend clung to him. "Is Marcos really gone?" When I nodded, he fished a couple of the red-white-and-blue presidential buttons from his pocket and held them up like I.D. cards. It was as if he was turning himself in to the police. "We're Loyalists," he confessed. "What should we do?"

I told him to start by throwing away the buttons. Then he could melt into the oncoming crowd and slip away. It was obvious that nobody would spot them without their markings, but the kids were too terrified to believe that it could be so simple. "It's like you said," the boy shivered. "There will be thousands of them coming. They will kill us if they find us." We walked them across the street and steered them away from the Coryites now gathering in threes and fours. They waved goodbye and hurried away, doing a terrible job of appearing inconspicuous.

By now, my jubilation had evaporated. Marcos had left behind a sad, sordid mess that showed every sign of turning violent. Typically, he had called in these die-hard supporters with an emotional plea to their nationalism and, above all, to their personal loyalty. He had armed them with clubs and vitriol, propped them up at the gates, then sneaked away without even bothering to inform them, much less doing anything to ensure their safety.

The treatment meted out to the Loyalists was actually shabbier than I guessed at the time. After Marcos left, soldiers of the Presidential Security Command (PSC) began to loot the Palace, their own barracks, the canteen, the media building, and many of the guest houses on the grounds. Realizing that the rabid pro-Marcos defenders would hold back the crowd for a while, they actively deceived the civilian Loyalists into believing that the President was still inside, to give themselves more looting time.

"But even that was partly bitterness on the PSC's part," according to Colonel Red Kapunan, the RAM leader who interviewed the Palace guards the next morning. "Marcos didn't tell them a thing. He didn't even have the courtesy to tell them he was leaving. To this day, many of them feel betrayed and misused. Even when they saw the helicopters, they couldn't believe he was leaving, because it would be unthinkable to do so without

informing the PSC. Eventually they had to figure it out for themselves –
obviously, before the [Loyalist] civilians did."

It was nearly 10 p.m. A few miles away, Aquino's speech-writer Teddy
Locsin was banging out an announcement of the Marcos departure on an
old portable typewriter, while his boss hovered impatiently by his shoulder. The new Channel 4, People's Television, was standing by to broadcast "President Cory" 's address to the nation.

The media had now descended on the scene in such numbers, and
with such an array of TV cameras, sound trucks, and arc lights, that it was
almost safe for us to return to Gate Four. But the mood remained ugly.
The Monster was a live wire by now, dashing around aimlessly with his
nail-spiked club raised for battle. And some of the more passionate Loyalists screamed at the press to remove the bright-yellow Cory I.D. tags we
had been wearing throughout the election and revolution. The tags had
Cory's photo at the bottom, causing one outraged civilian to rip it from the
neck of an American lady journalist. "Don't wear that face! We hate that
face!" screamed the Marcosian. But Cory's supporters were now numerous and brave enough to shout back. "You'd better get used to it," one
yelled. "She's the President."

From outside the Palace, an ambulance pushed slowly through the
throng and parked in front of the Gate. From inside the Palace grounds,
two Loyalists dragged out another over-eager Coryite who had hopped
the fence, this one also bearing multiple stab wounds. Oddly, the ambulance stayed in place after the man was helped inside. "We can't really
leave," explained an attendant. "We've heard that others are hurt inside,
and this is the only doctor around. We'll use the ambulance as a medical
station."

Most Loyalists were still convinced their President was in the Palace, and regarded the outsiders as a tactical device to divert their attention. One young man in a Marcos T-shirt called his group into a circle
behind the ambulance and offered his analysis of the situation. "We're
being infiltrated," he told them. "Identify yourselves as Loyalists to the
President, and get everyone else away. Don't give any consideration to
foreign reporters. They are the cause of all this trouble." The Monster
hurried over to second the motion. "Don't let yourself be brainwashed by
Enrile's men," he bellowed. "We're not going to surrender. Cory people
move out! We're willing to die for President Marcos. We're not here for
the money."

But the Loyalists were no longer powerful enough to simply dictate terms. Aside from the Aquino supporters, General Narciso Cabrera of the Western Police District had arrived with a handful of officers, who wandered through the crowd trying to gather up the clubs. Most of the owners refused to oblige, and the armed cops did not press the matter. Their reluctance was not surprising; General Cabrera was himself a Marcos appointee, and would soon be stripped of his post by the new government. "We're just here to keep order," he shrugged, when I asked why his men did not confiscate the clubs. "If we try to disarm them, there might be trouble." As it turned out, the clubs would soon be the least of anyone's problems.

A Marcos supporter in the familiar red-white-and-blue T-shirt approached me with a look of deep concern. He introduced himself as Rafael Casado, and said he wanted to present his side of the story to a foreign reporter. "I am a real Marcos die-hard," he insisted, "not one of those who are just paid to go to rallies. And I was willing to fight if there was something to fight for. But now . . . this is silly. Marcos is gone." Why didn't he explain that to the others? "I have tried," he said. "But many are fanatics. I told them he's gone and the soldiers have abandoned us. They just said, 'No, you are a spy,' and drove me away."

Crack! A sudden blast froze us all in our tracks.

"Was that a firecracker?" I asked Casado.

"No," he replied. "That's a gun."

Thunk! Another shot whistled through the gates, with the compelling authority of an M-16 attack rifle. We all began running down the cobblestone street leading to the Mendiola Bridge. Seconds later, the rat-a-tat-tat-tat-tat of a machine gun sent hundreds of us diving for cover.

I had Vangie by the hand and, spotting a concrete planter-box off to the left, we threw ourselves behind it. Just a few feet away we found a small indent in the high cement fence that lines the street. A half-dozen others immediately piled into the same shelter, crushing us into the smell of urine and garbage. It was a hell of a way to celebrate the fall of a hated dictator, but there was no time to ponder the irony. A machine gun inside the Palace grounds, high in the Media Affairs building, had us pinned down, pinging blue-white ricochets off the cobblestones. Very beautiful blue-white ricochets, I noticed.

The staccato bursts lasted for five seconds each, and seemed to continue for two or three minutes. But that estimate could be wildly off-base. Under fire for the first time, I discovered that standard concepts of fear do not apply. Instead of quaking in dread, you enter a realm of total concentration, where each shot seems to hang in the air forever, and the slightest sound or movement is greatly magnified. It is as if someone has slowed down the world and turned up its volume. On me, at least, the initial effect was oddly euphoric; Winston Churchill, I gather, once commented that nothing is more exhilarating than to be shot at, and missed. The ricochets were hypnotic, and the distortion of time created a false sense of security.

But that bubble quickly burst. "They'll be coming out after us," yelled a woman near by. "We'll be sitting ducks here. We've got to run for it." En masse, the whole crowd accepted this shaky logic and flew into a panic. We leapt to our feet, in a tangle of arms and legs, and tried to race down the avenue. Immediately a woman to my right tumbled onto the cobblestones and lay there. It was impossible to tell if she had been shot or had tripped and fallen. I slowed and turned, but someone screamed in my ear: "Don't look back. Just run!" Self-preservation won out as I joined a few hundred others in setting personal-best times for the 200-yard dash. The emotion involved required no explanation: it was pure terror.

Safety was a steel garage door one block away, where fear instantly turned to rage. "Why are the bastards still shooting?" someone demanded. "Don't they know Marcos is gone?" We sat around in glum outrage until the shots stopped and a woman on a second-floor balcony waved the all-clear sign.

A banker named Emanuel Montenegro had seen the whole episode. He was right against the fence at Gate Four when some teenagers had begun climbing it, and a nervous soldier atop a tank inside had opened up with an Armalite. That accounted for the rifle fire. The machine-gun bursts, he said, had come from the second floor of the Media Affairs building. "The first bullet just missed us," smiled Montenegro, hugging his ten-year-old son, Dennis. "But it's strange how things come around. When I was a student, Marcos was my enemy and I was in lots of demonstrations right here. Now I come back with my son and Marcos is still my enemy, and his soldiers are still shooting at us.

"Well, this is the last time. We made it, Dennis. Marcos didn't."

19 *THE FALL OF MALACAÑANG*

CAPTAIN RICARDO MORALES – the "supposed" Ricardo Morales, Imelda's coup-plotting military escort and instant TV star – missed the entire revolution. After his arrest on Saturday night, he spent the three days inside a windowless Malacañang prison cell, without a radio or even a watch, counting the nails on the ceiling and wondering when he would be lined up in front of a firing squad. The focus of international attention on Saturday, he had been totally ignored ever since.

About 9:30 p.m. Tuesday, however, two soldiers entered his room and addressed him formally as "sir". They informed him that General Santiago Barangan, chief of the dreaded Presidential Security Command, wanted to see him immediately.

"I tried to remain calm," he recalls. "But no, I was nervous, and I asked them, 'Okay, is this the time they are going to take me out and shoot me?' They said, 'No, sir. It's already surrender.' Surrender? I didn't know what they meant, but I suddenly remembered that a few minutes earlier I had heard military helicopters going overhead. I thought this might be true. But it might also be a trick. I didn't want to get my hopes up. I had already written off my life. If you start to hope . . .'' Morales was marched over to Malacañang's operations centre between the two escorts, and taken to General Barangan's office. He was astonished at what greeted him.

''The place was a total mess. There were Styrofoam food packages piled up everywhere, and every inch was littered with something. The General was drinking cognac when I reported to him. He looked at me and waited a moment . . . a kind of torture, I guess. Then he said, 'Get a glass.' I knew then that I was going to live and we had won.''

Morales gulped down some liquor and proposed a toast to peace. Then he wandered outside in a daze and tried to remember where he had left his car three days before. That mundane question, however, quickly gave way to more urgent considerations. The army was not going to shoot him now, but the growing crowd at the gates just might take him, a uniformed member of the Palace guard, and string him up from a lamp-post. That would be ironic, but also fatal.

"All the soldiers from the PSC were terrified," he discovered. "Some of the officers immediately came up to me and said, 'Dick, Dick, you'd better go to the gate because there's a mob out there. You'd better talk to them or they'll come in here and lynch all of us.' But I was afraid, too. I said, 'No, they'll lynch me first.' The PSC thought that everybody knew I was with the rebels, because they'd seen me on TV. They didn't realize that nobody believed it. I said, 'Look, that's all the more reason for me not to go. They might think I was part of some Marcos scheme.' "

Morales finally agreed to help his erstwhile captors. He carefully approached the nearest gate and found two priests who were leading the crowd. They, of course, had not the faintest memory of Captain Ricardo Morales, hero of the Revolution. But he somehow convinced them that there was nothing inside worth seeing and that the real action was at another gate. The churchmen hurried away, taking hundreds with them.

According to Morales, most of the PSC made an easy escape, in barges or trucks from the far side of the Pasig River, before the crowd arrived. The nervous soldiers left behind were hard-core presidential Loyalists who had waited too long and been trapped in the Palace grounds. It was they who opened fire at Gate Four. "The guys who shot were the last elements left there," says the rebel captain. "I guess they were trying to gain time and secure things before the mob came in. The idea was to keep you at bay while they were pulling out. They were shooting over your heads, or behind you. They were really afraid, I can tell you that. From inside, it looked like a really vindictive mob, and there was so much talk that they would lynch us."

After driving us away, the last few soldiers managed to change into civilian clothes and mix with the crowd. Some were in the vanguard of the "pro-Cory" Palace looters who appeared on worldwide television, burning and smashing the portraits of Ferdinand and Imelda.

The shooting was the last attempt to defend the Palace. After that, the dam burst and the human deluge swept towards Malacañang from all corners of Manila. President Cory Aquino had been on TV to make it official: "The long agony is over." Now eight million people were bursting to celebrate, and every one of them knew where the party would be.

This is what we had come to witness two hours before, but I had little taste for it now. The crowd had barely surged in from Mendiola when the first vicious beating began: a Marcos die-hard, still bedecked in ribbons and buttons but minus the club, was punched and kicked sense-less by dozens of jeering "celebrators". It was a classic Filipino *piranha* fight, where even passers-by put the boots to a defenseless victim. Such fights are a regular Saturday-night feature in the lower-class nightclub districts, but it was ugly and depressing in this setting. Four days of heroics had given way to cowardly sucker-punches.

A priest in a full-length white robe rushed to break it up. He would have made an extraordinary photograph as he lifted the victim in his arms, soaked to the knees in blood. The punks ran off, laughing and jeering, to terrorize others. One lady in her fifties was crying, and yelling after them: "Don't destroy our revolution! Don't shed the blood of Filipi-nos! The old regime is over!" Someone tore off his own jacket and wrapped it around the horribly battered Loyalist, who had begun shivering. A car arrived from somewhere and people helped the priest get the man into the back seat. They disappeared towards Mendiola, the car honking its horn, the priest leaning out of the window in his now-crimson robe.

Vangie and I edged back towards the Palace, staying behind the crowd in case of gunfire. But the scene at Gate Four had changed dramati-cally in twenty minutes. Hundreds had now scaled the walls and were standing on top, waving gigantic CORY IS OUR PRESIDENT banners and hurling fireworks into the air. Inside, the first looters could already be seen in the Media Affairs building, shoving sheaves of paper out of the windows. Bullit Marquez, an AP photographer who went in with the first wave, found a dead man lying in the lobby. Apparently one of those who leapt the Palace fence too early, he had been stabbed in the neck and side with an ice pick and his body had obviously been dragged some distance. The man was the sixteenth, and last, person to die in the Revolution.

The crowd in front of the gate had grown so large and boisterous that it was becoming difficult to stand upright. By chance, we were shoved into the arms of two friends who had just arrived, and hugs were exchanged all around. The noise made it impossible to talk, but their wide grins were infectious. Back in Toronto, it was only 10 a.m. and my dead-line was hours away. There was plenty of time to join the party and let it wash over us.

Joining the party was not easy. Everyone had the same idea, apart from those who were already trying to escape with their loot. One teen-ager came diving over the wall with an army boot in his hand, took a tumble on landing, and held it up proudly for all to see. "From inside," he grinned. It didn't look like much, but he was delighted. Typically, a few revolutionaries had stationed themselves atop the wall to help people over. I made it with a flying leap and a scraped elbow. Vangie, all five feet and one hundred pounds of her, was lifted over and deposited bodily on Marcosian holy ground.

Bedlam reigned inside Malacañang. The ground was soft from a recent rain shower, and the whole place was littered with Styrofoam food trays. A swarm of celebrants covered three abandoned tanks, trying to rip off their cannons with bare hands. People were running around with flags, photographs, books, TV sets, typewriters, reams of paper, Marcos speeches, phone bills, even plants torn from the flower beds – anything at all to show they had been there. Two young boys from the Mendiola Bridge gang were sitting under a tree, patiently forming strands of barbed wire into a Christ-like crown of thorns.

Many in the crowd had no idea of the Malacañang layout, and headed instinctively for the nearest big building. But that was just the media building, filled with offices and dark corridors. We opted for the Palace itself, a white Spanish-colonial wedding cake, its balconies lined with bullet-proof glass, a building that holds a nearly mythical symbolism for Filipinos.

Even from a distance, we could hear the shouting in Tagalog. "Malacañang is not your enemy! Only Marcos is the thief. Don't be thieves yourselves." Then the rolling chant: "Don't destroy! Don't destroy!" Unfortunately, the rabble crashing through an elegant bay window paid no attention to such high-minded urgings. Dozens of kids in jeans and T-shirts poured through the opening, and the sound of smashing chandeliers offered immediate evidence of their objectives. In moments, the vandals emerged onto the second-floor balcony – where Imelda Marcos had taken her farewell bow just ten hours earlier – and tried to hang a huge Philippine flag from the balustrade. This won a confused response from outside, where the multitude simultaneously hooted the looters and cheered the flag. An American TV crew pulled up, their camera mounted atop a Land Rover, just in time to send the next balcony scene into a billion homes. Did the vandals wait for the camera before lugging out a portrait of Marcos and hurling it over the edge? Probably not. But after their confederates below had set it on fire, they could not decide whether to stomp all over the fallen dictator or preen for the world TV audience.

By the time Imelda's picture was put to the torch, I was ready to go inside. It proved remarkably easy to clamber onto the wooden stage where Marcos had held his inauguration, and slip down a crowded marble corridor and into the ground-floor Presidential Library. That stately teak sanctuary was in the process of being ravaged by howling street toughs. It held nothing of value to them, just shelves of antique legal volumes and government records, so they vented their frustration by throwing books at walls and tearing out pages. I ducked a flying ten-pound tome on constitutional niceties, and drew an immediate apology from the hurler. "Sorry, ah?"

People were scurrying through the upstairs mansion, chased by self-appointed and powerless civilians. Tomorrow morning the new armed forces chief of staff, General Fidel Ramos, would apologize for the carnage. "We received word of Marcos's departure a little too late for us to make plans for the orderly takeover of Malacañang . . . then I was diverted to report to the President." In the meantime, there was not a soldier to be found – except the PSC plunderers in civilian clothes.

Nobody found Imelda's infamous collection of 5,400 shoes that night; the cache in the basement would not be discovered until a few days later. But hundreds of curiosity-seekers mounted the brown staircase to the Marcos family's dark, windowless private apartments, taking note of everything from the half-eaten final meal to the gallon jugs of "First Lady" perfume.

Everywhere there was evidence of a hasty departure. Drawers stood open. Empty jewel boxes, filing boxes, and stacks of documents were strewn all over the second floor. Imelda had obviously taken her two treasure trunks and loaded up everything else of great value. But there were dozens of velvet-lined cases spilling over with costume jewelry, five dozen boxes of Cartier silverware, a set of Russian crystal bells, and trinkets that seemed to be unused gifts. Her bed, at least thirteen feet wide, could have provided a spacious home for many of Manila's poor. An intricately carved wooden crown was suspended from the ceiling, enclosing the bed in layers of sheer curtains. A black stone "malachita" seance table, with a pentagram in its centre, was set at the foot of the bed, evidence of the First Lady's obsession with the occult. (Persistent rumors say Imelda had a seven-member cabal or "coven" that advised her on every political and personal move she made.)

The bedroom's parquet floors were covered with expensive Chinese and Iranian carpets. Rosewood, crystal, and silk filled the room. One of the Palace's twenty-two grand pianos was hidden beneath a snowdrift of photographs, all showing Mrs. Marcos, without her husband, greeting a cross-section of world political leaders and celebrities (classifying George Hamilton, Van Cliburn, and the Maharishi Mahesh Yogi as "celebrities"). Nancy Reagan held inordinate pride of place among the dozens of photos, captured with Imelda in every conceivable pose, beaming before a variety of impressive locales.

A walk-in vault had been virtually cleaned out, but papers still littered the floor. One receipt for $1,431,000 listed six pieces of jewelry from a store called Bulgarifor.

The First Lady's private bathroom reeked of the custom-made perfume that stood in gallon jugs. Each jug contained a supply of many lifetimes for most women, since no amount of dabbing behind the ears could possibly consume such a stockpile. Imelda apparently poured it into her bathwater. The mirrored ceilings reflected a sunken bathtub at least sixteen feet square. Towels were the size and thickness of carpets. Rows of Italian bathrobes hung in the adjoining dressing room, also mirrored, where the overpowering scent came from thousands of tiny perfumed soaps spilling out of wicker baskets. Here also was a collection of French perfumes, not of the "First Lady" brand. These were not in kegs, just convenient 1.5-litre bottles, like family-sized Pepsi.

As for the decorator's taste, a consensus among Manila society held that Imelda had created a "mirrored monstrosity . . . an expensive brothel". That haughty judgement, however, may have been prejudiced by the pornographic videotapes found stacked beside the two VCRs and the giant TV screen in her bedroom.

The President's quarters were comparatively modest, though his bedroom had the size and appearance of an intensive-care ward. Shelves of medicines lined the walls, and at least a half-dozen air filters were set up around the room. Beside Ferdinand Marcos's king-size bed was an electric-powered hospital bed, hooked up to an oxygen machine and an intravenous bottle. Near by stood a complicated piece of medical equipment called the Centurion Magnotherapy. For the benefit of laymen among the looters, Marcos had thoughtfully left a brochure explaining its function: to treat chronic and degenerative illness of the kidneys, lungs, and heart. Even stronger evidence of the President's rumored kidney ailment was found on the ground floor, where reporters stumbled upon a highly sophisticated operating theatre, with gleaming equipment far more modern than any available elsewhere in the Philippines.

Nor was Marcos content with traditional healing methods. Much of his ceiling was covered with little glass pyramids, their tips pointing down to his bed and desk. The strange alignment seemed to confirm rumors of his belief in "pyramid power". Philippine psychic healers later revealed that they, too, had often been summoned to treat him.

The fleeing dictator also left an intriguing assortment of reading matter on his night-table (*Self-Learning Course on Goat Raising* and Buckminster Fuller's *Operating Manual for Spaceship Earth* among them), along with an army helmet that appeared to be at least forty years old.

Near his desk, a solid-steel escape door was set in the wall, concealing a secret passageway to the back garden. It was painted dark brown and had apparently been concealed behind the bookcase now shoved to one side. Incongruously, there was also a battery-operated miniature Mercedes-Benz – a $7,000 toy that Captain Morales had helped Imelda lug home from one of her New York shopping sprees – parked in a corner of his bedroom. The sleek Mercedes belonged to grandson Borgy Manotoc, whose lifestyle would have stunned the ragtag children his age in the slums only a mile away.

Down the hall was an anteroom that had served as command headquarters for the operation against Camp Crame. A large, detailed map of the rebel camp was drawn on a wheeled blackboard identical to the ones General Ramos had used in his own office. And the President's generals had obviously kept score just as Ramos had. There were notations of various commanders supporting the rebellion, and estimates of possible strength in men and arms. As suspected, the bungling General Ver had greatly overestimated the forces arrayed against him, crediting General Ramos with artillery and firepower beyond even the rebels' wildest dreams.

The command post was of little interest to the rampaging young vandals, who swept through it to rip paintings and photographs off the walls and go whooping from room to room. Two stood in one of the bathrooms, repeatedly flushing the toilet with apparent fascination, while others wolfed down the remains of the Last Supper. The gang was particularly intrigued by the ornate conference room where Marcos so often held court on Philippine television. A huge Presidential Seal and the throne-like chair behind a microphone proved irresistible. The celebrants took turns posing in front of it, pretending to deliver speeches in that deep Ilocano accent ("I hereby order . . .") and shoving each other off the raised dais. Strangely, the television lights were still on, and the room had an almost blinding glare. A couple of toughs in heavy-metal T-shirts tried to pry the seal off the wall but were pushed away by the others. A skinny kid of about sixteen sat on the floor near by, mindlessly tearing Marcos's inauguration speech into shreds and tossing the strips into the air. Whoopee.

Back downstairs, the thugs in the Presidential Library had barricaded themselves inside, shoving bookshelves against the door. I was standing in the outer hallway, taking notes, when the first *New* Armed Forces of the Philippines soldiers arrived at about 1 a.m. They had yellow armbands on their camouflage fatigues, and most wore yellow-and-red "CORY!" headbands. All were smiling and waving to the crowd, who cheered and raised the soldiers' arms in triumph. A bright young lieutenant approached me with a yellow ribbon tied around the muzzle of his Armalite, and motioned to the library door. "Anybody in there?" he asked.

"Just the looters," I shrugged, and grinned at him. I was exhausted, light-headed, and strangely giddy; suddenly everything seemed terribly funny.

The lieutenant had the opposite reaction. At the mention of looters he was all business, shaking his head in disgust. He strode to the door, kicked it open, and motioned another soldier to follow him inside. Moments later they emerged with a column of shamefaced teenagers. "Let's all just calm down," urged a priest who had mounted a mahogany table in the hallway. "This is our place now, and we'll have lots of time to enjoy it. We're never going to give it to another tyrant."

Not that night, anyway. It was time to get back to the hotel and bang out something for the early edition of my paper. I found Vangie out front and headed for the gate, but within a few seconds we felt like salmon fighting upstream. People were still pouring over the fence in waves. Unknown to us, millions were marching towards the Palace from all over the city. Cars were abandoned in the streets for miles around as Manila traffic simply seized and stopped. For Cory's human barricade, the party had just begun.

"We marched all the way from Crame," says Karen Tanada, whose KASAPI group had kept the four-day vigil there. "And it was like a noise barrage from the beginning. We marched quickly, almost running in the excitement, and the city was just crushed with cars from a long way off. Even at Magsaysay Avenue they were so backed up that no more could come in. Everyone was honking horns and yelling as loud as they could. When we got there [the Palace] about 1:30 a.m., we almost had to push our way in. There was a jeep with a sound system – the Reformist soldiers – and they were telling us to get out. They told us there were still bombs planted there and they might explode. The guy on the PA was really berating the people about looting: 'Look, you call Marcos a thief and you're doing the same thing!' He said it over and over; after a while, the people got really mad at him.

"They kept sending us out, but we'd go back in. About 4:30 a.m. they sent everybody away because people started looting again . . . not the Palace, but the soldiers' barracks and canteen. So, later, the Ramos soldiers gave up and said, 'Okay, you can eat the food, but don't bring it out.' They set up inspection lines at the gate, because so many people were trying to smuggle things. They were trying to carry typewriters in a knapsack, and they'd just drop them when they saw the lineup. It got to be pretty funny. After a while there was a large pile of goods sitting there. It was like a customs area.

"At dawn, we held a big rally there in Malacañang Park, with speeches and prayers. It was just impromptu. People started yelling for the soldiers to get up and talk. When they tried, some of them just said a few words and stopped. They'd start to cry. A lot of people were in tears."

That is how People Power was supposed to end, in prayers and tears on the grounds of the Palace that had been Marcos's lair for so many years. And even President Corazon Aquino seemed to believe it was over. I was back at the Midtown, working on a room-service cheeseburger and a portable typewriter, when the lady in yellow-rim glasses smiled from the TV set. Her message was short – fifty-two seconds – and sweet. "We are finally free," she told the nation. "And we can be truly proud of the unprecedented way in which we achieved our freedom. With courage, with determination, and, most important, with peace. . . . A new life starts for our country tomorrow. A life filled with hope and, I believe, a life that will be blessed with peace and progress." She also had a message for the masses at Malacañang: "Please stay calm and observe sobriety for the sake of our country."

But the Four-Day Revolution could not yet be tied up in a neat yellow ribbon. The next face on the "new Channel 4" was that of the once-and-future Defense Minister. And for the celebrants tuned in, Enrile's bizarre message might just as well have been beamed from outer space.

Juan Ponce Enrile sat in the midst of this national jubilation, stared soberly into the camera . . . *and proceeded to thank Ferdinand Marcos for all he had done!* The praise was profuse, even gushing. Enrile told Filipinos he had never intended that things should turn out so badly for Marcos. Then he thanked the deposed ruler for sparing the rebels when they first assembled in Camp Aguinaldo. "The military under his control, or the portion of the military under his control, had the firepower to inflict heavy damage on us," said the minister. But Marcos's gentlemanly behavior had saved their lives. "And for that alone, I would like to express my gratitude to the President. As officers and men of the Armed Forces of the Philippines, we want to salute him for that act of compassion and kindness that he extended to us all."

I stood bolt upright, astonished, and shouted at the Sony Trinitron. What the hell was going on? The statement was patent nonsense, completely inexplicable. There were already strong rumors of Marcos commanders refusing orders to shell Camp Crame. Enrile must have known all about it. He certainly was aware of Operation Everlasting and the planned prison camp out on Caballo Island. He probably knew about Operation Mad Dog: a fake "guerrilla attack" on Manila that would allow Marcos to put Operation Everlasting into effect. So what was the game? What did this shrewd political chameleon Enrile have up his sleeve?

There was no way to find out in the middle of the night, and repeated questions over the next few days drew a blank. Because of the time zones, the Defense Minister's broadcast was seen by millions worldwide, but most Filipinos missed it. "Your guess is as good as mine," shrugged one political insider who did see the speech. "Maybe Enrile was just buying some insurance, in case Marcos comes back." In the post-revolutionary euphoria, there were easier things to write about. So it took me five months to get to the bottom of the story.

British journalist James Fenton was similarly intrigued by Enrile's bizarre statement, and concocted an elaborate conspiracy theory to explain it. In his book *The Snap Revolution*, Fenton surmises that Marcos "had seen that he had to go, and that the only way out for a dictator of his kind was exile. The point was to secure the succession. It could not go to General Ver, but Marcos was under an obligation to Ver, and therefore could not hand over the presidency to anyone else. In some way, whether explicitly or by a nod and wink, he had told Enrile and Ramos: you may succeed me if you dare, but in order to do so you must overthrow me and Ver. You must rebel."

The theory explained the lack of actual fighting. It also explained why Marcos made such a show of overruling Ver on television, and why the rebels never approached Malacañang until the President had left. The implicit Marcos bargain, Fenton postulated, went roughly like this: "I protect you from Ver; you protect my family and my reputation."

In fact, there was indeed a Marcos bargain behind Enrile's strange nocturnal tribute. But the reality is less intricate and much more logical than the theory. The key lies in our collective short-sightedness on that euphoric Tuesday night. Once Ferdinand Marcos left Malacañang, many believed that he was out of the country, and even those who knew he was at Clark assumed that his eventual departure would be automatic. Few stopped to consider that he was still a free man, still in the country, still with a die-hard core of military loyalists, and no longer surrounded by fanatic Aquino supporters.

The American military, of course, had no legal right to arrest or detain a Philippine president in his own country. They merely supplied transportation for his entourage to Clark, and a security detail to protect him there. A Philippine security unit also arrived at the U.S. base, but remained outside the main gates. In retrospect, it is clear that Marcos was free to go wherever he wanted at that point. And, by piecing together American pronouncements during the night, it is also clear where he was originally headed.

Associated Press, Agence France-Presse, and the American CNN TV network all quoted a "senior Reagan administration source" who disclosed that Marcos would spend the night at Clark and journey to his home province of Ilocos Norte. "He's not going to Guam right now and he's not going to Hawaii," the source told AP's Washington bureau. Neither the Philippine rebels nor the Americans were in any position to stop him. Although the small Filipino contingent at Clark had defected to the rebellion, the entire surrounding region was controlled by fiercely loyal Marcos generals. Even more crucial, the overland route from Clark Air Base to his beloved Ilocos was in the hands of such Loyalists as General Antonio Palafox and the commanders of Region Three. In a very real sense, Clark Air Base was about the *last* place the rebels wanted Ferdinand Marcos.

The fading President was, of course, quick to size up the situation – and to use it to his advantage. While the jubilant hordes were trashing his bedroom, eating his food, and hacking at his portrait, Marcos was on the phone to Trade Minister Roberto Ongpin in Manila. He started a broad philosophical conversation about his future, and informed his trusted advisor that he was thinking of going to Paoay. His wife Imelda, General Ver, and others were urging him to do so. What did Ongpin think? The minister was silent for a few moments, then answered quietly: "Mr. President, if you go to Paoay, this country will be plunged into civil war."

Hmmmm. Marcos conceded that possibility, and insisted that he wanted to avoid it at all costs. But what about his place in history? How would it look if he were driven from the country "like a stray dog from a market stall"? He could not bear to leave under such circumstances. Roberto Ongpin was well versed in the art of Marcosian indirection and immediately took the hint. "Let me talk to Enrile," he suggested. "I am sure he will tell the people of the Philippines that you are only leaving to prevent bloodshed. He'll be glad to secure your place in history." Seconds later, Ongpin was frantically dialling the emergency number of the Minister of National Defense.

"I was in this room, being interviewed on American television by

Ted Koppel," Enrile explained, after finally agreeing to unravel the secret. "That's when the call from Bobby Ongpin came in. He said that Marcos was in Clark . . . and he conveyed to me his request that I go on the air. Bobby told me that his reading was that if I make the statement [praising Marcos], then Marcos would leave the country. But if not . . ." The alternative was not explicitly spelled out, but Enrile required no geography lesson. At that point, says the minister, "he could very well have gone up North if he wanted to."

Enrile agreed to the request, but told Ongpin it might take a while to arrange. The ensuing series of urgent phone calls reveal much about the mental state of Ferdinand Marcos that night. It was less than fifteen minutes until Enrile received another call from Ongpin. Where was the announcement? The President had phoned back, and was waiting in front of his TV set. A half-hour later he called again. Then again. And again. And again. Manila's traffic had ground to a halt, so the Channel 4 television crew took hours to reach the Defense Ministry. It was an agonizing wait for the First Family.

"Bobby kept calling me up, because he was being called by Marcos," recalls Enrile. "And I said, 'Well, I'll do it. Just a minute. I'm waiting for the crew of Channel 4 to come.' And then I think Bobby must have called me several times more, until the crew arrived, and I went on the air." The minister insists the gushing tenor of his remarks was "not done to favor Marcos, really. I did it in order to give him the push to leave the country. . . . I made that statement in order to finish the whole thing once and for all, and avoid bloodshed."

President Ferdinand E. Marcos had been waiting, with growing impatience, for that one last pat on the head. He would not sleep, or decide his immediate future, until it was administered.

Immediately after the broadcast, Roberto Ongpin received one final phone call from Clark Air Base. This time it was Imelda on the line, sounding weary and emotionally drained. "The President has gone to bed," she said. "He wants to thank you and Enrile for your kind words. We will be leaving in the morning."

EPILOGUE

"Many of our members felt that if we revealed our 'naughty'
actions, some people would be afraid of us. They might figure
that, if we did it once, we are capable of doing it again."
– Colonel Eduardo "Red" Kapunan, September 1986

SOME PEOPLE MIGHT INDEED have feared the scenario that Red Kapunan so
candidly outlined to me. And some people would have been absolutely
correct. Colonel Kapunan, along with Gringo Honasan and many other
RAM insiders, were deeply involved in the abortive November 22 coup
attempt that finally drove Juan Ponce Enrile out of President Corazon
Aquino's fledgling government.

Ironically, it was none other than General Fidel Ramos who crushed
Enrile's second attempt at a military takeover, this one also scheduled for
2 a.m. on a Sunday morning. There was yet another Saturday-afternoon
discovery, and, apparently, a similar plea for Ramos's support. But this
time the General's answer was a resounding "No!". When he learned
that the Defense Minister's "special operations group" was again planning their favorite operation, Ramos issued an immediate bulletin to
every regional commander in the Philippine armed forces. They were
told to obey "only those orders issued by myself or by duly authorized
deputies of the general headquarters". The chain of command had taken
a sudden detour *around* Enrile.

The General's quick action was the exact opposite of Fabian Ver's
bumbling response nine months earlier. Ramos went immediately to
Camp Aguinaldo to meet Enrile, Honasan, and the other rebels, while
two truckloads of armed soldiers waited outside the meeting room.
Meanwhile, other forces surrounded radio and TV stations in the capital
and in several other key cities, and guards secured the telephone and
electrical companies. Six battalions of loyal troops were deployed around
Manila, while military trucks lined all roads to Malacañang and light
tanks poked their noses from the Palace gates.

Enrile had either banked upon Ramos's support or believed that he commanded the loyalty of most Philippine officers. Either way, it was an egregious miscalculation. The minister had cut a dashing figure in February with his Uzi and his flak jacket, and had later warned that he might "do a Rambo". But such macho threats masked an uncomfortable truth: Enrile was only a make-believe soldier – he was not going to kill anyone. When the crunch came on Saturday, November 22, it was immediately obvious the military would choose their own West Point general and "soldier's soldier" over the Harvard-trained lawyer.

Enrile missed the seven-hour cabinet session at which Mrs. Aquino demanded everyone's resignation. But he arrived at Malacañang for his own sixteen-minute meeting with the former housewife he was so eager to replace. He then emerged as an ex-minister, waving at reporters but declining any comment.

Honasan, Kapunan, and the other RAM colonels appeared tense and white-faced on Saturday night. But the whole affair was smoothed over in the familiar "talk-don't-shoot" style of the February Revolution. By Sunday, the Reformists were closeted with Enrile's successor, former general Rafael Ileto, and emerged with shrugs and smiles. "He asked for unity," as Honasan put it, "and we said yes." A few days later, Enrile himself presented Ileto with the keys to the Defense Ministry at a brief public ceremony, and noted that he was leaving "without rancor or regrets". The RAM security group he had always called "my boys" were also there, lounging in plainclothes with those little metallic bulges behind the hip.

The Reformists did not, apparently, plan to incinerate the Palace defenders at Malacañang Park this time. But it is not yet clear how "naughty" the November plan was. As usual, a number of scenarios were leaked to various media, which trumpeted them as the "inside" story. One version said the coup was code-named "God Save the Queen": a benign operation to remove Cory Aquino's left-leaning cabinet ministers and retain her as the figurehead of a right-wing government. But her own press spokesman, Teodoro Benigno, insisted that the plotters had intended to "bump her off".

If so, the military reaction was truly extraordinary. Honasan, Kapunan, and their men have been "reassigned" since Enrile's departure, but they have not been dismissed or charged with any crime.

It was Ninoy Aquino who best described his widow's quixotic quest as president of the Philippines. "The one who comes after Marcos is the one to pity," the late Senator said, just a few months before his 1983 assassination. "That will be an impossible job. After Marcos, the country will be bankrupt and ungovernable."

Aquino probably had himself in mind. At the time, his demure wife was merely serving coffee and cookies to the stream of political heavyweights who visited her husband in exile at Harvard. But it is Corazon Aquino who has lived to know the truth of Ninoy's prediction. Twenty years of Marcos's "kleptocracy" have left the nation virtually prostrate, its treasury looted and its economy comatose. Communist guerrillas of the New People's Army are too strong to be cowed by arms, and too wily to be lured from the hills. Provincial warlords still rule parts of the country as personal fiefdoms. And a clutch of political vultures continues to scrabble for every scrap of left-over power.

To throw an inexperienced housewife into that situation, say Mrs. Aquino's critics, is like feeding meat into a grinder.

Or *is* it? In her own gentle way, Cory Aquino has already established herself as something of an Iron Lady. She is obviously not from the mold of Margaret Thatcher or the late Indira Gandhi, but that gentle Filipina smile masks a core of tempered steel. President Aquino refuses to play political games, is direct to the point of bluntness, and simply freezes opponents with her absolute honesty.

The United Nations got a taste of that style in September 1986 when the General Assembly invited her to address them in New York. Instead of repeating the usual platitudes, Cory denounced the UN charter as an "invitation to hypocrisy" and mocked its grand pretensions. She also had pithy advice for any Third World nation that expects the UN to help in deposing a rapacious dictator: "You are on your own."

It has already become journalistic fashion to visit the Philippine slums, find potholes in Manila's streets, and write a neat "Nothing-has-changed-under-Cory" piece for the weekend paper. But that easy cynicism ignores the amazingly long list of Cory Aquino's genuine accomplishments. She has freed hundreds of political prisoners, restored the writ of habeas corpus, and set up a human-rights committee to investigate military abuses – all despite the vociferous objections of Defense Minister Enrile. The rule of law was reinvigorated by flushing Marcos-appointed hacks from the court system. The Philippine press is now as free and diverse as that of any Western country. Such formerly corrupt "milk cows" as the customs, immigration, and taxation bureaus have been placed in the care of squeaky-clean commissioners. Her determined peace offensive has wrested the moral high ground from the insurgent New People's Army and, in late November 1986, she achieved a major breakthrough by negotiating at least a temporary ceasefire.

The emotional and time-consuming task of writing a new constitution delayed fulfilment of her promise to restore democratic elections. But if Mrs. Aquino erred, it was in trying to have every conceivable point of view represented on the committee that hammered out a replacement for the old Marcosian legal code.

The economy remains a mess, largely because the political squabbles and the NPA insurgents have made the country such a risky place in which to invest. The new government counted heavily on an infusion of private capital, a strategy doomed by the stream of headlines shouting variants of: "Coup Rumored in the Philippines!" Still, the Manila stock market has boomed since the fall of Marcos, and economic shrinkage is down to one per cent of the GNP, after a ten-per-cent decline over the previous two years. The United States, Japan, and the International Monetary Fund have reopened loan and aid channels that had been sealed tight against the larcenous Marcos regime. And, most important of all, the current Philippine president is not piling up $10 billion in the Swiss bank accounts of "William Saunders" or "Jane Ryan".

Polls show that most Filipinos are frustrated by the lack of economic progress, and disgusted with their wrangling politicians. They do not, however, blame Cory Aquino.

"People complain bitterly about the government," says Manila newspaper columnist Max Soliven. "But none of that bitterness is directed at Cory. If anything, we tend to feel protective towards her. People say, 'Why don't they lay off her?' or 'Why doesn't she crack down on them?' Everybody seems to feel she is our best hope, maybe our only hope."

The cries for action rose to a crescendo as Juan Ponce Enrile – a member of her cabinet team – publicly criticized Mrs. Aquino for her "weakness" against the Communists, and repeatedly (if metaphorically) tweaked her nose in public. The Defense Minister claimed to be an "equal partner" in the government, and insisted he could not be removed without dissolving the new regime. Even the staunchest Aquino supporters doubted the wisdom of simply giving Enrile enough rope, and praying he would fashion it into a hangman's knot.

Yet, in retrospect, Cory's strategy seems brilliant. She could not dump Enrile earlier without making him a political martyr and the standard-bearer of all anti-Aquino forces. By allowing him to launch a coup, and then cutting him off at the knees, she has apparently deprived him of the martyr's role. The key to the gamble was knowing which way General Ramos would jump when the time came. Either Mrs. Aquino *did* know, or she got another enormous boost from the Supreme Commander who rules both her personal and her political life.

President Aquino's religious faith has only deepened since the February Revolution. She held a huge Victory Mass shortly after taking office, and told Filipinos exactly how they had ousted Marcos: "I believe that God actually came down and walked among us during those four days. There is no other explanation for what happened."

Such talk sends shivers down the spine of many hard-nosed international analysts, who see her peace offers and fractious cabinet as clear evidence of her weakness. If a political strong man with absolute powers could not defeat the NPA, how can Cory manage it? If she cannot even keep her ministers in line, how can she run a violent, corrupt, and sprawling Third World nation?

Others, however, see the same factors as evidence of Mrs. Aquino's inner strength.

"I say completely the opposite," argues economist Bernardo Villegas of the respected Research and Communication Centre in Manila. "All these dissenting voices are a great sign of strength on Cory's part. She is the type of person who refuses to surround herself with yes-men, the type who does not measure her own worth by how thoroughly she can dominate others. Obviously a political neophyte needs a variety of advice. It is the perfect formula for someone who has no background in government, yet has a very sharp political instinct. She has put together the best government she can. Whether it will be good enough . . . that's another question."

Cardinal Jaime Sin, of course, did finally have to answer to the Vatican for his audacious use of Filipino Catholics as a human buffer zone between two armies. But that March 1986 trip to Rome turned into a triumphal procession. The Pope greeted his Philippine cardinal – and oft-rumored successor – with public embraces and warm congratulations that put a stamp of approval on the overthrow of Marcos. Cardinal Sin explained the revolt as a fight between the children of light and the children of darkness; the Church, he insisted, had made the only possible choice. "The Pope bought it, and said: 'God bless you, my son,' " according to Felix Bautista, who accompanied his friend to Vatican City.

Sin's visit sparked much soul-searching among Catholic theorists, many of whom welcomed his bold gamble and suggested that the Church might learn a lesson from it. "What happened in the Philippines is a vindication of Cardinal Sin's outspokenness," said the Reverend John Navone, a moral theologian at Rome's Gregorian University. "Events have proved that he did not act too soon. Maybe the Church would do well to decry the injustices to Catholics in certain countries, like the Jews do. Perhaps in these matters we're really being overly political in our silence. And in these cases maybe we should be less political in speaking out for justice. Maybe the Jewish approach – don't let anyone get away with anything – is proving itself to be more valid.''

By coincidence, the highest-ranking Catholic dogmatists met that month to prepare an "Instruction on Christian Freedom and Liberation", another attempt to rationalize the Pope's paradoxical decree that priests shun politics while seeking justice for the oppressed. The paper was meant to reconcile diverse Church positions on Poland and Central America, while delivering another rebuff to advocates of liberation theology. But Cardinal Joseph Ratzinger, head of the powerful Congregation of the Doctrine of the Faith, knew a godsend when he saw one. His group hailed the Philippine revolt as an "outstanding example of active resistance" to oppression, exactly the sort of "non-violent and prayerful" overthrow the Church could wholeheartedly support.

Never mind that Vatican bureaucrats were appalled by the Philippine bishops' inflammatory pastoral letter, and had expressly warned Sin to "stay neutral" before his call to the barricades. No matter that the Southeast Asian nation is quite unlike Poland or Latin America. The "miracle at EDSA" had worked, and worked big. That was apparently enough for Cardinal Ratzinger's august congregation.

"The frightening part of it all," Bautista later conceded, "is that we were only allowed to get away with it because of my Cardinal's close friendship with the Pope. There is a great deal of trust between them, and that made all the difference. He [the Pope] knows the Cardinal is strongly anti-Communist and that there is a tremendous difference between us and the liberation theology in Latin America. Let me put it this way: if it had been any cardinal other than Cardinal Sin, then perhaps the Pope would have sided with the papal nuncio. And that would have been disastrous."

Despite outward appearances, the Philippine bishops never saw themselves as revolutionary firebrands. Nor did they ever consider an open defiance of Rome. All the bishops are obedient to the Vatican, and none would have challenged a direct papal order to scrap the famous letter. Their opposition to Marcos depended entirely on winning Pope John Paul's approval, or at least avoiding his outright censure. The Filipino churchmen, however, were devious enough to leave the Pope little time to take preventive action. If he had been intent on stopping them, he would have been forced to act instantly.

"Frankly, we hurried it out to the foreign press as soon as it was written," says one bishop who requested anonymity. "We knew the nuncio [Msgr. Torpigliani] would be outraged, and we could not afford a prolonged debate with Rome. It was submitted to the press and the Vatican more or less simultaneously, allowing for the time zones. Then we just waited to see if the Pope would lower the boom on us. He did not. He didn't approve it very strongly, but at least he gave us the benefit of the doubt."

The Pontiff's liberal reaction reveals much about the internal workings of the Roman Catholic Church. If you want papal approval for a political overthrow, it is apparently best to breakfast often in his apartments, have him visit your country and detest your First Lady – then beat him over the head with parallels to Poland, no matter how distant.

"Well, you know, the Pope was well aware of the incompatability between the Marcoses and the Cardinal. Whenever the Cardinal is in Rome, the Pope will call him up and say, 'Let's have breakfast at my place,' " says Bautista, who reads magazines in an outer anteroom while his Cardinal shares an omelette with the Holy See. "It's always absolutely private, and they were always joking, in a way like . . . 'Give my love to Imelda,' the Pope said once. The Cardinal gave him a look of consternation, and the Pope burst out laughing. Or sometimes the Pope would say, 'Look, I know the situation there. But try not to fight with them too much, huh?'

"Because, you see, the Pope knows how things are from his [1981] visit. His speech at Malacañang was very strong: If it comes to a conflict between the security of the State and human rights, then human rights must prevail. And the Pope was absolutely irritated with Imelda. He visited six cities in the Philippines and he took the plane. But Imelda made it a point to arrive in her own private plane, and she would touch down everywhere about ten minutes before he got there. There she would be, waiting to kiss his hand with the TV cameras trained on her, wearing a different outfit every time. When it came to the third city . . . well, the Pope had had a bellyful. He turned his back on her and ignored her. He wouldn't stay in the lavish Coconut Palace she had built for him, either. Imelda had to get Brooke Shields as the first guest. So the Pope, well, he understood the Cardinal's feelings exactly."

As for Poland, Cardinal Sin frequently exploited that soft underbelly in John Paul's stern admonitions. "I wouldn't say the Cardinal actually *manipulated* the Pope," Bautista says carefully. "But he is only human, and he realized the paradox. The Pope is always very outspoken that priests should not meddle in politics, but when it comes to Poland he does not hesitate to meddle. So that puts him in a quandary as far as the Philippines. When the Cardinal meddles, he just puts on his innocent face and says, 'But, your Holiness, it's the same situation obtaining in Poland.' And that would squelch the Pope.''

There are, however, limits to papal tolerance, and the Philippine Church has certainly tested them. The Vatican can ill afford to have Salvadorean bishops using their Filipino brothers as a precedent for dumping their own government. So the initial hearty approval has given way to subtle criticisms and even direct warnings. In the succeeding months, Rome moved to reclaim its authority over the Philippines and to rein in the outspoken bishops.

As early as April 1986, the Vatican warned that it would be ''criminal'' to misdirect the energies of popular piety towards an earthly plan of ''temporal liberation''. By June, the Pope had sent a special letter to all Roman Catholic bishops of the Philippines. It was written in plain English, and required no subtlety to decipher:

''The Church in the Philippines cannot forget that a large portion of the population finds itself living in economic and social conditions that are extremely difficult and at times unbearable . . .'' wrote the Pontiff. ''Preferential love for the poor . . . must become one of the principal lines of action of that ministry. This service of love and fidelity to man must, however, be in conformity with the nature of the mission of the Church . . . not of the temporal but the spiritual order. Not of the social, political or economic order, but of the religious one. This means, then, that the Church is called not to take positions of a political character, or to take part in partisan conflicts, but to give society the expert contribution which is proper to her, as the spiritual light and strength that can contribute to building and consolidating the human community.''

John Paul also told the clergy: ''To you . . . there is entrusted the promotion of effective and concrete national reconciliation. You have the mission not to provoke or to deepen divisions, but to help in overcoming . . . those that have been created, or that at least have emerged, among the population during the recent events.''

The Pope is a keen student of Philippine affairs. For his churchmen have indeed helped deepen the divisions of post-Marcos society. Even parish priests and nuns retain an acid contempt for cronies and officials of the *ancien régime*. And many among the clergy have ignored President Aquino's calls for national reconciliation.

''I think the Pope hit one of our soft spots with that letter,'' concedes one Philippine bishop. ''But I also think it's a letter that most of us will be able to obey. With Marcos gone, it is a lot easier to accept Vatican edicts about being non-political. When we were trying to overthrow a dictator, we had to file them away in a back cupboard for a while."

The United States expressed its "unequivocal" backing for Cory Aquino throughout the protracted showdown with Enrile. And American legislators interrupted her eleven times with applause in September 1986, during her eloquent address to a combined session of Congress. But underlying tensions between Washington and the new Philippine president remain. "You hit a home run!" Senate majority leader Robert Dole told Cory after her speech. She smiled sweetly and replied: "I hope the bases were loaded."

The irony might have been lost on Dole. But Filipinos got the point a week later when that same Senator led the Republican majority in voting *against* a $200-million aid supplement to the Philippines.

Relations have bumped along in that fashion – one step forward, one to the side, one back – ever since Mrs. Aquino assumed office. The strains were evident last June when Secretary of State Shultz arrived in Manila with the grand announcement that "the way has been cleared for a $200-million installment of U.S. aid to the Philippines." He added that the Reagan Administration had pledged to speed processing of the "grant", described as part of a $500-million "aid" package working its way through the bureaucratic pipeline.

Why all the quotation marks around Shultz's phraseology? Because those reports were greeted with groans and guffaws when they reached Aquino's ministers. "Aid?" asked Cory's executive secretary, Joker Arroyo. "What aid? Before we react with joy like jumping chimpanzees, we should know that what Secretary Shultz is bringing is rental money in payment for the use of the U.S. bases. It is not aid money, as people would make it appear." In fact, added Arroyo, the Americans were actually *behind* in their rental payments, and the $200 million was merely an overdue installment.

Two weeks later, Ronald Reagan weighed in with that marvellous assessment of Ferdinand Marcos quoted at the beginning of Chapter 14: "The one thing he did not want was bloodshed or civil strife. And so he left rather than permit that." Filipinos winced and shook their heads, while their new ambassador to Washington fired off a volley of his own.

Citing the 1991 renewal date for the U.S. bases agreement, Emmanuel Palaez warned: "The time for the U.S. to start winning back the hearts and minds of the Filipino people is now – not in 1991 or even 1988. If the U.S. adopts a wait-and-see attitude, it may be too late to overcome the residue of antagonism and resentment against the U.S. . . . the poison left

by Ferdinand Marcos, who expertly manipulated America's fears and
alienated her from the hearts of many Filipinos."

General Fabian Ver spent the early days of his Hawaiian exile earning a
reputation as a "cheap" tipper in various Honolulu restaurants. He has
since slipped from public view, although various "sightings" are reported
every few weeks. Last July, Enrile told the Philippine press that Ver had
entered the Malaysian state of Sabah to meet with Muslim dissidents of
the Moro National Liberation Front. Malaysia denied the story. Later, the
Philippine foreign ministry reported that a disguised General Ver had
been refused entry to Sabah by alert border authorities. He had arrived at
Kota Kinabalu airport with a false moustache, a wig, and a Lebanese
passport, but had aroused suspicion when he failed to respond to a Muslim
greeting.

At a rented beach house in suburban Honolulu, meanwhile, the Aquino
government's lawyers were allowed to question the former First Family
about Swiss bank accounts, New York real estate, disappearing aid money,
and other items of mutual interest. Marcos had opposed the interrogation
on the grounds that he was still head of state of a sovereign country, but a
U.S. federal district court ordered him to make a deposition. The October
session was not terribly fruitful, as Marcos invoked "the right not to
incriminate myself" a recorded 197 times. When presented with documents signed by "William Saunders", Filipino lawyers say the deposed
president examined them carefully but refused to answer any questions
about them.

 Imelda Marcos also invoked the Fifth Amendment, but her session
was reportedly much more animated. She burst into tears when asked
about her claim last September on the television show "60 Minutes" that
all the "Jane Ryan" signatures in the Swiss bank documents were forgeries.
And she rained invective upon the government lawyers when they asked
embarrassing questions about her wealth.

 Back in Manila, Marcos supporters have begun circulating a letter
from their hero to his son Ferdinand Jr. (Bongbong). The letter is in
Marcos's own handwriting and appears to be authentic. It is worth quot-
ing in full:

  To my son Bongbong and to all the sons of the Philippines
 of his generation: I will soon hand over to your hands the flags of
 battle for the mystic cause of our freedom and honor. For this is
 turning out to be your battle. I shall quietly wage the last vigorous

campaign, but must soon ask you to take up and follow the only cause that youth willingly dies for – the Search for [sic] Galahad for our own Holy Grail.

As a young man like you, I looked up to the heavens and swore to pursue this mystic cause of freedom even unto death. I look at your generation and I know you will swear to the same persevering faith to shield our people's freedom, with your wounded body to your dying breath.

Go, then, son and claim this honor.

Affectionately, and with prayers.

Your father,

Ferdinand E. Marcos

CHRONOLOGY OF EVENTS

1965 – Ferdinand Marcos is elected the sixth president of the Philippines.

1972 – Marcos declares martial law and arrests thousands of his opponents, including the charismatic opposition leader Benigno Aquino.

1980 – Aquino is released to undergo triple-bypass heart surgery in the U.S. Upon his recovery he takes a job at Harvard University.

1981 – Marcos officially lifts martial law, but retains most of his dictatorial powers.

1983 – Amid reports of President Marcos's serious illness, Aquino returns to the Philippines. He is shot dead on the airport tarmac. Hundreds of protest demonstrations are staged, and the country's economy begins a sharp decline.

1984 – The Agrava Commission investigating the assassination finds that a military conspiracy was responsible. It names chief of staff General Fabian Ver, one civilian, and two dozen military men as prime suspects.

– General Fidel Ramos is named acting chief of staff while Ver is on "leave" to face charges, but Ramos is given little power to effect real changes.

1985 – U.S. Senator Paul Laxalt arrives in October with a personal letter to Marcos from President Reagan. The two discuss the possibility of a "snap" presidential election.

– Marcos announces the election on Nov. 3, during an American TV interview.

– Cory Aquino, swayed by a million-signature petition, announces her presidential candidacy.

– General Ver, acquitted in December along with all the other defendants in the Aquino murder trial, is immediately restored as chief of staff.

ELECTION CHRONOLOGY – 1986

Feb. 7 – The day of the presidential election is marred by widespread violence and fraud: A promised "quick count" grinds to a halt amid contradictory claims.

Feb. 9 – Computer operators at the government vote-counting centre walk out, claiming fraud.

Feb. 11 – Cardinal Jaime Sin appears at the independent NAMFREL counting headquarters to praise its beleaguered volunteers.

Feb. 14 – The Catholic Bishops' Conference issues a pastoral letter which denounces the election as "tantamount to forcible seizure".

Feb. 15 – The Marcos-controlled National Assembly concludes its canvass, and declares Marcos the duly elected President.

REVOLUTION CHRONOLOGY – Feb. 22-25, 1986

Saturday, February 22:

11:00 AM – Colonel Red Kapunan informs RAM insiders that their plan to storm Malacañang Palace has been "compromised".

11:30 PM – Kapunan and Colonel Gringo Honasan inform Defense Minister Juan Ponce Enrile of the problem. Enrile's reaction: "Let's go fight".

5:00 PM – Captain Ricardo Morales, security escort to Imelda Marcos, is arrested in the Palace guards' lounge.

6:45 PM – Defense Minister Enrile and General Ramos hold a startling press conference to announce their breakaway from Marcos.

9:00 PM – Cardinal Sin appeals on Radio Veritas for Filipinos to guard the rebel camp and avert violence.

11:15 PM – President Marcos appears on Channel 4 announcing an apprehended coup plot by RAM. Captain Morales confesses his role to a disbelieving national television audience.

Sunday, February 23:

1:00 AM – Marcos reappears on television to assure the nation the situation is under control.

3:00 AM – Enrile holds another press conference, and is near tears when told that thousands are massing outside his camp.

5:00 AM – The Radio Veritas transmitter in Malolos is destroyed. The station is reduced to using a small backup unit in Manila.

2:15 PM – An armored column with two Marine brigades under General Tadiar leaves Fort Bonifacio to attack the rebels. It is stopped at the corner of EDSA and Ortigas Avenues, and engulfed in a sea of civilians.

2:45 PM – Enrile and his men cross from Camp Aguinaldo to join General Ramos in Camp Crame.

4:20 PM – Marine commander General Tadiar issues an ultimatum to the civilians he will attack in 30 minutes.

6:00 PM – Marine tanks retreat from EDSA. One brigade attempts to attack Camp Aguinaldo on foot.

7:00 PM – Radio Veritas goes off the air.

12:00 PM – Marcos delivers a passionate harangue on Channel 4 and threatens to "sic the artillery" on the rebels.

Monday, February 24:

12:05 AM – Radio Bandido suddenly appears on the air, with June Keithley at the microphone.

5:55 AM – A Loyalist anti-riot squad disperses defenders at a Camp Aguinaldo gate. Marines under Colonel Balbas move in and set up artillery for an attack on Crame.

6:08 AM – At sunrise Colonel Sotelo leads eight helicopters from the 15th Strike Wing to the rebel camp.

6:30 AM – Radio Bandido announces that Marcos and his family have left the country. Tens of thousands celebrate the "false victory".

9:01 AM – Colonel Balbas is ordered to fire artillery at Crame. He does not comply.

9:30 AM – Marcos holds a televised press conference to prove he is still in the country. Ver and Marcos have a heated argument over dispersal of civilians.

9:56 AM – The Channel 4 transmitter is hit by rebel fire. The TV station goes off the air.

10:30 AM – The Rebels send a lone Sikorsky gunship to attack Malacañang. The helicopter fires six small rockets into the Palace grounds.

11:55 AM – Three rebel gunships destroy the Loyalist helicopters at Villamor Air Base.

1:00 PM – Colonel Balbas and his troops retreat from Camp Aguinaldo.

6:55 PM – Marcos appears on Channel 9, promises a fight to the finish, and imposes dusk-to-dawn curfew.

Tuesday, February 25:

3:00 AM – Marcos phones Senator Laxalt in Washington.

5:00 AM – Laxalt tells Marcos to "cut, and cut clean".

9:05 AM – Marcos phones Enrile, offering to form a provisional government.

10:00 AM – Cory Aquino is inaugurated as the seventh President of the Philippines at Club Filipino.

11:55 AM – Marcos is inaugurated as President on the Malacañang Palace lawn. The broadcast is cut short when the transmitter is struck by Sikorsky machine guns.

5:30 PM – Marcos phones Enrile and asks for a U.S. security escort.

9:05 PM – U.S. helicopters take the Marcos family and others from the Palace lawn to Clark Air Base.

ACKNOWLEDGEMENTS

The *Globe and Mail* has been remarkably tolerant of my obsession with the Philippines, and gave me the time to write this book. My special thanks to Norman Webster.

Several Filipinos provided endless help in the research process, including Ike Joaquin, Roger Cleofe, Lucy Orara and Teresita Rodriguez. I am also deeply indebted to "insiders" such as June Keithley and Red Kapunan for their willingness to tell the whole truth, whatever the cost to themselves.

I am grateful for some marvellous quotes from *People Power*, a verbal history published by the Reuter Foundation, and from Nick Joaquin's *The Quartet of the Tiger Moon: Scenes From the People-Power Apocalypse*.

My wife Evangeline and Cora Baron served as living Philippine encyclopedias during the writing stage, and prevented me from making dozens of mistakes.

Finally, with affection and esteem, I thank Douglas Gibson, my editor, for his deft transformation of a manuscript into a book.

B. J.

INDEX